CUT & RUN

CUT & RUN

SAYING GOODBYE
TO THE LAST GREAT FORESTS
IN THE WEST

GRACE HERNDON

WESTERN EYE PRESS
TELLURIDE

CUT & RUN
is published by
Western Eye Press
Box 917
Telluride CO 81435

ISBN 0-941283-11-9

Printed in Dexter, Michigan
by Thomson – Shore, Inc.
on recycled paper, using
soy-based ink, an environmentally
sound alternative to traditional
petroleum-based inks.
Designed by Lito Tejada-Flores
on a Macintosh SE computer
and set in 10 pt. New Baskerville.

Western Eye Press is a small
Colorado-based publishing adventure
primarily dedicated to publishing
works on the Rockies & the West.
Other Western Eye Press titles include
the photo-art books: *HIGH COLOR,*
Spectacular Wildflowers of the Rockies,
by Linde Waidhofer;
RED ROCK, BLUE SKY,
Mysterious Landscapes of the Southwest,
also by Linde Waidhofer, and
La ROSE, An Intimacy of Roses,
by True Redd. We've also published
YELLOWSTONE TO YOSEMITE,
Early Adventures in the Mountain West,
a historical reprint from the 1880s
illustrated by Thomas Moran,
and a series of skier guidebooks
to Colorado, Utah, New England
and the West Coast.

This book is lovingly dedicated to my mother, Katherine Barrett Jaynes, a consummate citizen-activist who, at the age of 90, still demonstrates her long-held conviction that in a democracy, one citizen can make a difference.

Grace Herndon

CONTENTS

AUTHOR'S PREFACE

No Tree Hugger

Although I am acquainted with a number of more or less certified tree-huggers, I do not count myself among them. I am, rather, an interested latecomer to the question of National Forest timber policy.

Individual interest in a particular issue is frequently shaped by circumstances. As a child, growing up in the 1930s on a tree-shaded boulevard in an older residential neighborhood in Chicago, trees, for me, came in two classes: Christmas trees and trees that dropped their leaves in the fall. Both had special meaning: the evergreen for its traditional holiday overtones; and the huge oaks, elms and maples for the riotous fun we children had diving into the big, crunchy piles of leaves they provided each autumn.

Later, when I became involved with Western Colorado's cattle-ranching scene, U.S. Forest Service policy still did not attract my particular attention—not until the 1980s. I think my experience may well parallel that of other non-tree-huggers who, for the most part, have always had a generalized sort of faith in the professionalism of the Forest Service and the district rangers who were seeing to it that forests across the American West would last forever.

And while I, too, have had my moments of forest awe—in the midst of the golden glow of aspens in fall, a touch of new snow underfoot giving the whole grove a hushed, other-worldly magic—I could never qualify as even a fledgling naturalist. But, as a reporter with years of experience covering Western Colorado issues, and as a member of a ranching family affected by natural resources issues, timber policy ultimately rose higher and higher on my personal priority list.

I offer this book as a contemporary overview of what is generally regarded as a critical time for federal forest management in the American West. The facts and opinions outlined here are based both on research and interviews, by phone and face-to-face, with a broad cross-section of people on all sides of the public-timber issue.

Natural resource policies are, in a very large measure, what the American West is all about. Timber policy on public lands in the West is just one aspect of this larger picture, closely related to the others—water, wildlife, grazing, mining and recreation. Nor is the story limited to Forest Service policy. Public timberland in the West is owned and managed by official bodies other than the National Forest System. These include the different states, Indian tribes, and the U.S. Bureau of Land Management, a major manager of public forests in Northern California and the Northwest. But my inquiry focuses primarily on National Forest timber policies. This is the heart of the matter. The Forest Service and the way it performs will determine the future of the last of the West's great forests. In the 1990s, the American West will burn with timber policy issues every bit as hot as the flames that, in 1988, consumed thousands of forested acres in Yellowstone National Park and its ecosystem.

Like the author, readers will not have to be card-carrying eco-terrorists or emotional tree-huggers to understand that everyone in the American West has a stake in how much of the West's great forests will survive. This is much more a political and social question than a scientific one. While foresters, ecologists, biologists, silviculturalists, naturalists, and all the other "ists" involved, seldom agree on any single timber management thesis, the timber industry clearly stands poised to cut the last great forests in the West before the end of this century. This is a story that's only been addressed in bits and pieces, region by region. If this book has a contribution to make, it is in looking at public forest policies and problems across the widest canvas we have—the whole of the American West.

Books like this are not written in isolation, in a vacuum, or in an ivory tower. I want to thank all those who helped me track down and understand this subtle and complex story. Thanks, too, to Lito Tejada-Flores and Peter Shelton for hours spent with this manuscript; to friends near and far who provided critical encouragement as the book took shape. And special thanks to my husband and life's partner, Steve, a staunch and faithful accomplice in this endeavor.

INTRODUCTION

"Clearing the land" is a hallowed phrase in American history. Among our heroes since colonial days have been the men who cut a path through the forests and later felled the trees and cleared the land for planting. So, it is something of a surprise that in the 1990s, 500 years after Columbus first set a European foot on America's eastern shores, we are seriously questioning whether we are clearing too much of our forests, too rapidly.

We still honor the true man of the forest, the logger. The mythological giant, Paul Bunyan, as much as Uncle Sam, is a part of our collective heritage, a member of our national family. Indeed, the popular idea of the Northwest—Oregon, Washington, and Northern California—as one infinite and beautiful forest, its redwoods and evergreens forever a sturdy symbol of soaring might, is also part of that myth. As America struggles to comprehend the fact that its resources, from oil to timber to untamed open space, are finite, developing new strategies to manage and protect those resources will involve some fundamental rewriting of the American myth.

Timber, of course, is at least theoretically a renewable resource. Unlike oil, or gold for that matter, trees can and are being cultivated. So timber policy—and we are talking here about public land and public forests—is concerned neither with preserving nor destroying, but rather with *managing* timberland.

Before the turn of the century, enlightened America leaders, from the great conservationist John Muir to Gifford Pinchot and Theodore Roosevelt, among others, contributed to the idea of a National Forest. With little fanfare, exactly 100 years ago as this introduction is being written, Congress passed a bill authorizing the president to designate Forest Reserves on public lands.

In 1897, Congress passed the Organic Administration Act, establishing administrative authority for management of those new reserves. Legislation followed which added more definition to these federal reserves and their purpose, but it was the appointment of Pinchot in 1898 as the head of the new Department of Forestry, initially under the Department of Interior, that set the direction of forest management on public lands.

Pinchot's classic, *Breaking New Ground*, traces these and other significant stages in the development of the U.S. Forest Service, as we know it now. In 1905, the new federal Forest Service was transferred to the U.S. Department of Agriculture, with Pinchot as its first chief. He provided powerful leadership, implementing and expanding policies which reflected his "conservation" and forest management credo, choosing for the agency the goal of managing the nation's National Forests for "the greatest good for the greatest number for the longest period." In time however, it became clear that Pinchot's initial ideas linking "conservation" of public forests to timber production and other wise "uses" were open to interpretation.

Enter John Muir, Aldo Leopold, and the wilderness movement. In 1924, Leopold's new concept of wilderness preserves or set-asides was adopted as an administrative policy by the young U.S. Forest Service. Leopold, an assistant forester in the Southwest, proposed the first wilderness area for the Gila National Forest in New Mexico, while the great naturalist, Muir, is forever linked with the creation of Yosemite National Park in California.

Today the concept of preserving wilderness is embraced by millions of Americans as an enlightened principle that ranks alongside democracy, civil rights, and freedom as a fundamental tenet of our society. But to those who still see the West as an untamed empire crying out for exploitation, wilderness is a dirty word.

Many forest industry leaders and forest professionals with state and federal agencies make a sharp distinction between conservation and preservation. These analysts often describe diehard wilderness advocates as "romantic" and inflexible preservationists. Perhaps the late Edward Abbey, the magnificently irreverent and highly regarded author (*The Monkey Wrench Gang* and *Desert Solitaire*) and current Earth First!ers wouldn't take offense at that.

In any case, by the 1980s recreational use of public lands had became a national priority. Hunting, fishing, camping, hiking, skiing and the seductive seclusion offered by over 90 million acres of designated wilderness, are today vital to the American psyche.

The U.S. Bureau of Land Management (BLM), created by the consolidation of the U.S. Grazing Service and the General Land Office in 1946 to manage millions of acres of semi-arid and desert land in the American west, has also been forced to factor-in recreation as a principal use on the lands it manages.

BLM land was generally the west's leftovers after the National Forests boundaries were drawn—often desolate, unfriendly, treeless land, characterized by one Colorado rancher as scraggly range capable of supporting nothing but "rocks and lizards." By the 1960s some of the most awesome of BLM's holdings were being set aside as the great national parks in eastern Utah that we know as Canyonlands and Arches. So much for rocks and lizards.

As the West changed character, so has the nation's understanding of its natural values. National legislation has attempted to set management rules for public lands which protect those values. Traditional industries based on consumption of natural resources, particularly mining and ranching as well as timbering, have been the life blood of the west's high, dry regions—a zone that author Joel Garreau (*The Nine Nations of*

North America) calls "The Empty Quarter."

Coupled with a greatly increased market for timber from western forests after World War II, conflicts have steadily accelerated over how public lands should be used (or not used) and who should use them. Both timber industry leaders and their critics, from foresters to economists and conservationists, predict that the final battle over what remains of the great forests of the American West will take place in this decade. The rhetoric is predictably brisk.

As the National Forest System celebrates its 100th anniversary in 1991, it is highly appropriate to look into timber management policies on federal lands. This book centers its attention on the National Forests of the American West. Beginning in the 1980s, National Forest timber policy issues hit the front pages of national publications from Time and Newsweek to the New York Times.

Those who cared about National Forests in the American West in the last decade of the 20th Century had more than timber policies to worry about. Grazing, mining, and oil and mineral developments were bumping up against a new public lands constituency—more and more these people were urbanites who looked to public parks, forests, wilderness and special reserves for recreation, as a sanctuary, and for those special benefits—the sense of awe and of discovery—that only unspoiled wild land can provide.

The rise of the environmental movement, starting in the 1970s, has focused new attention on the importance of managing public lands to protect water and air quality, as well as protection of the nation's treasured landscapes. Many citizens no longer see the Forest Service as the trusted stewards of the public land. Forest Service leaders acknowledge that timber policies are at the heart of this debate over good stewardship. In fact, until recently the Forest Service was the most highly respected of all the federal agencies. But today Forest Service leaders publicly concede that this proud image is now seriously tarnished.

Some forest management professionals advise us that for most of this century critics have periodically predicted American would be crippled by a "timber famine." This dire forecast hasn't come true. Timber supplies (two thirds domestic, one third Canadian) have so far been quite adequate to meet the country's hearty appetite for wood and wood products. This lack of a timber shortage, according to these pro-logging forest managers, shows "we must have been doing something right." Others vigorously disagree, arguing that timber is indeed running out and that the nation's forests are increasingly being trashed. And these voices are growing. The public uproar over timber policies on National Forests can now be heard from coast to coast.

But most of us shake our heads and wonder aloud how to make sense of the charges and counter charges in the national debate over federal forest management. Where should citizens who are concerned about National Forest timber policies go for factual information? The forest science community itself is carrying on a furious debate over every facet of timber management. Forest management is recognized by nearly everyone now as a global issue.

The environmentalists, the "Greens," provide an important and compelling point of view, which, in turn, is regularly attacked by those whose conclusions are shaped by a different set of values. Economists tote up figures to support "facts" presented by every side. The timber industry, powerful and important, sees itself as a basic ingredient in the American economic mix.

It is clear that members of Congress have had, and will have, the final word on National Forest timber management policies for decades to come. These policies are political issues. They will be decided in a political arena; yet they will affect what the West's National Forests will look like for generations.

During the course of my research for this book, timber policy experts everywhere—from universities, the industry, the Forest Service, and conservation groups—talked to me about National

Forest issues in terms of "values" and "changing values." At first I found these words off-putting. They sounded bureaucratic and condescending.

"Values" also seemed to signify money—economic values. Many people I talked to do, in fact, measure the value of forests solely by the board foot. Others in industry and government, however, were saying that a growing number of citizens now believed that forests were highly valuable for a whole host of reasons other than producing commodities—not just for lumber, minerals, oil or grass for livestock. More and more Americans "value" National Forests for recreation—hunting, fishing, camping, and what's called the "non-consumptive" wildlife experience (watching and photographing the forest's creatures).

I came to understand that in this context "values" and "changing values" referred very broadly to how the American West is changing—what its place in the global scheme of things will be. These changes add up to what many are calling "The New West."

In the 1980s, America's western timber industry understood very well what was ahead. Old-growth timber was running out—1000-year-old trees don't come along every day. The Northwest, the American West's big timber-producing region, was at the eye of this timber-supply storm. But, for the most part, the average citizen had little idea that all other western states—except Nevada with virtually no commercial timber industry— faced the same forest issues. It was just a matter of scale. Citizens in Arizona and New Mexico "valued" their nearby National Forests for exactly the same reasons as their counterparts in Montana or Oregon or California. Timber in those states was falling at an alarming rate, as well.

The timber industry, its goals and purposes clear, understood perfectly what could be done in a changing world and a changing forest. Changing technology meant lumber mills that could produce almost twice as much usable wood—planks, chips, pulp, whatever—from a single tree. Mechanization in the woods brought hot-shot chainsaws and the *feller-buncher.* Looking like a second-cousin to a lunar lander, this mobile machine has powerful arms that grapple and clearcut clusters of trees and undergrowth and transport the bunched material to a central loading point. Like hay-balers and other modern agricultural harvest equipment, feller-bunchers, which can replace four loggers, speed "harvesting" and eliminate jobs.

But when questioned, industry leaders, and a significant number of USFS timber managers I talked to, say it's the American appetite for wood products—from low-cost housing to the posh, second-home market, to a never-ending supply of high quality paper products—that is responsible for accelerating timber harvesting both in the American West and globally.

Inevitably, accelerated timber harvesting involves clearcutting, a practice that has become an integral part of managing National Forests as tree farms. High "fiber" production, for everything from paper to planks, is the goal. Forestry scientists (silviculturalists) are developing hybrid trees, "super trees" that will grow bigger and faster than native species. As native, old-growth forests are cut, forest scientists and timber managers put their heads together to decide what kinds of commercially valuable trees to replant.

Most timber professionals in both the Forest Service and private industry vigorously defend clearcutting, accusing environmentalists of shortsighted and naively unscientific reactions to this admittedly ugly practice. Some timber industry supporter go so far as to claim that environmentalists are really to blame for blatant clearcutting in recent years along scenic highways. They say the specter of increased government regulation over forest practices, both on private and on publicly-owned timberland, has simply forced timber industry managers to accelerating their clearcutting into more visible areas.

Clearcutting has everything to do with tree farming or "plantation forestry." Farmers clear the land, plant a crop, cultivate it, and harvest it. When producing timber became the prime activity of the U.S. Forest Service, forestry departments in American universities soon responded by backing the formerly despised practice of clearcutting. One older forester I talked to mused about the change, saying that when he was a young forestry student the phrase "clearcut and burn" had been a sarcastic slam about shoddy forestry practices.

In addition to its focus on clearcutting, the current public forest debate swirls around such issues as the massive Forest Service road-building program (which of course, is part of the agency's timber program) and whether to open up millions of acres of roadless National Forest timberland (including some ancient or old-growth forests) to logging. Also under fire is the widespread practice of selling federal timber below cost to help subsidize "timber dependent" communities dotting the rural American West.

The rise of timber exports to Japan and other Pacific Rim countries has added a new and incendiary issue to this timber-policy debate. Federal laws restrict the export of raw or "round," unprocessed logs cut on National Forests. But no one seriously disputes the fact that the log export trade has had a profound affect on western timber supplies, on federal timberlands and privately owned forests as well. The public must decide how much federal timber it is willing to provide for a timber industry which sends one of every four logs cut in the Northwest overseas.

Prime private timberland in the West is also being converted to real estate development—often subdivisions—at a fast pace. In the eastern and southern U.S., the timber industry has already sold off much of its own first class forest land.

Western forest-products industry leaders are also nervous about holding onto their share of the building materials market. If consumers find wood products too scarce or too costly, they will turn to alternative building materials. Once the timber industry loses its present market share, it will be very tough to win it back, industry forecasters warn.

Threatened with new and stricter controls on where and how

timber can be cut, on both private and public land, the timber
industry in the 1980s and early 1990s has tried to stay one jump
ahead. Timber managers have lined up timber sales well in
advance. The tempo of logging in the Northwest has hit high
gear in hopes of cutting great old-growth stands that might later
be set aside as habitat for the infamous northern spotted owl, the
benign, but now officially "threatened" forest bird that has come
to symbolize the debate over balanced forest management. Even
in Southwestern Colorado, in the summer of 1991, old-growth
conifer stands on the San Juan National Forest were falling at the
rate of 30 trees every 45 minutes.

On the 100th anniversary of the National Forest System, this
frenzy of logging activity gives new and urgent meaning to the
phrase "cut and run." This epithet was once used to describe early
American timber operators who ruined one forest, then quickly
moved on to another. Sadly, this description may be truer than
ever.

Part I
WESTERN TIMBER BASICS

CHAPTER ONE

Will There Be Enough Timber in the West?

A war of words is raging over timber management policies on public lands in the West. It centers around future timber supplies and the huge western timber industry that feeds on public forests. Currently, the National Forest's annual cut is pegged at 11 *billion* board feet—*nearly double the volume targeted 10 years ago!* Much of that will come from the American West. ("Annual cut," incidentally, is a basic term used in this timber war. So are "even-flow" and "sustained yield," once hallowed forest-management principles that seem, for now at least, to be mothballed.)

From scientists to elected representatives to industry officials to environmental groups, western leaders speak of a crisis in U.S. Forest Service timber management policies. Some are fighting fiercely to save what remains of the American West's ancient forests; others argue in support of the industry's view that timber supplies should last almost indefinitely.

Wood, as the industry is fond of saying, is America's favorite building material and the Forest Service, historically, has committed itself to supplying huge amounts of National Forest timber for an industry that is as old as time. Or almost. What forest management policies, we can ask, will insure a continuous supply of domestic wood for untold decades to come?

The range of views is startling.

Western timber industry spokesmen proclaim, reassuringly,

that at present logging rates timber supplies in the U.S. are in fine shape. Not so, say environmentalists, who point to evidence that the forest products industry has pushed the Forest Service into selling far more public timber than its forests can reproduce. They argue that the principle of the *even-flow* of forest timber to provide a *sustained-yield* has been scrapped for fast profits and global markets. (Today, timber supplies and timber prices are influenced as much by international as by domestic factors.) Traditional forestry, still steeped in the can-do attitude of the frontier West, tells us that science has conquered the multiple mysteries of growing great forests. Professionals foresters assert that it is possible to "manipulate" a forest to produce any desirable feature—wildlife habitat, more water, "merchantable" timber or whatever. Others vigorously maintain that global warming, acid rain and polluted air, among other factors, may make all those arguments moot.

Entering the 1990s, however, the Western Woods Products Association in Portland says, charitably, that it is "mostly well-meaning people who mistakenly believe America's forests are endangered." The Association's current *Timber for Products – Action Kit* (with accompanying video) asserts: "In the American West alone, right now there is more than 1.36 trillion board feet of timber. That is a forest reserve so immense" that if it were all turned into lumber products, it would build homes "at the rate of 1 million per year for the next 160 years." And, they add, because those immense forests are, in the purest sense, naturally renewable, "that forest could continue to hold 1.36 trillion board feet."

The Association's informational "kit" is, in fact, a call for political action to oppose National Forest timber management plans that could result in federal timber harvest reductions "equal to more than four billion board feet of western timber each year." And while it doesn't claim to tell the whole story, the Association's pitch clearly focuses on impending political decisions which threaten the industry's timber supply.

"There is no timber supply crisis at this moment," Western Wood Products leaders warn. "But there is a timber supply time-bomb ticking, ready to go off sometime in the 1990s. That's when federal forest plan reductions will strike ... if we don't do something about it." The Association adds reassuringly: "America can have its outdoor recreation, timber, income for the treasury and an array of other benefits all by keeping forest lands in production for products." In this best of all worlds, America has conquered its environment, tamed its forests, preserved its mythical Paul Bunyons, and is assured of a never-ending supply of beautiful wood to grace the homes of its happy, prosperous families.

But other industry voices are more cautious. William Dean, a senior editor for Random Lengths Publications, Inc. of Eugene Oregon, warns that the supply of sawlogs is shrinking and that "the 1990s will require a difficult adjustment to a changing timber base." Random Lengths is a well regarded, 50-year-old lumber and plywood market reporting service that tracks the marketing of wood products produced in North America and publishes reports on forest products markets, including an analysis of conditions affecting them.

In a special report titled: "The 1990s—The Final Decade: Boom or Bust For Wood Products?" Dean offers significant insights for timber planners in the 1990s. And while Dean does not side with industry critics on questions such as timber harvest limits on the National Forest, he does warn about trouble ahead for the forest products industry.

"The industry in the Northwest was founded on the use of large old growth logs," and while it is making the transition to smaller logs, "the industry is anxious to continue logging old growth as long as it lasts," Dean reports. The supply, he notes, is variously estimated from 20 to 50 years at present rates of logging. Old-growth timber stands in the Northwest have become a major public issue—a national *cause célèbre*, thanks to the northern spotted owl. Loggers in the Northwest see harvesting old-growth timber as their birthright; but public outcry has put the future harvest levels in old-growth forests (also described as "ancient" or "native" forests) in doubt.

The rest of the West, meanwhile, is discovering that old-growth stands are also on the federal auction block nearly everywhere. In high and dry New Mexico, for example, the wood products industry has developed a hot new export market for what used to be a low-value tree, Englemann spruce. The Japanese, it turns out, love the pale, good-looks of Englemann spruce, as it reminds them of traditional woods no longer available to today's Japanese home-builders. These towering giants are found across the southern Rockies, in New Mexico's steep mountain canyons, and in Colorado's dark green high country.

But the current debate over future western timber supplies has indeed tended to focus on the Northwest because, like the South, this region is so conducive to tree farming. Future timber supplies in the Northwest, Dean and his publication, Random Lengths, acknowledge, have been compromised by recent premature logging of "juvenile" second-growth stands that hadn't reached their optimum size and volume. While this has taken place on thousands of acres of privately-owned commercial forestland, it has nonetheless created intense pressure to increase National Forest harvests to keep the industry supplied.

Kirk Ewart, a well-known timber industry spokesman and Boise Cascade corporate official in Boise, Idaho, denies the charge that, following World War II, the timber industry scurrilously "raped the land." This is a powerful phrase and it has become generic to the fight over western forests. "Did we overcut on a sustained yield basis? Yes, we did," Ewart explains. But this dramatic rise in timber harvest on commercial timberland was a response to a national need—houses for returning war veterans—and was part and parcel of a booming post-war economy.

If the timber industry hadn't responded to the nation's need by overcutting its private forests, the U.S. Forest Service itself would have been obliged to "accelerate the harvest" (a term Ewart vastly prefers to "overcutting") on the public's own forestland. Ewart sounds a patriotic note when he expresses these ideas. He wants to convey the notion that the timber and wood products industry is acting in the national interest. "Now," Ewart says, "it's the Forest Service's turn" to provide the sawtimber American home builders demand.

For their part, National Forest policymakers also see problems ahead. In a formal statement before a Congressional subcommittee in the spring of 1990, Forest Service Chief F. Dale Robertson told House members that, while long-term timber supplies "appear to be in good shape....there exists a serious shortage of softwood sawtimber in the mature age classes over the next 20 years or so." A shortage of mature timber on many private commercial lands exists "because we looked to these lands in the past to meet our growing needs for timber. The National Forests "now have nearly half of the [the nation's] standing softwood sawtimber," and as a result the "age-class imbalance on other lands greatly enhances the value of the National Forest softwood sawtimber..."

Chief Robertson said that, in the coming decade, the Forest Service faces perhaps its most difficult dilemma: that of balancing timber management with the other "roles we should be fulfilling." These other roles involve recreation, wildlife and water; as well as managing for ecological values like biodiversity; and preserving unique assets such as old growth and rare plant and animal species.

Timber industry leaders bristle at such talk. So, too, do many foresters who support "traditional forestry." They generally see stands of old uncut trees as "decadent" forests that testify to a colossal waste—a waste of thousands of acres of public land which could (and should, they say) be cut so they can produce a new crop of trees.

Over and over, timber-industry voices tell us that "the best forest is a managed forest." Frank Gladics of the National Forest Products Association, like some other trained foresters, is certain the public simply hasn't gotten the proper technical information to understand how forests live and die. Traditional foresters grumble about public interference in forest management decisions best left to "professionals."

They tend to gloss over a whole litany of mounting public concerns about National Forest policy. And, increasingly, a growing number of professional foresters, educators and other experts who make up forestry's scientific community are saying that the Forest Service is so biased toward "commodity production" and the timber industry, that it literally can't see the forest for the trees. University of Northern Arizona Professor of Forestry Richard H. Behan says matter-of-factly that if the West keeps cutting its forests at the present rate, by the end of the decade there won't be enough left to argue about.

CLOSEUP
Jerry Franklin's New Forestry and Its Warning

Jerry F. Franklin, a University of Washington ecologist and researcher who has been called "the nation's foremost expert on ancient forests," is one of the most sobering voices in the forest debate. In scientific papers and speeches at conferences and symposiums, Dr. Franklin trumpets the alarm about global climate changes and how these changes may affect the way trees grow.

"Global change is a significant issue we tend to ignore," Dr. Franklin writes, "reflecting our tendency to view forests and forest environments as immutable. They are not! Global warming is occurring and the only real argument among scientists is how much and how fast."

He points out that past fluctuations in climate have caused "profound changes" in the northwest's vegetation, and these climate changes were much smaller than those projected in the next 40 years. "For example, the maximum temperatures experienced during this interglacial period were only two degrees warmer than those at present, yet lowland areas of the Pacific Northwest were apparently more sparsely forested than at present."

Scientists are now predicting temperatures for that region which will be two to five degrees Celsius higher than they were at the beginning of this decade. Equally troubling is the fact that additional rainfall isn't expected to accompany this rise in temperature. "Increased catastrophic disturbances are almost a certainty," Dr. Franklin observes, if such predicted global changes occur.

Dr. Franklin and his forestry colleagues have written: "Perhaps the most profound effects of global climatic change will be on disturbance regimes—frequency, intensity, scale, and locale of wildfire, wind and rain storms, and the outbreaks of pests and pathogens. In some cases, altered disturbance regimes will create a 'doubly whammy,' as the existing forests are destroyed and hotter, drier conditions make tree regeneration even more difficult.''

And Franklin's is not the only warning voice. Stephen Schneider, climatologist with the National Center for Atmospheric Research in Boulder, Colorado, points out that the theory of global warming is based on strong scientific evidence which suggests "that the injection of invisible greenhouse gases is likely to cause unambiguous global-scale warming by around 2000 and create unprecedented climatic change sometime in the 21st century." While the media, Schneider says, has hungered for specifics—when and how much—and critics have protested that the theory is too vague to justify serious counter-action now, scientists agree climate changes lie ahead.

Jerry Franklin's other "New Forestry" views, especially on such practices as clearcutting and the value of pristine wilderness preservation, do not please everyone. But he and his team of researchers at the U.S. Forest Service Pacific Northwest Research Station, are widely recognized as leaders in the field of ecosystem studies. These studies are producing revolutionary new evidence of the critical need to manage forests as a whole ecologically-interdependent system. "Already we are learning that parts of the forests that we have never considered seriously [from tiny fungi to downed and rotting timber] are proving significant, even essential to ecosystem functioning. And through this new information, we are finally recognizing the many fallacies and weaknesses in our traditional forestry dogma."

The importance of saving what we are beginning to recognize as old-growth forests is a whole new concept. On a 1990 field trip across Colorado's Grand Mesa National Forest, Wayne Shepperd, a Forest Service researcher, told me: "We're plowing new ground. For research and management this [concern with old-growth forests] is a new direction."

Federal forest management, focused sharply in recent decades on high production and fast profits for timber industry constituents, has taken on the style of corporate farming. While it's possible to argue that corporate-style tree farms may be appropriate for industry-owned commercial forest land, scientists and an increasing number of enlightened federal foresters are calling for a halt to over-simplified, single-species tree-farming on National Forests in the West. Can long-term site productivity on these so-called "even-age" tree plantations be maintained? Franklin has his doubts. While mimicking intensive agriculture, silviculturalists "have been wondering how far the system can be pushed." Their answer has been, "Don't worry—we can fix it later."

Given unknowns like global warming and what Franklin calls "our woefully inadequate knowledge of forest ecosystems, we must ask ourselves: have we been proceeding prudently? The answer, inescapably, is no."

CHAPTER TWO

The Environmental Opposition

Dick Whitmore doesn't have a good word to say about Lighthawk, a small conservation-minded group of pilots who take politicians, civic leaders and other decision-makers aloft for a bird's eye view of the West's massive clearcuts and other environment horrors. "The Wings of Conservation," as Lighthawk calls itself, and its eye-witness sky tours, have been highly effective in the political battle over forest management. But to timber-industry honchos like Whitmore, these pilots and their flying machines are just one more maddening aspect of the growing environmental opposition—an opposition they accuse of unfair tactics, irrational bias and unrealistic expectations.

I found Dick Whitmore in his office in Bellingham, Washington one fall morning just as the sun was breaking through the remnants of the first big rain of the coming Northwest winter. Whitmore heads Mt. Baker Plywood Inc., a bustling, 40-year-old, employee-owned company that manufactures hardwood plywood. Railroad tracks run right by the company's front office door. Its yards and clusters of mostly windowless industrial structures back up to Bellingham Bay, in the far northwestern corner of Washington state, a region of green and misty rainforests.

Whitmore is a big genial man in chinos and a muted plaid shirt, who looks as if he'd be entirely comfortable in the woods, or anywhere else. He confesses, as we talk well into his lunch hour,

that he can happily spend hours discussing timber issues. Like so
many others I talked to during my quest, Whitmore is a trained
forester. His career began with a seven-year stint in U.S. Forest
Service. Then, starting in 1980, he spent six years in Central
America where he was involved in logging and exporting
hardwood. To understand all sides of the timber and forest
products issue, Whitmore, who is perhaps in his mid-40s, says
confidently, "You have to look at the world—the big picture."

He's also dead sure environmentalists and other ecosystem
worriers aren't really calling for better management of National
Forests, but want "non-management," instead. He scoffs at the
idea that the Northwest is losing wildlife. ("Critters," we agreed, is
a satisfactory term for both the vertebrates and the invertebrates
conservationists believe are threatened.) Whitmore says: "I don't
think we're losing species." He sees traps which tell him "they're
still trapping pine marten." Whitmore's voice gains intensity.
"And the pileated woodpecker *lives* right here in Bellingham," he
says, shaking his head and leaning back in his chair for a quick
upward roll-of-the eyes. Both the pine marten, a tiny fur-bearing
mink-like mammal and this forest-dwelling woodpecker are
frequently cited as woodland species that may be declining.
(Biologists say, although pine martens and goshawks, for
example, are used by the Forest Service as indicator species,
inventories and important on-the-ground monitoring is lacking.
As a result, USFS guesswork often substitutes for hard data about
habitat requirements.)

Whitmore says his examples are clear proof that there is "no
basis" for claims by many wildlife biologists that these, and other
forest critters, are threatened by loss of habitat. He knows a few
biologists who think the way he does; the rest he dubs "biostitues."
(He pronounces his newly minted word "by-ost-i-tute," and
definitely relishes this little joke.) Still he ultimately concludes
that more money should be spent on scientific inquiry and less "in
courts and in Congress" arguing about management practices on
the National Forest.

Whitmore, like his environmental counterparts, is clearly an experienced combatant. His answers come like tanks in a military parade—manned by a waving, smiling trooper, they roll out without a hitch. "What we have here is a certain group of people who have an aversion to forest management or harvesting timber. They don't like it and they want to see it stop. It doesn't matter if it's federal land or state land or private land; and they'll use any ways or means to do it.... We see it daily.... We don't see this death and destruction that some of these Johnny-come-latelys are talking about."

Whitmore says the Forest Service is now "dysfunctional," paralyzed by environmental politics. In the face of this political opposition, Forest Service Chief Dale Robertson, whom Whitmore once worked for, is "playing dead." Whitmore allows that "we have overcut some here," but he blames that on environmental groups who "locked up" timber on public land through timber sale appeals and court action. And today he's absolutely incensed over a short film by Lighthawk. "That thing is so full of lies and innuendoes and no way of proving what you're looking at—it's ridiculous." There's something basically unfair, he suggests, about Lighthawk's overflights.

Whitmore's views on environmentalists—the opposition—are typical of the entire "timber community," the forest industry plus a number of hard-headed Forest Service types as well. And the themes he touches on are recurrent elements in every forest debate.

Fairness, for example, is a word fired across many a battle line in what one writer calls this "War in the Woods." In my talks about western forest management issues with people across the spectrum, the question of fairness came up as consistently as the sunrise. Each side accuses the other of using unfair tactics, distorted figures, and information that runs from inaccurate to blatantly unscientific. Every hallowed symbol has been used—from the wholesome, hardworking logging family to the sacred, cathedral-like qualities of California's shrinking redwood forests. Still, despite years of verbal sparring, insults and indignation, by the 1990s neither side, environmentalists nor the industry and its allies, had successfully won (and held) the moral high ground.

I was surprised to find that each faction in this fight generally claims that it is poor and the other side rich.

In recent years, surely one of the poorest and most ragtag of the groups, and easily the most notorious, has been *Earth First!*, a left-handed off-shoot, led by defectors from the highly circumspect *Sierra Club* and *The Wilderness Society. Earth First!'s* headline-grabbing guerrilla tactics and acts of "eco-terrorism," such as tree-spiking, along with its bold rhetoric, have outfoxed the timber industry's more polished media campaigns and outraged many traditional westerners, including some Forest Service officials. (Tree-spiking, not necessarily endorsed by many EarthFirst!ers, involves driving spikes into old-growth trees to snarl chainsaws.)

However, one USFS staffer I talked to, a wildlife biologist with close to 20 years in the Service, had no trouble understanding the frustration of people like Dave Foreman, former Wilderness Society staff member who ultimately gave up on the more gentlemanly forms of environmental combat to help found *Earth First!* "I don't blame them [the Earth First!ers]," this biologist told me on an early summer day in Colorado as we picked our way over downed timber in a patch of fine old Englemann spruce and alpine fir.

Twenty years ago, this man had been part of the research team that sounded the first warning about the decline of the northern spotted owl, an "indicator species" which pointed to the ecological decline of the ancient forests of the Northwest. The USFS and other government agencies buried this telling information, and for the next two decades chose instead to accelerate clearcutting of the great old-growth forests in Washington and Oregon. This fact undermines the timber industry's contention that forest management decisions should be based on science. No wonder serious-minded forest professionals like this biologist can feel sympathetic to the most radical eco-protest groups.

While more mainstream environmental groups may distance themselves from their notorious *Earth First!* cousins, their words are no less combative. As the political stakes rise, so does the rhetoric opposing sides use to describe the issues, and each other. Like most political battles, this one has its special twists. Over and over we hear and see tell-tale signs of a *class war.* Timber industry spokesmen—like Frank Gladics, a top staffer with the National Timber Products Association in Washington D.C.—accuse environmental groups of spewing "propaganda," of over-simplifying the issues in order to draw support from a vast pool of rich and innocent city dwellers. Leading voices in the conservation movement reply that the industry's political dialogue amounts to everything from petty "sloganeering" to wholesale distortion of the facts.

The near century-old *Sierra Club,* for example, charges that the U.S. Forest Service has been on a $2 billion "decades-long road-building spree" and that it has plans for 40,000 miles more during the 1990s. This means "the timber corporations are reaping a subsidy of over half a billion dollars annually," the *Sierra Club* claims in a fund-raising pitch. Not so, says the Forest Service and the industry. These roads provide broad public benefits and therefore fulfill the agency's multiple use mandate.

Logging communities in the Northwest are hardcore centers of anti-preservationist sentiments. The word there is: "Don't wear any Sierra Club buttons in the bars." Taking their cue from the beleaguered western sheep industry's bumper-sticker slogan: "Eat Lamb—A Million Coyotes Can't Be Wrong," Northwest timber-cutters flag their pickup bumpers with the message: "Eat a Spotted Owl—Save a Logger's Job."

Workers fighting for their jobs are primed to think of environmentalists as the over-educated, non-working elite. Feelings among the so-called "working class" are so strong that workers in other industries (like fishermen), by way of introduction, state disdainfully: "I'm not one of those tree-huggers."

Gladics characterizes wilderness and preservation as "white, upper-class issues." He observes that while hunters were once in the front ranks of those who took a collective stand on management policies involving wildlife and public lands, today national environmental groups with different agendas have eclipsed the hunting lobby. The AARP generation *(American Association of Retired Persons)* thinks wilderness is a walk from their "Winnebago to the campground outhouse."

It's hard to tell precisely when such views switch from demographic observations to social or economic class baiting. But there are plenty of barbs to go around. Backpackers and other recreationists are often pictured as snobbish, self-centered, non-producers who oppose Forest Service road building programs that would provide access to many more acres of public land which is now inaccessible to the less hardy majority. Critics of the USFS, of course, reply that the Forest Service's road-building binge is tied to the agency's timber bias.

*Earth First!*ers, however, are trying to reach across presumed class barriers by using the log-export issue to forge new links with lumber mill workers who are losing jobs because the industry is exporting "round" or unprocessed logs to Japan. In 1989, the U.S. shipped nearly 1.5 billion board feet of timber to Japan, about 2 million board feet more than the previous year. The U.S. exports a total of more than 3 billion board feet of wood, but Japan is by far this country's biggest overseas customer.

"Stop Job Exports'" and "USA and Japan: Stop the War on Nature," banners proclaimed during a 1989 *Earth First!* "action" protesting log exports. The timber industry itself is so divided on the matter of exports and this issue is so hot that timber industry lobbyists simply dance around its fire.

Sometimes the rhetoric drowns out the arguments. "Arrogant and high-handed" are terms one small mill operator in the Northwest uses for both sides, preservationists and wilderness-types as well as the big-timber corporations, caustically lumped together as "Big Timber."

In the American West the environmental movement's actual political clout varies from state to state. But by the 1990s, environmental groups had developed a distinctly layered look. On the top layer are the big national groups: the *National Audubon Society*, the *National Wildlife Federation*, along with the *Sierra Club*, the *Wilderness Society*, *Defenders of Wildlife* and literally scores of others. Sharing national ranking are national sportmen's groups such as *Trout Unlimited*, plus *The National Resources Defense Fund*, the *Environmental Defense Fund* and the *Sierra Club Legal Fund*, all organizations which specialize in legal and legislative action.

On the bottom tier are the grassroots groups. This strong new force in resource conservation politics—the local grassroots group—first appeared in the 1970s. In just about every western state, tags such as "Alliance," "Save" and "Friends of" identify local citizens' organizations built around the relentless watchdogging of a specific place. In eastern Wyoming it's *Friends of the Bow*, a group fighting for reforms on the Medicine Bow National Forest. California's *Save the Redwoods League* and the *Kern Valley Wildlife Association* both monitor what remains of the giant sequoias in the Sequoia National Forest. And today there are similar groups active in every western state.

Sometimes conservation organizations function simultaneously on the national and grassroots levels. Over a Saturday morning breakfast at Arliss's, a pleasant eatery in Bellingham, Washington, David Schmalz, painting contractor and environmental activist, talked to me enthusiastically about *Audubon's* local "Adopt-a-Forest" program. Schmaltz's group monitors the nearby 1.8 million acre Mt. Baker-Snoqualmie National Forest (the same forest that plywood manufacturer Whitmore is concerned about, from a very different point of view). *Audubon*, one of this nation's oldest conservation groups, announced in the summer of 1991 that it was restyling its image—considered outdated and fusty— to meet the challenges of the new decade.

In the spectrum of conservation groups, *The Nature Conservancy*, an international organization with offices and a professional staff in each state in the U.S., is in a class all its own. The richest of the lot, *The Conservancy* single-mindedly searches out and buys one-of-a-kind tracts of land to help preserve the planet's "natural diversity"— the plants, animals and ecosystems special to a threatened place. And *The Nature Conservancy*, non-confrontational and quite at home in Fortune 500 boardrooms, successfully taps into corporate millions to buy and preserve the 5.5 million acres it now protects in North America.

Midway between local and national groups, dozens of regional coalitions, umbrella groups, and state-wide organizations in the West perform a variety of mid-level tasks, often acting as coordinator, and/or moderator in the complex multi-player game of environmental politics. This level includes groups such as the *Idaho Conservation League* and the *Wyoming Outdoor Council*, the Spokane-based *Inland Empire Public Lands Council*, and the *Colorado Environmental Coalition*.

The *Southern Utah Wilderness Alliance* had few forest issues on its agenda during the 1980s, but is widely respected for the clout it's developed in desert and canyonlands issues. SUWA will probably be looking at more timber issues in the '90s; Utah state forester Gary Cornell says Louisiana-Pacific is eying vast acres of aspen in the beautiful La Sal Mountains near Moab. (Forester Cornell by the way, like Mt. Baker Plywood's Whitmore, has little regard for most environmental groups.)

The *Western Organization of Resource Councils*, based in Billings, Montana, ties together local groups from the Dakotas, Idaho, Montana, Wyoming, and Colorado. In the Northwest, *The Native Forest Council*, of Eugene, Oregon, works energetically to save the last of the nation's native, virgin forests wherever they exist. *Save America's Forests*, a Washington D.C. organization, is a coalition of national forest reform interests, and specializes in tracking legislation pertinent to this movement.

According to Charles "Chuck" Keegan, who directs forest industry research at the University of Montana's School of Business, Montana's forest products industry doesn't have an easy time of it because "environmental groups are so effective in this state." The Bozeman-based *Greater Yellowstone Coalition*, for example, is a powerful force watchdogging logging and other environmental concerns on the five National Forests and two National Parks in what they call the "Greater Yellowstone Ecosystem." These forests—the Beaverhead and the Targhee in Idaho, the Gallatin in Montana, the Shoshone and the Bridger-Teton in Wyoming—have for decades supported major logging industries in all three states. Opponents of the *Coalition* reserve a special kind of venom for this group of environmental warriors who regularly take on the industry in public debates.

The *Oregon Natural Resources Council* lists 60 member-organizations within its fold and is considered Oregon's leading environmental voice. In a state where timber is still called king, Andy Kerr, the Council's conservation director, is the Oregon timber industry's number one enemy. Kerr, a rogue knight, has boldly and successfully attacked Oregon's King Timber through the USFS timber sale appeals process, creating what Time magazine called "a legal logjam" in unresolved timber sale cases. Nevertheless, most forest reform leaders think environmentalists are still the underdogs in the fight to save more of Oregon's forests and watersheds. Few that I talked to in almost two years of interviews for this book were optimistic for the short term. During the early 1990s, they all concluded, ancient trees would keep falling at an alarming rate—185 acres of irreplaceable old-growth forest each day, according to the *Native Forest Council*. "America's remaining virgin forests, some of which are the last temperate rain forests on earth, are concentrated on publicly-owned lands entrusted by the citizens of this nation to the care of our government," the Council warns. And they're going fast.

Women's organizations, too, have staked out their own environmental territory. In Montana, I discovered a Livingstonbased group called *Women in Timber* which backs timber workers and logging communities. In Cedar City, Utah, a fledgling organization conceived by Susan Pixier and several like-minded outdoor-types calls itself *Great Old Broads for Wilderness.*

While opposition to timbering-as-usual is stiffening all across the West, the battle for public and political support still had no clear winner as America entered the '90s. But the U.S. Forest Service lay bleeding on the battlefield for all to see. With its credibility under fire from every side, the Forest Service itself looked like a wounded dinosaur. Still, no one believes this bureaucracy will fail to survive. The question is simply how. And can it, or will it reform its traditional, and now controversial pro-timber policies and practices?

However, leaders from all three sides—the environmental organizations who fiercely oppose current timber management practices on public land, the timber industry itself, and the Forest Service—all agree on one thing: Congress and elected officials in each western state will continue to decide the fate of the West's great forests. Those decisions won't be made on either ecological or economic considerations alone; they will be made on the basis of potentially powerful political pressure—or lack of it— from the voters of America, both east and west.

CLOSEUP
Jack Pera, Born Again Activist

Environmental activists are not cast from a single mold. Some come to the environmental movement from a background in ecology or the natural sciences; others grow into the role naturally, out of their own life experiences. Like Jack Pera.

In Telluride, a mountain town full of newcomers, Jack Pera has the very decided distinction of being a third-generation native. This Southwestern Colorado community also knows something about natural resources. Once a booming, turn-of-the-century mining town tucked high in a gorgeous pocket of the San Juan

Mountains, Telluride is now a fast-growing ski resort that prides itself on historical preservation and brilliantly successful summer festivals like the internationally acclaimed Telluride Film Festival.

Realtors, entrepreneurs and big money from both coasts, along with a few aging true believers from the '60s, give Telluride its present-day social texture. Among this social mix, "oldtimers" like Jack Pera and his wife, Davine, draw unique respect. The Peras have made a particularly graceful personal transition during Telluride's 20-year transformation from a fading mining town in 1970 to a dressed-for-success resort that markets its glorious scenery with the élan of a polished Park Avenue jewel thief. The Peras belong equally to Telluride's past, present and future.

Now 53, Jack Pera is a short, sturdy, straight-arrow of a man with slightly strawberry blonde hair, steady pale blue eyes and a quick, friendly manner. He is the grandson of a Finnish immigrant miner. Mining, like ranching and small-time logging, is a way of life in the Rockies. For decades, it was simply a given that boys growing up in mining communities would follow their fathers down into the mines. Jack's father, however, worked for the local power company, which may explain why during the 14 years Jack worked for the Idarado Mining Company, it was above ground, in Idarado's big warehouse and materials section. In the '50s, Jack also worked for the U.S. Forest Service on a massive spruce beetle control program in the nearby Lone Cone Mountain area.

Then in 1969 Jack and his wife Davine opened Timberline Hardware in an ancient store space on Telluride's main street that had been unoccupied for 40 years. The Pera's timing was excellent. Telluride was just beginning its rebirth as a mountain resort; and hardware store and resort prospered together. The sale of their business in 1980 (it's still the only hardware store in town) gave Jack and Davine the financial independence to chase other dreams. Jack, already a skilled outdoor photographer, edited a lifetime of inspired nature photography into a nightly multi-media program, "Mountain Splendor."

And it's here, in his passion for nature, that one discovers the

essential Jack Pera. In the same way that certain people are said
to be "born artists," Pera is a born naturalist. Like a territorial
animal, Pera has spent a lifetime roaming the forests, climbing
the mountainsides and photographing wildlife around Telluride.
"I have a deep affection for the natural world—not just the trees,
but the plants, the animals, the birds—I care about everything,"
Pera says. From caring to activism was, in Pera's case, but a short
step. Jack is also the founder/leader of a grassroots
environmental group that stopped a planned, National Forest
timber clearcut along Telluride's southern gateway. The success
of the drive to "Save Sheep Mountain" is absolutely unique in
Western Colorado, and most likely elsewhere in the West as well.

In 1987, a small public notice appeared in The Telluride Times,
the oldest of Telluride's two weekly newspapers, announcing a
U.S. Forest Service plan to log millions of board feet of old
growth spruce and fir on Sheep Mountain. This notice changed
Jack's life.

The southern route into Telluride takes travelers from the small
ranching community of Dolores, up the beautiful Dolores River
canyon into the heart of southwestern Colorado's most dramatic
mountain terrain. Colorado Highway 145 tops out at over 10,000
feet on Lizard Head Pass, a wind swept alpine opening dominated
by the silhouette of 13,188 ft. Sheep Mountain. Inexplicably,
U.S. Forest Service timber planners had no reservations about a
Sheep Mountain timber sale that would shave bald the face of this
massive, densely forested mountain. Dark and primitive
Englemann spruce marched up its flanks, providing, as they have
for decades, prime elk habitat and an established elk calving
ground.

For years, Pera had been watching timber activities creeping up
toward Rico, a moribund mining town on the other side of Lizard
Head Pass. The scars from a big logging program in the Rico area
some 25 years before, along with acres of a failed spruce
replanting effort in an even older fire-scarred area, had convinced
Pera that the Forest Service didn't have a handle on how to

successfully regenerate a spruce forest. Ultimately, in some areas, the Feds just gave up and replanted Douglas fir where, along the Molas Pass, Rico and Lizard Head routes, towering alpine spruce forests had formerly held their ground all the way to timberline.

Jack says it was almost an accident, glancing at the fateful Sheep Mountain timber sale notice. "This is horrible," he recalls thinking. He did two things. He went out on Telluride's main street with a petition. And then he went to see Jim Davidson, a Telluride area native and a longtime friend who also happened to be the editor and publisher of an upstart weekly, The Telluride Mountain Journal. It seemed as though all of Telluride wanted to sign Jack's petition opposing the Sheep Mountain logging plan. The few that Jack missed, standing in front of the post office on main street, were fired into action, sooner or later, by "all those wonderful stories Jim wrote."

Full of high-energy, politically savvy citizens, Telluride in the late '80s provided the perfect ideological soil for a hot local environmental contest. And the U.S. Forest Service, unwittingly, had become the perfect target. Its past failures lay strewn across the terrain from Telluride south to the New Mexico border. By mid-1988, the Sheep Mountain Alliance was a fearless and well-financed political force. Jack Pera, not surprisingly, was elected SMA's first president, a job he still held as the organization neared the end of its third year.

Soon after the the initial "Save Sheep Mountain" effort got underway, it was hard to find anybody in Telluride who'd admit to being pro-logging, and most certainly not for the sort of clearcutting the Forest Service planned for Sheep Mountain. People understood that loggers from the Dolores area might be hurt by the loss of a timber sale, but as Jack Pera explains now, timber operators must learn "they can't take everything."

Heavy lobbying by Sheep Mountain people followed a disheartening series of negotiating sessions between SMA and the Forest Service. So, SMA and people like Jack and Davine were almost caught off guard when, in August, 1989, the U.S. Forest

Service announced that the agency was withdrawing plans to log some 3.1 million board feet of old growth spruce and fir on Sheep Mountain. Moreover, for the next 10 years the agency would manage the region as a semi-primitive roadless area and wildlife habitat.

It was a stunning victory. But from the outset of the Sheep Mountain affair, it was clear that Jack Pera was emerging as a true, grassroots preservationist. Since then, he's devoted part of almost every day, studying issues, writing letters or talking on the phone, and educating himself about silviculture and forest management.

"You know, sometimes the Forest Service doesn't tell you the truth," Jack says, without the slightest reservation.

A few months earlier in Durango, Colorado, when I met with the National Forest Products Association's Frank Gladics, this Washington-based lobbyist knew all about Jack Pera. Gladics had worked with logging interests who were on the other side of the Sheep Mountain fight. The timber industry lobbyist suggests that Pera probably isn't a pure, dyed-in-the-wool environmentalist. Gladics thinks the main reason Pera came unglued over the Sheep Mountain timber harvest plan was "because it was in his own back yard."

Most people who know Jack would disagree.

By the beginning of the new decade, Jack was studying an out-of-control pine beetle infestation that was threatening to destroy thousands of acres of ponderosa pine forests on the Uncompahgre Plateau, a high tableland about 50 miles west of Telluride. "I want to learn about beetles.... I have to ask: is this abnormal?" He is also looking for evidence of old fires. Bug infestations and wildfires, of course, greatly affect forests, their health and ecological balance. And they play a large part in forest management programs.

Jack thinks a growing shortage of mature timber and the tangled economics of logging "must be addressed." But he has no doubt that with the U.S. Forest Service, "when it comes to logging, all other values go out the window."

Today, payments from the sale of his hardware store are running out, which means Jack will soon be looking for a regular job. What he'd really like to do is become a full-time environmental lobbyist, or a professional staffer for a group working to save Sheep Mountains everywhere. His wife Davine is concerned that this might not work out because Jack's forestry knowledge is largely self-taught. On the other hand, loggers and timber industry spokesmen would have a tough time tagging Jack as an eastern elitist.

Almost two years of timber policy research has shown me that the American West is full of Jack Peras, dedicated and informed people like him who are saying: "Whoa, the timber industry can't have it all."

CHAPTER THREE

The Stewards, Foresters and Forestry

Timber industry spokesmen—and they do mostly seem to be men—often identify themselves as foresters first and members of the timber industry second. Whether by longstanding design or for personal enhancement, forestry school graduates tend to take on a mantle of sanctity, as if they have joined some great and secret forest fraternity. This rather closed guild-like society of foresters tends to speak with authority for both the timber industry and the U.S. Forest Service. So, perhaps we shouldn't be so surprised by National Forest timber policies dominated by what the timber industry wants and needs—policies that frequently view the National Forests more as tree farms than shrinking national treasures

In *Timber and the Forest Service* author David Clary, the former chief historian for the Forest Service, describes the Forest Service as "a group of mere mortals who for a long time believed themselves to be burdened with a sacred mission... [national timber production]." This forestry mystique, both inside and outside the Forest Service, reverently promotes the image of an ancient and highly honorable priesthood. Whether foresters are speaking of the science of growing trees (called silviculture—the name itself sounds noble) or the infinite complexities of National Forest timber management processes and the timber "market," their tone is frequently that of teacher to pupil, wise adult to innocent child.

In fact, brotherhood, and a certain elitism within the Forest Service, is a matter of agency policy. In *Public Lands Policy* Paul Culhane points out that Forest Service personnel are by selection, training and patterns of socialization, a fraternal group. Frequent transfers of USFS personnel disrupt potential local ties and tend to replace them with built-in friendships within the service. Those who don't fit comfortably within this pattern of social and professional conformity drop out early.

But those who remain are fiercely loyal. A "voluntary conformity" takes over. Service policy becomes a way of life. Ninety percent of Forest Service line officers are trained foresters whose education has given them "a common professional value system," and a reverence for the service, its history and its lore. Over and over, foresters advise members of the public that forest management decisions should be left "to the professionals." These matters are "very complex, very difficult," they say solemnly. Like other professionals, foresters have also adopted a professional vocabulary designed to dazzle as well as intimidate the unknowing. Ancient priesthoods used similar techniques to keep the peasantry in subjugation.

Although public criticism of the Forest Service has accelerated sharply in the last 30 years as values have changed, at one time the local forest ranger's professional views were virtually gospel. During the first half of this century, the U.S. Forest Service enjoyed an unequaled reputation as a select corps of public servants, a reputation that culminated in the myth-like image of the "ranger on horseback," dedicated to a pure and noble cause.

The ranger wasn't the only myth-like figure on the Western landscape. In those early days of the National Forest system cowboys were our main mythical heros. And predictably, grazing interests dominated public land policies in the American West. Cattle ranchers were close personal confidantes of district rangers and their Forest supervisors. Then, after timberstands east of the Mississippi had been depleted or "slicked off," the timber industry moved west in earnest, and the logger became the next mythic figure in the Western landscape. Today loggers and cowboys, like miners, still have a role in the West's modern mythology of rugged frontier individualism And of course, grazing and timbering are still dominant uses on thousands of acres of public land.

The post-World War II era, however, saw a huge increase in the demand for lumber to build new homes for millions of returning war veterans. As logging accelerated and other uses like public recreation blossomed on the National Forests, the myth of the "ranger on horseback" began to wear thin. Managing National Forests to meet what was assumed to be America's grand post-war vision, set the stage for mounting public concerns about the future of federal forests.

But as citizen activists soon discovered, the Forest Service has always had "a timber bias," an unwritten doctrine which led to an enduring marriage between the timber industy and the National Forest system. The doctrine of "timber primacy" is described by one authority as the tenant that "timber is the chief product of the forest: all else is secondary: water, forage, wildlife, recreation and all the rest."

Forestry schools taught forest management for timber production. The Forest Service saw itself, first and foremost, as the manager of a vital commodity. (The American West alone holds some 58.8 million acres of National Forest timberland.) One disenchanted forestry student, who has since become an internationally recognized consultant on raising hybrid corn, says his forestry school studies carried a clear message: "Trees are dollars." And while this sort of indoctrination helped insure a close relationship between the U.S. Forest Service and the nation's timber industry, that message ran counter to new expectations about public lands. Recreation and conservation led the list.

These expectations, and growing conflicts with federal timber policy dictated from Washington, D.C., helped to give rise to a

broad new environmental agenda, and the citizens' organizations
that spoke for these new values. The first Earth Day celebration
in 1970 symbolized these values.

In the late 1960s and the 1970s, Congress enacted a series of
laws which zeroed in on National Forest conflicts. These new laws
set up standards and procedures which were specifically designed
to curb runaway timber practices, and to provide specific ways for
the public to monitor the National Forest planning process.
Major issues were wilderness preservation, clearcutting, the use of
herbicides to kill off less merchantable trees, and below-cost
timber sales.

Starting in 1960 with the Multiple-Use Sustained Yield Act, federal
legislators passed the Resources Planning Act in 1974, following
that with the comprehensive National Forest Management Act
(NFMA) two years later. These last two pieces of reform
legislation, hammered out through intense political negotiations,
outlined strict forest planning procedures which were supposed
to make timber policies on public land something of an open
book. Logging's major negative impacts would be dealt with
through the National Environmental Planning Act (or NEPA) and
its environmental impact statement requirements.

Mindful that they were managing the public's land, Forest
Service officials have always, employed a variety of techniques to
tap public opinion—even before such reforms. District rangers,
in fact, were expected to keep a list of "key men," community
leaders outside the agency who rangers more or less cultivated
through frequent contacts. Today, we recognize this practice as
networking, as in "the good ole boy network." Nevertheless, the
public at-large has felt increasingly powerless to affect National
Forest policy. A University of Idaho study a few years ago found
that the Forest Service often conducted elaborate public
participation and information-gathering sessions but that, in the
end agency personnel were reluctant to share any decision-
making power. Another study notes that despite extensive public

meetings about National Forest issues, "there was no indication that participants believed that better public participation led to greater direct influence on local land managers' decisions."

Over time, the Forest Service has devised increasingly elaborate and costly systems to spur public participation and promote the idea of a democratic process involving public land-use decisions. Few proved satisfactory and some were spectacular failures. For example, after the passage of the Wilderness Act of 1964 brought designation of an initial 9.1 million acres of wilderness preserves, the Forest Service, responding to a Congressional directive, began studying thousands of acres of unclassified roadless areas on federal Forests and BLM to determine both their extent and their suitability for possible future wilderness designation.

The resulting "Roadless Area Review and Evaluation" studies—RARE 1 and RARE 2—were a sweeping attempt to take public testimony at the local or ranger district level on the future of these roadless areas. The results satisfied no one and during RARE 2, raised a firestorm of conflicts among a new and prickly assortment of local special interests from snowmobilers to backpackers.

In their book, *The Angry West,* former Colorado Governor Richard Lamm and journalist Michael McCarthy are sharply critical of the part the timber industry play in this public process. They write:

"During the RARE hearings the timber lobby deluged the West with propaganda and misinformation, often through industry-sponsored newspaper advertising, and almost always its assertion was that RARE would swell America's [by then] 14 million wilderness acres to 350 million. In some areas companies sent letters to employees suggesting that wilderness would cost jobs. Virtually every lumber mill closure in the West was blamed on wilderness. And on occasion the industry lent tacit support to the disruption that made a mockery of many RARE hearings. In every way it could, the industry in general created and sustained an atmosphere of crisis."

By the beginning of the 1990s, the Forest Service still hadn't developed acceptable ways to resolve land-use conflicts on the National Forests it managed. The agency also had to face the fact that congressionally mandated multiple-use land reform policies, adopted since the 1960s have been increasingly at odds with timber industry expectations. Members of the public, more and more dissatisfied with National Forest timber management policies, began turning to the courts for help.

The National Forest Management Act required the nation's 156 separate National Forests (over 80 of those forests are in the western states) to develop comprehensive 50-year forest management plans, which would be revised every 10 years to produce a current 10-year forest plan. These plans, costing something like $200,000 each, for openers, have turned out to be a legal and financial nightmare for the Forest Service, as well as a serious threat to the timber industry's domination of forest uses. By the spring of 1989 there were over 300 active appeals to forest plans. A substantial number of these appeals have been filed by parties other than environmental groups, including timber and mineral interests, off-road vehicle organizations, and state and local governments.

In fact, some forest management plans were so flawed that USFS Chief Max Peterson, who headed the agency in the mid-1980s, flat out rejected or "remanded" final plans for four western forests— the Black Hills National Forest in Wyoming and South Dakota, the Grand Mesa, Uncompahgre, and Gunnison (three forests combined administratively), and the San Juan National Forest, both in Western Colorado: and Eastern Colorado's Arapahoe-Roosevelt. All four Rocky Mountain Region (R-2) remands, critics suggest, should be laid at the feet of former Regional Forester Ray Evans who, they add, saw forest mostly in terms of timber sales. Five plans in other areas have also been remanded or withdrawn. Evans has since retired.

During this same period, the Forest Service entered the new world of computer technology. Coupled with the agency's growing conviction that science and technology could transform both the art of growing trees as well as the complexities of timber management, the Forest Service teemed with high tech excitement and a renewed spirit of elitism.

To develop computer models of forest plans and management projections, including economic values, Forest Service planners use FORPLAN, a computer program so obtuse that "only a few FORPLAN experts outside the Forest Service" can comprehend the information, according to independent forest economist and author Randal O'Toole (*Reforming the Forest Service*).

Arizona's Game and Fish Department, which mounted an unprecedented public challenge in the late 1980s over planned timber harvest levels on three National Forests in that state, noted in a 1990 white paper that "FORPLAN is so large and complex as to be virtually impossible to understand." Outside experts, from universities to specialists with other agencies, say the FORPLAN program is a poor planning tool as well, unsuited for the work it's supposed to do.

National Forest management plans, clearly, aren't written for the average user. Largely unreadable, the plans feature hundreds of pages of *forestese*, that are nearly indecipherable to those outside the brotherhood. Still, NFMA-required forest plans have provided a powerful legal tool that environmental groups, and their newly-acquired fleets of experts, are using to challenge forest management policies. Teaming up, grassroots groups, along with national environmental organizations, have been devastatingly effective in these legal challenges, which are often centered on projected federal timber harvest levels.

Despite the rise of the environmental movement in the 1960s, and a new set of forest values associated with it, many traditional foresters today, both within the service and without, remain baffled and largely frustrated by the idea of a wilderness forest. To them uncut timber is wasted timber. Wilderness is bad land use because wilderness is land which has been taken out of "production." To these foresters and to the logging industry in general, wilderness forests make about as much sense as an unharvested garden, or fruit fallen to the ground in a country whose citizens are going hungry. Although the Forest Service itself originated the idea of wilderness preserves in the 1920s, 40 years later the agency had adopted a strongly anti-wilderness stance.

One state forester I talked to turned noticeably huffy when I used the term "conservationists," in reference to environmental groups. "Please don't call them conservationists." he said disdainfully. "I'm a conservationist—they are preservationists." His reaction, it turned out, was typical of many a forester, certain of his credo and what it stands for. It involves long held values about conserving natural resources *in order* to use them. Forests and trees are to be nurtured, "conserved" in a properly *managed* forest setting, to be used, as the first Forest Chief Gifford Pinchot put it, "for the benefit of the many, and not for the profit of the few."

As the Forest Service grew during the post-World War II era, schools of forestry steadily turned out more and more foresters, trained in the values and policies of the bureaucracy they were to serve. Forestry graduates joined the Service already indoctrinated in the agency's traditional positive response to the industry's demand for more and more public timber. By the late 1980s when the Reagan Administration had convinced the world that happiness came with a market economy, the market "demand" for timber had become part of the gospel of the Forest Service brotherhood.

Despite opposition often led by the timber industry, the nation had, by the 1990s, set aside over 91 million wilderness acres, public land which includes everything from fierce and wonderful deserts and canyonlands to alpine timberland. Unsettled issues involving roadless areas and their timber (including old growth forests) are still at the heart of many western timber disputes. With pressures from more and more users for more and more "special uses" the Forest Service has become entangled in an ever-tightening multiple-use bind. The dilemma has been compounded by the fact that the Forest Service is administratively geared up for timber production. Its harvest targets and quotas, set by Congress and the political process, are aimed at providing a steady flow of timber to insure "community economic stability."

This well-documented policy, which virtually promises the timber industry a steady flow of logs for its western sawmills, surfaces whenever National Forest timber policies are discussed. As its production capacity increased, the timber industry confidently expected the supply of logs from the National Forests to keep pace, while the U.S.Forest Service on all levels continues to talk about the need to sustain timber industry jobs in the American West. In a 1989 speech in Eugene, Oregon, Forest Service Chief Dale Robertson said, to accommodate the growing demands on the nation's federal forests, "What we need to do is make a bigger pie."

In the face of mounting public concern, USFS officials cling to their long-held belief that National Forest decisions are a matter for forestry "professionals." In the view of one high-level, Forest Service official in Portland, the public thinks that "the plural of anecdotes is data." Foresters, timber organization officials, and others aligned with the timber industry, repeatedly told me that timber issues in the American West, are largely "a public relations problem." National Forest Products Association spokesperson, Frank Gladics, who points out that he also is a forester, is convinced that the industry can counter what he calls environmentalist "propaganda" simply by "educating" the public. This should be done, he explains, by presenting "the cleanest, most scientific explanation" of forest management issues. Among other things, Gladics thinks the public should understand that advances in silviculture now make it possible "to design a forest to mimic any [features of nature] you want. It's all do-able." Perhaps such techniques will, in the next decade or so, produce something we'll come to recognize as "designer forests."

Historian Samuel Hays has written at length about American industry's remarkable ability to line up scientists, economists, attorneys, and other professionals to support industry's status quo. Non-profit organizations such as The Tobacco Institute, for example, found plenty of experts to argue that there was no connection between smoking and lung cancer. And the American Forest Institute has had no trouble generating statistics that show that future demand for wood products makes further wilderness designations impractical. One reviewer calls this public matching of scientific wits, a "good science versus bad science" public relations gimmick. But it's clear that in public debate the credibility of professionals and experts is somewhat tarnished.

In the debate over the future of western National Forests taking place as we enter the 1990s, traditionalists in the forestry brotherhood continue to argue, sometimes angrily, that forest decisions are best left in the hands of trained foresters who are singularly equipped to use their best "professional judgment." True, a new breed of young rebels within the forestry profession are now questioning that professional judgment, but such rebels are still a minority. Most foresters are far more conservative.

CLOSEUP
Bob Kenney, Hard Working Forester

Bob Kenney, 49, has been a forester all his professional life, much of it spent in Colorado. He is admired by his co-workers for the role he takes on as a mentor to new USFS employees. More than once, this veteran forester has intervened with higher-ups on behalf of beleaguered summer crew workers when they run afoul of some obscure (and most likely foolish) agency rule.

When I ask this veteran what he thinks about "Inner Voice," the dissident insider publication put out by Jeff DeBonis, the rebel U.S. Forest Service timber-sale planner, Bob Kenney allows that he's heard about DeBonis, but has little personal concern about the issues De Bonis has managed to splash all over the media. No, he says, he and other staffers in the Grand Junction office of the Forest Service never really talk about the sorts of issues that DeBonis is so upset about. Their beat is the Grand Mesa, Uncompahgre, and Gunnison National Forest, a 5,000 square mile forest in Western Colorado. And, according to Kenney, "lots of those issues don't really pertain to Colorado." This National Forest's acronym, GMUG, is pronounced "Ga-mug," an exceptionally ugly sound for these rugged and sweeping high altitude forests of ponderosa pine, quaking aspen, spruce and fir.

We are talking on a sunny Friday afternoon, in a small, jammed space that serves as Kenney's office in Grand Junction, a city so named because it is situated at the confluence of two great rivers that pour west from the Rockies, the Colorado and the Gunnison.The whole suite of GMUG offices is drab and somewhat cluttered—clearly a no-frills operation. Kenney says that on this forest the biggest problem is a shortage of staff. An empty desk in Kenney's office cubicle used to be occupied by another forester, but after he left, the vacancy hasn't been filled—an example, says Kenney, of this district's ever-shrinking budget. Instead of the issues De Bonis talks about—overcutting and preserving the diminishing inventory of old-growth forests—Kenney says about his National Forest: "The thing I hear is, we still have the same amount of work to do but less people to do it with."

His tone is weary, frustrated. Bob is a pleasant, no-nonsense kind of a guy. Of medium height, with thinning dark hair, he looks exceptionally fit. His thick upper body suggests that perhaps he's been working out with weights. In any case, he doesn't look like the desk-bound paper pusher that USFS foresters say planning demands are making them into.

Waving a hand toward a wall of files and standing floor racks that hold up layers of maps, mylars and graphs, Kenney says planning "is a nightmare." What about claims that the Forest Service is seriously behind in its timber base inventories? And what about charges that the Forest Service uses dangerously outdated numbers, which are fed into its computer modeling program (FORPLAN), resulting in skewed and inaccurate forecasts that favor the timber industry and fatten Forest District budgets?

Oh, that doesn't happen on *this* forest, Kenney responds. There was a time when GMUG, like a number of other forests, tended to take the answers the computer models spewed out "as gospel." But this forest, he says, recently took a different tack. Now, each district "factors in" whatever special problems or circumstances its foresters have encountered during the last 10 years.

Kenney says he knows "this forest has done an inventory within the last 10 years." He suggests the inventory process is pretty much an ongoing thing. Right now his office is working on a 10-year timber action plan, plus reworking GMUG's 50-year forest management plan. Like so many others, this plan raised a firestorm of protest, and ultimately was remanded to the local forest by the U.S. Forest Service Chief.

But despite his close involvement with timber planning, Kenney also allows that he "has no idea what volumes [of timber] we will cut" on the areas he's been covering. All the district's accumulated information is sent to the Forest Supervisor's Delta office where those future timber-cut volumes are formulated. (Final timber volume "targets" or quotas, come down from Washington D.C.)

Kenny assures me his boss, GMUG supervisor, Griff Greffenius "wants a quality job done" on timber management and sales. "I work closely with the biologists—we design the sale" to avoid sensitive areas, says Kenney, suggesting that clearcutting is generally out of favor. Yes, on the San Juan Forest there *were* some horrendous clear cuts. "It's coming back [the forest] but it's very, very slow." The San Juan is the National Forest bordering the GMUG on the south. Kenney shakes his head, and sends a little laugh toward the ceiling. "Yeah, we've made some big mistakes. Now, the only species we clearcut is aspen," and beetle-infested pine because "it's already dead."

Kenney leans forward. "Insect money is very political," he confides. He is referring to the way political pressures from elected officials can affect Forest Service budget allocations.

Then later he adds that the government also favors clearcutting "old-growth spruce." These stands, he says, are "so decadent there's no choice—clearcut or let it fall down."

As our conversation moves on, Kenney talks about indicator species, either birds or animals, that are regularly used to measure the health of the forest. Funny, somebody, perhaps on the San Juan, reportedly caught sight of a relative of the notorious spotted owl, the critter that blew the lid off the old-growth logging controversy in the Northwest. As a matter of fact, Kenney seems to remember, either the Forest Service or possibly the Bureau of Land Management is "doing a spotted owl survey" somewhere in Western Colorado. To protect designated indicators such as the Aberts squirrel in pine forests, for example, he tells me that foresters may well " design a timber sale that's not economical." This was one of the rare excuses I heard for controversial below-cost timber sales.

Kenney conveys the idea that the demands placed on the U.S. Forest Service, by the public, the Congress, the agency's budget, and the complexities of modern life, make the job of managing the public forests impossibly difficult—or maybe just impossible. He's recently gone through another in a series of "half-assed sessions" in which everybody—the whole staff—gets together to figure out collectively how to "streamline" the process. Kenney's voice sags with disbelief. Clearly, he thinks the whole thing is a waste of time.

But those who've known Kenney over the years regard him as a fine forester who is serious about his role as a protector and preserver of the public's vast western lands. A half dozen years before, it was Kenney who broke federal ranks to call for a war on hordes of mountain pine beetles that were eating their way through Uncompahgre Plateau pine stands to the south.

Kenney was called into the head office over that breach of

discipline. He seems relieved that a resurgence of that beetle epidemic is now somebody else's problem. "Insect money is *very* political," he repeats.

Kenney mentions that his wife, a professional nurse, and his daughter are vacationing in Mexico. He reminds me, only a casual acquaintance from several years ago, that his teenage daughter, Carrie, barely survived a terrible automobile accident a few years ago and will never fully recover. Her brain is forever damaged. "We'll have to take care of her the rest of our lives," he says in flat tones, swallowing the pain.

Bob Kenney is just six years from retiring from the U.S. Forest Service. It is four o'clock on a Friday afternoon and he's ready to go home.

Part II
THE NORTHERN ROCKIES

CHAPTER FOUR

The Black Hills,
Where Western Timber Sales Began

The Black Hills National Forest, about 5000 square miles in western South Dakota and eastern Wyoming, holds a unique place in the history of federal timber management. Acre for acre this National Forest today is more intensively managed for timber production than any other in the Rocky Mountain region. Its lower elevation, longer growing season and other highly favorable forest conditions, have made Black Hills forests phenomenal producers of ponderosa pine, one of the most-favored of western woods.

The location of this great pine forest, literally at the edge of the western frontier, has shaped its special destiny. This is where, a century ago, the fledgling U.S. Forest Service sold its very first western timber. In 1899, the U.S. government agreed to sell 14 million board feet of Black Hills ponderosa pine to the Homestake Mining Co. This historic transaction is now referred to as "Case No.1," the first federal timber sale in the West. The sale came just two years after the passage of the 1897 Organic Administration Act which authorized the federal government to take charge of much of the West's unclaimed timberland.

"Ninety years ago," the U.S. Forest Service explains, "selling timber from the Forest Reserves was a novel idea. Today, timber harvest is an accepted way of achieving land management objectives, thanks in part to the success of Case No.1." All the more reason, conservationists say, for the Black Hills National Forest, with its superior growing conditions, to have an exemplary record of wise timber management.

But despite this National Forest's natural blessings and its long historic record, Black Hills forest management is today under sharp attack for everything from overcutting to misleading budgets that tend to bury timber-related costs. Critics say that in the 1980s a runaway road-building program laced the Black Hills with miles of near-boulevards in sections long recognized as "high value wildlife areas" (a strangely awkward but much used phrase in forest planning matters). In any case, the Black Hills National Forest averages a rather incredible two and a half miles of roads for each square mile of forest. Critics suggest that in the 1980s a cozy relationship between a well entrenched timber industry and federal forest managers—plus a lack of attention from environmentalists—created a golden opportunity for abuse.

Black Hills National Forest officials, however, point out that communities such as Spearfish and Custer, South Dakota; and New Castle, Wyoming, are strongly dependent on the 2700 jobs created by the Black Hills logging industry. Federal timber managers also assert that the Black Hills, with some $9 million in annual timber sales, hasn't had a deficit timber sale since 1986-87. But independent economists hotly disagree. Today, these same managers claim, the Black Hills has an effective "balanced" multiple-use forest management program.

Contradicting such rosy official claims, in 1989 a broad range of citizens groups from conservationists to outdoors enthusiasts were fighting a planned timber sale in the Norbeck Wildlife Preserve. This 34,873-acre preserve lies in the heart of the most intensively used recreation area in the Black Hills. Forest plans called for harvesting 33.4 million board feet of sawtimber over a 20-year period, accompanied by 6.2 miles of new roads plus rebuilding almost 50 miles of old roads. Forest managers claimed that "wildlife habitat will be improved through a combination of commercial timber harvest, prescribed burning, and thinning...."

Opponents of the Norbeck timber sale plan saw it as an outrageous and out-of-balance proposal that favored the timber industry.

Two years later, as Black Hills National Forest planners work over revisions in the Black Hills Forest management plan, the future of the Norbeck Wildlife Reserve remains unsettled. But without the equivalent of the Northwest's headline-making northern spotted owl, such Black Hills public timber controversies have gone largely unnoticed by a national readership caught up in the trauma of "owls vs. jobs" taking place in the rainforests of Washington and Oregon.

But the fact is, according to critics, that politics, not prudent forestry, has driven decision-making here, just as it has on all the great public forests in the American West. Indeed, the Black Hills National Forest provides a remarkable example of much that's gone wrong on the National Forests in general, offering us a 100-year case history of evolving public-timber issues all across the West. Most of the problems—potential abuses, multiple-use conflicts, below-cost timber sales—seem to be present here despite this National Forest's nearly ideal timber-producing environment.

Even in the Black Hills, timber sales have been money-losers. How can federal timber managers explain away this history of below-cost timber sales, coupled with rampant road-building in an area so favorable to timber production?

Analysts like Randal O'Toole—a leading forest economist and a relentless critic of the Forest Service—say the agency's budget is to blame for much of what's gone wrong on the Black Hills National Forest (and other federal forests across the West). Forest Service budgets, he says, have little to do with real forest management and have everything to do with sustaining the huge Forest Service bureaucracy. O'Toole's and his researchers ("Cascade Holistic Economic Consultants" or CHEC) take aim at public forest policies with the same sort careful scrutiny and relentless statistical firepower that "Nader's Raiders" used so effectively on Detroit and the American auto industry in the 1960s and 1970s. In analyzing the Black Hills. O'Toole cites an obscure but detailed 1984 study *by the Forest Service itself* which found that this Forest "had the greatest negative cash flow of any National Forest."

So it turns out that the Black Hills, for all its exceptional timber growing potential, is a forest beset with troubles. And these troubles include timber inventories set at *250 million* board feet which, forest managers now acknowledge, are overstated by perhaps *100 million* board feet.

Foresters tell us that such inventories begin with aerial surveys and much later, as demand requires, are firmed up by on-site counts. These are done using a variety of formulas and computer programs. National Forests are required to plan timber sales around an annual (or allowable) sale quantity based on sustainable-yield principles and the Forest's inventory of its standing timber.

Veteran forester Gordon Robinson, who managed industry timberland for 30 years before becoming the Sierra Club's staff forester in 1966, notes that in recent years, "foresters have applied computer technology to the problem in hopes of improving the accuracy of their predictions." But he adds: "I have observed that with each new development in forest technology, estimates of sustained yield increase." Such overly optimistic predictions, and corrections made far too late in the timber management process, have inevitably led to "a consistent decline in quality and sustained-yield capacity."

How is it possible that in the Black Hills National Forest, where federal timber sales first began 100 years ago, timber inventories were *overestimated* by an astonishing two-thirds? This is no minor goof, or shrug-of-the-shoulder slip. And once again the Black Hills reflects a wider reality—in the early 1990s, inflated, inaccurate National Forest timber inventories were turning up all over the American West.

Some National Forest supervisors are already recognizing the implications of such errors, but elected officials from governors who use their political influence to hold onto jobs within their states, to members of Congress—the people who actually set annual timber harvest levels on National Forests—have taken little notice of the problem. Like so many other timber issues, it's a problem that won't go away.

By the end of the 1980s, local environmental organizations, such as those that developed around the Black Hills, were among the first to realize that National Forest timber sale planners "didn't know what they had" on the ground. As updates of National Forest 10-year management plans come due in the mid-1990s, grossly overestimated federal timber inventories are coming to light on first one National Forest and then the next. In some cases the task of developing new and accurate timber inventories is so daunting, forest managers are even calling on citizen volunteers to help count trees in the public forest. Soliciting assistance from self-taught amateurs, is clearly a major departure for a federal agency that, for 100 years, has prided itself on its professionalism as managers of the nation's public forests.

The Black Hills National Forest and Case No. 1, rich with history and present day timber conflicts, seemed an ideal place to begin our state-by-state quest for a fuller understanding of Western timber issues. The story of the Black Hills is not reassuring. Nor is it unique.

CHAPTER FIVE

Idaho,
First Signs of Forest Reform

Logging towns in the American West are, in a sense, feudal. They are often rural, single-industry communities with social and economic relationships that make them seem more like forested medieval fiefdoms than modern societies.

Some of the bitterest timber-supply battles at the beginning of this decade rage around timber stands within millions of acres of roadless areas on federal lands in Montana and Idaho. This is where wilderness values and commercial logging meet head on. Fueling the fight, according to the University of Montana's Charles Keegan, is the fact that "the 10 counties in Northern Idaho and the nine western-most counties in Montana, are arguably the most timber-dependent counties in the western states."

U.S. Forest Service policy itself has fostered the development of these single-industry logging communities, especially in the inland states of the American West, where federal lands are virtually the only source of timber. The result is an insidious co-dependency between government and industry that only perpetuates this timber feudalism.

Economist Keegan agrees that the question of timber dependency is "at the core of why this whole debate is so nasty." To make his point, Keegan explains that in states with highly diversified economies, such as California and Washington, the timber industry represents a much smaller share of the state's economic pie. So, although Idaho and Montana are *not* among the nation's leading timber producers, they still rank third and fourth as the nation's most timber-dependent states. Maine, on the country's northeastern seaboard, is a huge timber-producer and also has the nation's most timber-dependent state economy. Oregon, also a major producer, is the nation's second most timber-dependent state; and Washington, a big timber producer but with great economic diversity, is fifth. (Keegan and his colleagues at the University's Bureau of Business and Economic Research are also, arguably, the best and sometimes the only source of comparative regional economic information on the logging economy.)

Oregon's and Washington's lumber output is more than three times the volume produced in Idaho and Montana; yet these two inland states are probably more critically affected by changes in National Forest timber policies.

Federal policy is the key to the future of western forests and those who shape this policy are the key players. Until his surprise retirement in 1990, Idaho's powerful three-term Republican Senator, James McClure, was timber's reigning champion. His successor, Republican Larry Craig, is expected to closely follow McClure's legendary pro-development stance in western politics. McClure held sway as the senior Republican on the Senate Energy and Natural Resources Committee and the Senate appropriations subcommittee, and was chairman of both groups when Republicans held the majority in the Senate.

It is not surprising then, that for the past decade most public land and resource legislation affecting the West (and policies resulting from that legislation) bore McClure's imprint. As the Idaho timber industry's best friend, McClure helped scuttle a 1984 proposal aimed at reforming the widespread practice of below-cost National Forest timber sale. Had the measure passed, Idaho's federal timber sales would have suffered the deepest reductions.

McClure has also stood solidly in the way of a second round of Idaho wilderness bills dealing with National Forest roadless areas. These disputed areas include some 2.2 million acres of Idaho timberland earmarked as suitable for commercial timber operations. Idaho, with its rugged and inaccessible interior, now has more potential wilderness that any other state in the lower 48. Timber industry leaders fume over the idea that conservationists have successfully held up logging in these roadless areas, and have converted them into "de facto wilderness." Court cases have made it clear that until Congress passes added wilderness designation bills, timber stands in roadless areas in the eleven western states are mostly off-limits to logging. But, as the West's available timber supply shrinks, more and more timber sales and new access roads are being planned for roadless areas within National Forests.

In Idaho, the timber industry, fighting hard for access to timber stands in roadless areas, is clearly alarmed about where its future timber will come from. An industry publication advises that: "While the timber industry and the Forest Service disagree on the amount of timber which should be available from each national forest, there is no disagreement that a significant portion of that timber must come from roadless areas....We in the industry along with the Forest Service count on these roadless lands to meet short-term needs."

Overcutting on privately owned commercial timberland, industry leaders acknowledge, means the next privately owned crop of trees in the West won't be ready to harvest before 2000 *at the earliest.* The net result is what U.S. Forest Service Chief Dale F. Robertson has called a significant 20 to 30 year "gap" in the orderly flow of sawtimber. But it's curious that in almost all of the western states, regardless of who owns the privately-held timberland or how much there is, the timber industry still looks to federal forestlands to supply ever bigger volumes of sawtimber. (Idaho contains 14.5 million acres of commercial timberland, defined by the industry as "land which is biologically capable of growing repeated crops of timber and is not dedicated to another non-timber use.")

The University of Idaho's Jo Ann Force, a professor of forestry policy at the University's College of Forestry, Wildlife and Range Science in Moscow, Idaho, says she's not sold on the view of some forest economists who believe timber shortages will drive prices so high the Forest Service could be induced to open up more of Idaho's roadless timberland. "The American public would have to be willing to have less wilderness," she says. Surveys, she notes, continually show that support for wilderness remains strong.

Dr. Force says it's impossible to generalize about timber issues in Idaho because "each forest is different." But her statement underlines a major stumbling block in the national timber debate: Forest Service leaders tend to use these real regional differences in what amounts to a very successful informational shell game.

As more and more citizens formed grassroots organizations during the 1980s to look into matters on nearby forests (from *Friends of the Dixie National Forest* in southern Utah, to the *Kern Valley Wildlife Association,* a Sequoia National Forest watchdog group in central California) Forest Service officials in greater numbers began taking shelter behind an informational stonewall. This lack of candor, which many see as the ultimate bureaucratic con game, has helped destroy the USFS's once proud image as dedicated stewards of public land.

National Forests within Idaho account for 9.7 million acres (66 percent) of the state's total timberland. The timber industry and other private owners hold another 3.6 million acres, while Indian tribes and the state account for about 1.7 million acres of Idaho's publicly-owned (or communally-owned) timberland. During the 1980s timber cutting in all western states accelerated sharply. In Idaho, production rose a stunning 61 percent. Idaho's National Forests—forced to meet unrealistic annual timber targets dictated by Congress and the bureaucracy—sold timber like hotcakes.

The timber industry, however, prefers to credit this dramatic rise to "consumer demand for the finished wood products made from that timber." But in part, this increase is also due to a lodgepole-pine beetle-timber salvage program on eastern Idaho's Targhee National Forest. This program allowed the industry to gorge itself on a huge 80 million board foot annual cut during the 1980s. Now that "bug timber" is running out; and in the early '90s the Targhee's yearly timber sale volume will drop by more than half.

Management policies on the Targhee have come under fire from all sides. Environmentalists say the Targhee presents a particularly outrageous example of ham-handed clearcutting. In the Ashton, St. Anthony and Rexburg regions of eastern Idaho smaller timber operators complain that they were forced out by a cozy relationship between the U.S. Forest Service and bigger operators who became the prime beneficiaries of the Targhee timber sales bonanza. Since 1979, 46 small mills and log-home operations have been squeezed out, leaving just 14 still active. Now the two biggest players, Idaho Forest Industries, owners of the St. Anthony mill; and the Louisiana-Pacific Corporation at Rexburg, are looking for ways to avoid shutdowns themselves, since the Targhee's salvage timber is running out.

Louisiana-Pacific began eyeing stands of Douglas fir growing on steep, unstable slopes within the Targhee's off-limits roadless areas. But in a 1989 editorial, The Idaho Falls Post-Register said the wilderness value of those areas outweighed their logging values. Warning that trees wouldn't grow again in such inhospitable terrain, the editors said the government's timber management dollars would be better spent in more productive areas.

Still, conservationists in Idaho aren't hopeful about stemming the flow of federal timber any time soon. Craig Gehrke is a tall, athletic sort, a likable professional environmental activist who could have easily ended up working for the Forest Service. Like so many other professional activists, Gehrke looks to be

somewhere in his late 30s or early 40s, a baby-boomer. He studied
at the University of Idaho to be a forestry range management
specialist. Gehrke talks about university classes that emphasize
"commodity" production on public lands and is shocked as he
now recalls how his own classes focused squarely on intensive
"production of grass and forage for cows." Since then, he's heard
a different call, ending up instead as head of *The Wilderness Society*
regional office in Boise. He says Idahoans are generally slow to
change but "even conservative Idaho people want clean air and
water," and the majority of Idaho's citizens want to leave roadless
areas pretty much unchanged.

He's pessimistic about the future, given the agency's "timber
bent" and its longstanding allegiance to production of
"commodities," grass for livestock grazing as well as timber.
Gehrke rocks back, raising the front legs of his chair a good two
inches off the floor. He talks about a major bug infestation
currently facing Boise National Forest timber managers. What to
do about controlling both bugs and fires is under hot debate in
Forest Service circles. Still balanced on the back legs of his chair,
he laughs: "And guess what the answer is? Their answer to both
fire suppression and bugs is 'go cut some more trees.'"

He concludes that forest management is a highly inexact
science, and that forestry schools often specialize in turning out
"federal employees" trained to make public lands produce salable
commodities. In the Northwest, Oregon's universities are said to
be famous for training foresters to USFS specifications. In
Washington, the state university, I was told, is widely known as
"Weyerhaeuser U." Evidence suggests, Gehrke adds, that in Idaho
and elsewhere in the West, public timber managers have been
"cutting faster than their knowledge was increasing."

A somewhat different, more optimistic view is offered by David
Adams, a longtime forester who now teaches silviculture at the
Idaho University's College of Forestry, Wildlife and Range
Science. "There is no lack of knowledge.... I think knowledge is
way ahead of practice." Colleges and universities are indeed

turning out well-trained foresters. But when those somewhat idealistic young foresters "enter the real world" of commercial forest management, Adam explains, they're likely to be told: "We don't do things that way here." New and better practices are often ignored, Adams suggests. For example, new rating systems, based on 15 years of research and computer technology, help identify the risk of bug infestations in various timber stands. But this new method has yet to be used in the field. Adams also claims it's no longer true that forestry schools are academic assembly lines for the U.S. Forest Service and other public agencies. However, he concedes that 20 years ago the charge was true; Colorado State University, where Adams once taught, used to be widely thought of as "a ranger factory." But public interest in National Forest management in recent years is prompting a change in the way federal forest lands are managed, he observes. In contrast to most other professional foresters and timber managers I talked to, Adams claims foresters now see conservation-minded citizens as allies who are "allowing foresters to do what they want to do." He says foresters view this as a happy turn of events, collectively saying, "Ah, finally!"

Adams, however, isn't overly impressed with some of Dr. Jerry Franklin's "New Forestry" techniques. Franklin has developed an impressive reputation as the guru of "old-growth forestry" who warns that forest management must change in order to protect complex and critical forest ecosystems and the precious biological diversity within them. Adams says certain of these practices may be new in the Northwest, where Franklin is based, but many are "common practices here" in Idaho.

Franklin's shelterwood system—leaving select trees in an otherwise clearcut patch—"is not a new silviculture method. We're already doing it here." And while "clearcutting is a very satisfactory method" [to use] when you're growing new trees," public outrage over this ugly business, plus what Adams calls "more knowledge" about clearcutting's drawbacks, means clearcutting will be used less frequently in the future.

The Forest Service tends to use clearcutting more than it's used on private timberland, Adams says. This is the result of "an unfortunate regeneration policy" built into the controversial 1976 National Forest Management Act; this law requires evidence of replanting or regeneration of the forest within five years. To stay within the law, National Forest timber managers can't afford to wait for natural reseeding to take place. Thus, the preferred cycle has been clearcutting, replanting, thinning, and often application of chemical fertilizers, pesticides and herbicides. We've come to call these easily recognizable non-forests "tree farms" or plantations.

Adams says cheerfully: "This is an exciting time to be in forestry," a popular observation among the career foresters I talked to. The 1990s will see new forestry research devoted to "looking more at [forest] systems. Computer models can simulate the results of research, so the next step is to try to fully understand why these systems interact in the way that they do," says Adams.

Even though not everyone gives him full credit, there is overwhelming evidence that Dr. Franklin, one of the fathers of the ecosystem approach to forestry, is among those leading the way down this neglected forestry path. And so is Chris Maser, another highly regarded forest scientist and sometime member of Franklin's research teams. Maser's written words are gentle, forgiving and persuasive. He describes the intricate links—fungus, tiny seed-carrying rodents, mysterious bacterial changes and the like—that exist in great old forests. He joins Franklin and others on the leading edge of forest ecology in warning against haste, arrogance, and what amounts to politically motivated forest management. Maser writes: "Nature designed a forest of long-term trends: we're trying to design a forest of short-term absolutes." The timber industry's own scientific team dismisses Maser's ideas, charging that his work, *The Redesigned Forest*, "suffers from an abundance of inaccurate and selectively-chosen information" and fails to "speak to values and philosophies of forest management."

While forest scientists publicly thrash out their opposing views, the politics of National Forest management in Idaho and the West is the day-to-day stuff of federal timber policy. Industry leaders in Idaho say that annual timber sales on National Forests in Idaho have been seriously curtailed by the 1976 National Forest Management Act (NFMA), the landmark federal law requiring each National Forest to develop comprehensive forest management plans. This law has provided a new avenue for public participation in federal forest management. Former closet conservationists are suddenly active in groups such as the *Citizens of the Teton Valley* and the *Idaho Conservation League.* These, along with a dozen or more regional and national environmental groups now keep a watchful eye on the nine National Forests within Idaho's borders, and the on-going game of timber politics and the management of the public's natural resources in the American West. Not everyone applauds their efforts.

Idaho-based Boise-Cascade, a major player in the wood-products industry easily qualifies as "Big Timber." Boise-Cascade official Kirk Ewart told me: "I think the National Forest System was created to yield a stable amount of raw material for dependent communities." Environmentalists, he suggests, are getting in the way of this policy.

A case in point involves efforts by conservationists to save what's left of the Northwest's native fish population. Timber and threatened salmon spawning habitat met head on when environmentalists challenged plans to cut timber along the South Fork of the Salmon River in the Payette National Forest in west central Idaho. In October, 1990, USFS Chief Robertson overturned rulings by local and regional USFS supervisors approving the timber sale plan. Robertson's decision was "hailed as a victory for summer chinook salmon and water quality in the controversial South Fork drainage," Boise's Idaho Statesman reported. But industry leaders said they'd been deprived of an important opportunity to demonstrate new logging techniques, including hauling logs out by helicopter.

It's certain that growing efforts to protect native salmon and their habitat in Idaho (and across the Northwest) including the implementation of the Endangered Species Act, will significantly affect regional timber policy in the coming decade.

CLOSEUP
The Renegade Forester of the Nez Perce National Forest

"Anadromous" isn't a term most of us use on a daily basis. But it's one Nez Perce National Forest Supervisor Tom Kovalicky tosses out with ease. He speaks of the Nez Perce in North Central Idaho's panhandle region as an anadromous forest—its rivers and streams providing critical spawning beds for summer steelhead and spring chinook salmon in the Columbia River Basin. Anadromous, from the Greek for "running up," refers to fish such as these, which swim upstream from the sea to spawn. From the earliest days, tales of this spectacular aquatic migration have awed adventurers and enhanced the region's rain-forest mystique.

Tom Kovalicky, part P.T. Barnum, part born-again forest manager, is outspokenly critical of the federal forest management system he serves and he takes pride in being called a U.S. Forest Service system maverick. "I never signed on to be a lackey," he tells me in a no-holds-barred telephone interview in early November, 1990. I am astounded by his candor. Kovalicky, unlike many foresters and timber industry leaders I've talked to, has nothing but good things to say about Jeff DeBonis, the young U.S. Forest Service revolutionary who quit the system in early 1990 to fight for reform from without. "Jeff has some absolutely bonafide concerns," Kovalicky assures me.

DeBonis, it turns out, worked for Kovalicky on the Nez Perce a few years before. Here where his ideas found a welcome audience, "He did a heck of a job." At that time reform was already underway on the Nez Perce, says the manager of this 2.2 million acres of public forest and prime wildlife habitat. But the

Willamette National Forest in Oregon, where forest planner DeBonis went next, provided the requisite friction to ignite Jeff's reformist agenda. (DeBonis now leads his fledgling reform movement from outside the agency.)

Nearly half of the Nez Perce is classified as wilderness and its managers promote the whole resource as a "fish factory." They estimate the value of recreational sport fishing, together with the commercial value of salmon and steelhead produced there, at close to $7 million. Trout fishing adds another $1 million to the cash flow this fish factory generates. Public relations handouts tout these accomplishments. "The Nez Perce National Forest manages a significant portion of the fisheries resource in the Clearwater River Basin—a total of 2000 miles of fishing streams and 1200 acres of high mountain lakes.... The anadromous fisheries alone represent roughly 10 percent of all the summer steelhead and spring chinook salmon produced in the entire Columbia River Basin."

When did Kovalicky hear the reformist call—a summons that, for most Forest Service regulars, would amount to an environmental siren song? As far back as 1985, in a talk before the Society of American Foresters, Kovalicky reported that the Nez Perce had "rejected the philosophy that timber is king." It had also rejected "the old approach that wildlife and fish must be used like a commodity to be considered useful." For a traditional, timber-producing National Forest such as the Nez Perce, this radical change required leaders with "a certain boldness," men and women "who dare to be different, who dare to challenge some of our cherished allegiances," he advised this august gathering of the forest fraternity.

This is strong stuff for a bureaucrat whose agency was already under siege from all sides.

Six years later, Kovalicky, now in his fifties and nearing retirement, sounds even more reckless. The Forest Service, he says, is only belatedly recognizing the values of old-growth forests and their complex and still mysterious ecosystems. He explains this lack as a painful sin. His tone is confessional:

"We were slow to recognize the values of old growth, including myself, [because] we never saw old growth as an issue. We only saw old growth as a commodity,....We never saw it as a national treasure; we only saw it as boards. We made a terrible mistake by not standing back in the '70s and saying, old growth is more than a commodity."

His tone changes. He is now the advocate. Reform within the Forest Service will be slow, he suggests, because "the top people weren't trained to see [the forest] holistically.... they saw it only as a commodity." As a result, the U.S. Forest Service in Washington, D.C., and on the regional level is run by forest managers who were "trained to see functionally." Viewing the forest as a whole ecosystem remains a radical and dangerous approach within the ranks of a tradition-bound brotherhood.

Many forest managers both inside and outside the USFS scoff at the concept of managing federal forests as a whole ecosystem. This new view of forest management, Kovalicky says, "is in its infancy. No one can adequately identify it or describe it." The ecosystem issue involves a conceptual limb he's not ready to crawl out on. "Holistic" is his term. So is "biodiversity," short for the biological diversity, from tiny bugs to big game, which characterizes a rich, varied, older and well-preserved forest. Both terms are at the heart of the current forest management debate.

Why has the art of forestry or the science of silviculture been so slow to connect with the idea of managing the forest as a whole? Kovalicky doesn't hesitate. "You can blame a lot of that—the lack of intelligent research—on the universities and the Forest Service research factories. The universities and the government researchers as a whole do not put their energies into the future of an ecosystem; they put their energies into a product."

Speaking about the values of old growth and the importance of balanced forest ecosystem management he continues:

"Researchers eventually saw it, but they didn't see it quick enough to see the social and political explosion that would occur in the

'80s and '90s." Kovalicky talks about the dilemma that federal
forest managers face when they're forced into meeting
irresponsible annual timber harvest quotas, "targets identified for
us by the political process." These unrealistic timber quotas have
resulted in what Kovalicky calls "destructive forestry." During the
past 10 years, Idaho and the rest of the Northern Rockies have
seen more than their share of bad forestry. Logging 100 to 200
year old lodgepole pines that cling precariously to the steep
mountainsides is a harsh and unsightly practice that he says
amounts to "mining the trees."

Fish habitat in the Nez Perce National Forest "has suffered in
the past from a lack of knowledge [about] the effects of
management on fish habitat requirements," Kovalicky told the
Society of American Forestry in 1985, adding that forest managers
there had now instituted the "strongest fisheries program in
Region 1."

Explaining this five years later, he says: "In this part of Idaho,
water usually came last." An avid fisherman himself, Kovalicky
was among the first to see the light. He and his team of federal
forest managers have gone through "hell and pain," but they've
put together a forest planning document "built on water quality."
Timber and other uses are evaluated according to how they
"respond to water quality." Excessive road building and what he
describes as "indiscriminate logging" had meant lost wildlife
habitat, lost big game shelter and lost spawning beds for those
anadromous steelheads and chinook salmon. The annual timber
cut on the Nez Perce—the "political cut," Kovalicky calls it—has
been pegged at close to 120 million board feet. "It should be at
75 million right now," he tells me. We continue in the
confessional mode.

On the questions of timber inventories, he tells me that
inventories used in the Nez Perce were based on "soft data" and
amounted to "guesswork." My own personal experience with the
agency has led me to believe that many a USFS forester—God
forbid they should be thought to be computer illiterate—have

embraced the idea that computers and programs like FORPLAN meant that hands-on forestry was virtually obsolete. While it's true that just as many USFS staffers complain that mountains of paperwork keep them in the office and out of the woods where they really should be, computerized analysis and its conclusions have clearly driven forest planning in the '80s and early '90s.

Today—five years into the first 10-year segment of the Nez Perce's 50-year forest management plan—Kovalicky says "we're discovering just how bad our data was." Sampling techniques "which can give you the answer you want" are being discarded. Instead crews are being sent out "to measure" what's actually there. "After five years of cutting 100 million board feet a year, we'll now have a good handle on what this land can produce." A number of agency foresters I talked to danced around this subject of inventories and university analysts suggested it was a hush-hush subject, but no one inside or outside the agency addressed the question in more straightforward terms. Kovalicky sounds like a man with a mission, grandly unafraid. And how can this cause— conserving western forests—advance? "Pray to the saint for hopeless causes," Kovalicky shoots back.

Can Forest Service Chief Dale F. Robertson lead a heroic charge, take a dramatic and public leadership role, perhaps sacrificing his career in order to fire public indignation over this "destructive forestry?" (One conservationist had told me the times called for "a suicidal chief.") No, no, says Kovalicky, suddenly sounding grave. "Dale Robertson is in a very dangerous leadership role. He can be replaced [at will] by the Secretary of Agriculture." That replacement, Kovalicky says, could turn out to be a hopeless and repressive reactionary. The political game of managing the nation's National Forests and their resources is an intricate and sometimes ruthless business. "The only thing we can hope for is that he [the Chief] has the courage to keep moving ahead."

In Idaho, the unorthodox programs Kovalicky has put together to rebuild fish habitats within the Nez Perce National Forest haven't always pleased the state's Fish and Game Department leaders. They've questioned both the program's technical merits as well as its money source—up to over a $1 million annually for habitat improvements from the Bonneville Power Administration, the huge hydropower utility responsible for seven dams in the Columbia River Basin. Idaho's powerful, pro-timber senior U.S. Senator, James McClure, twice publicly singled out Kovalicky for criticism during the year before his retirement from the Senate in 1990.

Environmentalists and recreationists hail Kovalicky's approach to a more holistic "anadromous" forest, but, not surprisingly, timber industry leaders see him as a turncoat who's sold out to the other side. Kovalicky, however, sounds blithely confident about the direction he's chosen for the Nez Perce. The worst "they" can do "is promote me," he chuckles. Apparently, Kovalicky and Robertson understand each other. In fact, this Forest Chief has cited the Nez Perce for excellence. In 1989, the Nez Perce was named "the most successful National Forest in the implementation of its forest plan." The following spring, the Chief himself presented Kovalicky and his management team with a plaque commemorating this achievement. Kovalicky's tone is pure delight as he describes the presentation ceremony in Washington D.C.

The Nez Perce forest plan, implemented about 1986, initially faced eleven formal challenges. Only three appeals remain unresolved: two ask for higher annual timber cuts which Kovalicky thinks is a lost cause, and a third involves " a technical appeal," dealing with the way fish numbers are calculated.

In a bureaucracy where conformity makes for successful careers, Kovalicky is clearly a happy outlaw. He and his managers see themselves as modern and progressive policymakers who admit past mistakes, then "fix the sucker and make sure it doesn't happen again." Critics say, beware of Kovalicky's "happy talk." Others generally agree that Kovalicky doesn't indulge in the evasive stonewalling which is so typical of most official Forest

Service spokespersons.

Back to the matter of reform, Kovalicky cautions: "If the Forest Service wants to survive as an agency, reform *must* come from within." But there is also no substitute for public concern and public action. "Right now the system is in the hands of the politicians."

CHAPTER SIX

Montana
Jobs *and* Wilderness, a Compromise

Montana runs on a few basic industries and is handicapped by a troubling lack of economic diversification. The state's economic pie is simple and straightforward: it shows the timber industry holding down an unmistakable 16 percent share of the state's economic base during the 1980s. Montana's leading industrial contributor is the federal government, followed by agriculture (which includes timber in statistical compilations), "other manufacturing," mining, railroads, and tourism. Timbering and government activities grip Montana's 10 intensely timber-dependent western communities in an economic stranglehold. Together they account for 65 percent of the business in this region, famous for big sky and tall timber.

But northwestern Montana is also the home of the Lolo-Kootenai Accords, ground-breaking federal timber agreements negotiated between organized labor (itself a nearly extinct species in the timber industry) and two other sometime opponents, sportsmen and conservationists. The accords, unveiled in June, 1990, back compromise solutions to the timber sales vs. roadless wildlands stalemate in the Lolo and the Kootenai National Forests in Montana's northwest. (The Lolo and the Kootenai forests are Montana's top timber producers.) These unprecedented grassroots agreements came after some three months of secret negotiations between select groups representing moderates on both sides of the 10-year-old feud. Many of those involved had come to see the stand-off as a politically-inspired stalemate.

Both wilderness and jobs came out winners here, negotiators agree. The accords envision setting aside as wilderness more than 670,000 acres of roadless National Forest land, while releasing 532,000 acres for logging, mining and other development.

John Gatchell of the Montana Wilderness Association, a lead player in the Lolo-Kootenai affair, says that these negotiations were a case of "taking the issue back to the people." He and unions leaders agree that strident political rhetoric plus the 11th-hour Reagan veto of a Montana wilderness bill in 1988 "polarized the dialogue on wilderness." But he adds, "We've broken through that....We saw we were both being used."

U.S. Senator Conrad Burns, a conservative Republican and wilderness foe who is linked to the James Watt-Joseph Coors wing of the West's arch-conservative Republican party, is blamed for much of the polarization. In contrast Democratic Representative Jim Williams, who handily won re-election to Congress, has doggedly supported wilderness settlement and is something of a patron saint in these matters. Brian Erhart, a millworkers union representative in the Bonner-Missoula area, says recent re-election sweeps by both Williams and U.S. Senator Max Baucus in the seven counties affected by the accords demonstrate overwhelming local support for the Lolo-Kootenai agreements.

Following their mid-summer debut, the accords were variously hailed as a brilliant, democratically-inspired end run around obstructionist politicians, or else condemned as an underhanded, undemocratic operation designed to exclude all but a few interested parties. Senator Burns, for one, immediately attacked the agreements. But editors at Helena's Independent Record were soon advising critics to "Stop whining, you guys...[and] join in to help, not fight!" The Idaho Falls Post Register said: "Idahoans frustrated by the impasse over a wilderness prescription for the state should monitor Montana's area-by-area experiment to settle its wilderness dilemma."

But Montana's Congressional delegation has remained fiercely divided on wilderness in general and these accords in particular. And six months later, no one could say with certainty whether the accords would ultimately become law by themselves, or become part of a new statewide wilderness bill.

Still, the Lolo-Kootenai accords are, without argument, historic. Consider the participants: for the Kootenai forest, the *Kootenai Wildlands Alliance*, the *Libby Rod and Gun Club*, the *Kootenai Flyfishers*, and the *Cabinet Resource Group*, representing conservationists; and the timber unions, represented by the *Lumber, Production and Industrial Workers Locals #2581* of Libby and *#2719* of Thompson Falls. The Lolo negotiators were the *Missoula Back Country Horsemen*, the *Montana Outfitters and Guides Association*, the *Great Burn Study Group*, and the Missoula-Bitterroot Chapter of the *Montana Wilderness Association*; and for the unions, there were four locals of the *United Brotherhood of Carpenters*, a local of the International Woodworkers of America, and the *United Paperworkers International* local.

The accords soon won support from nearby Forest Service officials, Champion International (operator of mills at Libby and Thompson Falls and the region's biggest employer) and ASARCO, a mining company with interests on these National Forests. Don Wilkins, a Libby union official who worked on the accords, told the San Francisco Examiner his members supported the accords because they recognized that rapid timber cutting to maximize corporate profit might not be in workers' long-term interests.

"There's some apprehension (among the workers) about what these companies have done in the last five to six years with their own lands, just wiping it out down to the pavement. And now they're going into the public land," Wilkins told the Examiner. The accords also broke through the barrier of "owls vs. jobs," fighting words that have become national symbols for the struggle over the future of the Northwest's last great forests.

Don Bachman, a longtime environmental activist from Crested Butte in Western Colorado who now works for the *Greater*

Yellowstone Coalition in Bozeman, thinks other Montana timber workers should consider what millworkers in Libby and Thompson Falls have to say. The failure of timber managers (on federal forests and elsewhere) to provide for a truly sustainable flow of timber, Bachman says, may mean "this could be the last generation of timber workers" in Montana as well as other parts of the American West. As big companies like the Plum Creek Corporation and Champion clearcut the last of their giant private timber stands, they'll join in the competition for what's left of Montana's federal timber. Bachman and others suggest the competition could be bloody.

Plum Creek is infamous in conservation circles as the timber company spawned by the Northern Pacific Railroad to log the millions of acres of prime timberland the railroad acquired as federal grant land during the western expansionist years following the civil war. Union representative Erhart says the accord team is continuing to work together on other forest management issues, and is determined " not to let Plum Creek or Champion do what ever they want to do on the National Forest."

The *Greater Yellowstone Coalition* (GYC) in Bozeman keeps an eagle eye on timber affairs in the five national forests within the Greater Yellowstone ecosystem. Forest economist Randal O'Toole was hired by GYC in 1987 to look into the economic realities of the five forests. He concluded that the "economically efficient level of timber harvests from the Yellowstone forests is near zero." Management of forests in such "a vast complex of lands, resources and management programs" is difficult at best, he suggests. "Timber, grazing, and recreation all lose money."

In his 1988 book, *Reforming the Forest Service,* O'Toole uses two Yellowstone ecosystem National Forests, Montana's Gallatin and Beaverhead, as examples of how "forest managers commonly assume that timber price increases of the future justify money-losing timber sales today." To U.S. foresters, O'Toole explains, wood is second only to food as an essential for existence, thus rising price trends make sense to agency planners. He then says:

"The Forest Service claims it needs to maintain the timber program for 'community stability' and to ensure that mills will be around to consume the wood in the future when prices increase. Yet it would probably be cheaper for the Forest Service to buy the mills and pension off the workers than continue the losses. If the Gallatin prediction is correct—and it may be an underestimate—*taxpayers will lose over $61,000 per year for each of the 71 people whose jobs are supposed to depend on the Gallatin National Forest timber sales.*" [italics added]

O'Toole argues forcefully that the best way to reform the Forest Service is through the agency's budget process, a system so skewed toward timber production that it rewards forest managers for continuing to sell federal timber below cost. Road building is another "budget-enhancing" activity, which explains why the U.S. Forest Service has become this nation's *number one road builder.*

Twenty-two years before the Lolo-Kootenai Accords demonstrated the power and the possibilities of grassroots environmental action, earlier Montana leaders had made forest policy history of a different sort. By the late 1960s, the U.S. Forest Service had adopted wholesale clearcutting as its dominant method of harvesting timber, and the public was aghast at the results.

Montana's Bitterroot National Forest (where the agency bulldozed terraces for replanting following clearcutting) provided particularly outrageous examples of the Forest Service's out-of-control timber production drive. Guy Brandborg, retired Bitterroot Forest Supervisor, spoke out first, and successfully lobbied Senator Lee Metcalf, who instigated a study by the University of Montana, known as the Bolle Report. The 1979 report—named for Arthur Bolle, then dean of the School of Forestry—stood then and stands now as an outspoken indictment of traditional forest management practices. The report said that "multiple use management, in fact, does not exist as a governing principle on the Bitterroot National Forest" and charged the agency with "mining timber" on timberland not suitable for commercial logging.

The Bolle Report helped open the way for new federal legislation in the 1970s, such as the National Forest Management Act, which conservationists hoped would end such destructive practices (it hasn't fulfilled that promise). Although one year later, the 1990 Lolo-Kootenai Accords still have not been adopted by Congress as part of any new Montana wilderness plan, the Montana coalition that produced these historic agreements shows that local opponents in a decades-old timber dispute can, indeed, find common ground.

CLOSEUP
Sara Johnson, A Quiet Fighter

Montana wildlife biologist Sara Johnson could become famous someday.

After all, whoever heard of Jack Ward Thomas before the now notorious Thomas Report in 1990 which said that, to save the northern spotted owl and maintain the forest's ecological balance, the U.S. Forest Service must stop systematically logging thousands of acres of old growth forest in the Northwest.

But Sara Johnson isn't looking for fame. It's justice she wants. After 14 frustrating years with the Forest Service, she quit in 1980 to join the fight from the other side. Now a paid staffer with *American Wildlands*, an environmental organization based in Englewood, Colorado, Johnson uses her time selectively.

She specializes in writing technical appeals to National Forest management plans and timber sales—the kind of legal appeals that have stopped many a timber cutting plan in its tracks. She says the Forest Service is an easy target. In setting up these controversial timber sales, the agency simply hasn't adhered to the National Environmental Policy Act (NEPA) and the National Forest Management Act, laws that "finally gave the public a way to combat" runaway timber sales on public lands. The 1969 NEPA legislation, for example, requires all federal agencies to prepare detailed statements about "major" actions which will have a significant effect on the environment.

While each appeal is unique, Johnson says most Forest Service planning documents have fundamental flaws. Forest Service planners regularly claim, falsely, that timber sales "will increase wildlife habitat." And when it comes to questions about adequate protection for "cavity nesters" (birds and mammals that live in tree hollows and the like), the agency simply has "no answers." Also USFS timber planners devise sale plans based on the agency's standard 80-year forest regrowth cycle, or rotation. While the 80-year rotation formula may be a convenient planning tool for foresters, Sarah points out that many slow-growing trees don't reach maturity in 80 years.

Johnson, a tall, lean lady with the high cheekbones and classic good looks of her Scandinavian forebears, isn't pulling any punches. "I think the Forest Service is corrupt," not an unusual condition for government, she notes. "I'm amazed the information on the spotted owl ever came out."

Although the Forest Service boasts that wildlife biologists are regularly members of the agency's timber sales planning teams, Johnson says their views are largely ignored. During the 14 years she worked for the Forest Service, Johnson says: "None of my recommendations were ever used—except to close a road."

The anger is still there. Clearly, Sara Johnson is a fighter. And she doesn't like to lose. She recalls a particularly frustrating experience involving a proposed timber sale on the Targhee National Forest in Northern Idaho. Her cautious recommendation, to leave less than one percent of the planned sale area for wildlife habitat, infuriated the likely timber buyer and prompted a royal row between Johnson and her superiors.

The agency arranged a field trip to the sale site, where Sara and the timber buyer went head to head over saving what Sara saw as a minuscule but critical part of forest. "My boss sided with the timber buyer. I was so mad I didn't speak to my boss" at all during the long ride back to the office. The anger etched a permanent notch in the mental record she was accumulating against the agency she believes abandoned its principles and buried the evidence of its destruction of irreplaceable wildlife habitat.

Now, she has the law on her side. "The Forest Service doesn't have a leg to stand on. There's too much biological evidence. If the Forest Service doesn't do a good job [meeting the National Environmental Protection Act requirements], they can't justify those timber sales in court."

Sara isn't your run-of-the laboratory scientist. Or litigant, for that matter. She grew up on a ranch in Gregory, South Dakota ("cows, wheat and corn") and hoped to be a veterinarian. Instead ended up with a Masters Degree in general science. She and Tom Glorvigen met during their graduate school days at the University of Eastern Montana at Bozeman. Tom earned an advanced degree in fisheries management biology, but for the past 15 years has owned and operated the KOA campground near Three Forks, Montana, where they make their home.

Three great rivers, the Madison, the Jefferson and the Gallatin, join nearby. For history buffs, it can be a profound experience to climb the bluff on a bucolic day in early fall, as my companion and I did, and look down upon the spot where, in 1805 the Lewis and Clark expedition made camp—after successfully establishing that the merging of these three rivers formed the long sought-after headwaters of the mighty Missouri.

Sara Johnson and Sacagawea, the legendary Shoshone woman who courageously guided the American discoverers across thousands of miles of fierce and unknown territory, have a lot in common. Each studied the land in great detail, closely observed every feature, recorded those observations (each in an appropriate way) and then made critical conclusions based on their training and experience.[1]

Three Forks, about 40 miles west of Bozeman, provides plenty of the tranquility Johnson needs for her work. The task involves endless amounts of reading "to keep up" with both the scientific and legal aspects of forest plan and timber sale appeals. "I don't do this alone," says Sara. Bozeman is a center of environmental activity, and Sara regularly consults with several other wildlife biology specialists there. In addition to her work for *American Wildlands*, she also does consulting on a volunteer basis for other conservation and environmental groups who are out to save what's left of their particular forests. The demand is strong. "I could work 80 hours a week if I wanted to," she confides.

We are sitting across from each other at a table near the window in the KOA's big office room. Sara unfurls a map with dark patches here and there. These, she says, represent grizzly bear recovery areas on a portion of the Gallatin National Forest. (The Gallatin, incidentally, is one of the West's chronic timber management money-losers, costing taxpayers $4 million a year in below-cost timber sales.)

In 1975, facing compelling evidence that grizzly bears were threatened, the Forest Service developed special forest management guidelines for protecting grizzly bear habitat. However, the guidelines allowed "other activities" to supersede the guidelines requirements — and they often did. Leaning forward, Sara Johnson declares: "The Forest Service is *very* anti-bear." In the eight years she worked in Montana's Gallatin (adjacent to Yellowstone Park's northern border), Johnson says she was "never once consulted about grizzly bears." In the 1980s, biologists' comments were regularly dropped from the final environmental assessment on timber sale proposals.

In one case, according to Johnson, it took a Freedom of Information Act filing to uncover one wildlife biologist's comments involving a proposed timber sale on the Beaverhead National Forest. The biologist's findings had simply been blacked out. Sarah tells me that while the Forest Service made a big show of employing staff biologists to protect wildlife and its habitat, the agency has routinely ignored or suppressed their reports about the great gray owl, the pine marten, the Williamson sapsucker, the northern three-toed woodpecker, wolverine, lynx, and other species that live in what she calls "mature and over-mature forests." Just the kind of trees the timber industry covets, the kind of big, old-growth trees that can be cut into a great many profitable two-by-fours or studs or beautiful veneers.

"Species are being lost on all National Forests. I truly believe if people understood what is really happening, they'd be outraged. But the Forest Service has such a [pure] image," people still think of the agency as the true defenders of the forest and its wondrous creatures.

For all its frustration, her 14 years with the Forest Service provided invaluable training and experience. She's studied everything from grizzlies to deer mice. As a field scientist she's seen other abuses of public land. In some areas, she tells me, "grazing has totally changed the small mammal population....There are no flowers, once sheep have grazed."

Can the Forest Service be reformed from within? Sara Johnson sees a few hopeful signs. A recent environmental assessment of a timber sale slated for Idaho's Targhee National Forest included observations by the staff biologist about a noticeable decline in the great gray owl population. But, given what the Forest Service historically "likes to do best, build roads and cut trees," Sara Johnson isn't sure internal reform will come in time to save the few precious remnants of the West's once glorious wildlife habitat.

"I feel a sense of urgency. In another 10 years, it seems like it will be hopeless." Clearcutting, for example, means that remaining stands of old-growth timber "are all edge," a bonanza for predators. To survive, the forest's interior songbirds (and other forest dwellers as well) require large forests where they can find both food and shelter from their enemies. Now predators— such as cowbirds—simply "patrol" the vast, straight edges of clearcuts, easily downing birds or small mammals trying to make a run for the nearest patch of hospitable habitat. Sarah adds, "Cowbirds love clearcuts, and the other birds [who are their prey] are paying for it."

It was late September when I visited Sara and Tom, just a few days before the campground would close for the winter season. Watching Sara stride across the mostly empty parking lot one morning, amber hair hidden under a well-seasoned cowboy hat, bridle in hand, heading toward the back fence and her grazing horses, I thought to myself: Sara Johnson seems like an unlikely fanatic. Researching issues and writing formal appeals to forest management plans and timber sales which threaten habitat on publicly-owned National Forest is simply what biologist Johnson likes to do best, what she thinks is most important. With a little chuckle, she describes the start of a new appeal project. "I get so excited. I can feel my cheeks turning red," she says, sliding an open hand upward on each cheek like a flustered schoolgirl.

In between forest issues, Sara writes romance novels. Another unlikely occupation. Both occupations, she suggests, are extremely satisfying.

Sara has no qualms about taking federal forest issues to court, if the administrative appeals process fails to rule for her side. If the Forest Service "does a good NEPA job," she believes, "they can't justify these sales." She is "thrilled" by a new court ruling overturning a Congressional ban on forest timber-sale appeals in the Northwest, one of the minor skirmishes in the greater battle over owls and old-growth forests there. In contrast, timber industry people I talked to were horrified at the idea that judges, who "know nothing about managing the forest," are making decisions "best left to trained forestry professionals."

Sara Johnson worries that politicians and timber industry leaders might find a way to persuade the U.S. Congress to pass laws "legislating the cut." She's speaking about the annual cut, central to all timber harvest controversies, which is now set by some unfathomable interior Forest Service process. (Even University of Colorado law professor Charles Wilkinson, a leader in the Forest Service reform movement, tells audiences he hasn't been able to track the decision-making process used by the agency to determine each year's "annual cut.")

The U.S. Fish and Wildlife Service, the federal agency

responsible for monitoring endangered species, is, according to Sara, "a waste of taxpayers money." Several other ecologists and biologists I talked to agreed with that point of view, although others say this agency's work is often choked by political constraints. Wildlife issues, most agree, are politically hot. Sometimes too hot. Like other bureaucrats, U.S. Fish and Wildlife staffers know that their jobs are on the line, should they speak out at the wrong time on the wrong issue.

That's another reason why Sara Johnson likes the view from outside the Forest Service. "Governments always get corrupted," she offers. She pauses a moment and looks out the window at Montana's lovely fall landscape as she considers my question about the message she'd like to send out to people who wonder what's happening to their National Forests. She leans forward, gives a little shrug as if what she says will sound deceptively simple. It is. "The only way public land will remain valuable [as a public resource] is through public involvement."

---

[1] *Author's note: My friend, Doreen Yellowbird, a former Washington, D.C., administrator who now directs radio and newspaper communications for three North Dakota tribes, recently provided authoritative information on the question of how to pronounce the name, Sacagawea. Various writers and historians disagree on the question, but I have taken Doreen Yellowbird's advice in this matter, saying it "Sa-COCK-a-wea." Other modern authorities also prefer the "ga" spelling over the more familiar Sacajawea. In any case, this grand historical figure, whose name means Bird Woman, is a particular heroine of mine.*

CHAPTER SEVEN

Wyoming
"...Flat Run Out of Trees"

Wyoming is both blessed and cursed. Blessed with an exquisite abundance of scenic beauty and natural resources. Cursed by the fact that so much beauty and the exploitation of so many resources—from mining, oil and timber to outdoor recreation— are often in conflict. With the state's economy in the doldrums in the 1980s, and the Reagan Administration encouraging a "grab it now" attitude toward natural resources, it's not surprising that Wyoming seemed to welcome a stepped-up timber harvest on the 2.2 million acres of National Forest timberland within its boundaries. (Federal ownership accounts for over 30 million acres in this state, but only a fraction of those acres grow marketable timber.)

Wyoming's four National Forests—the Big Horn in the north, the Bridger-Teton and the Shoshone in western Wyoming, and the Medicine Bow toward the southeast, along with a portion of the Black Hills National Forest—provide the bulk of timber for the state's timber industry. But close to one-third of the state's 4.3 million acres of timberland is held privately, contained within Wyoming's big, sprawling cattle ranches—ranches that lend a special historical character and real western flavor to this rugged, often unforgiving region. Rex Johnson, Wyoming State Forester, says Wyoming's ranching families are seldom willing to sell their trees for sawtimber. And only a comparative scrap of commercial timberland is owned by the forest industry itself, which means that Wyoming's timber operators must rely almost exclusively on federal lands for sawtimber.

State officials say the timber industry's place in the state's economic base is, by itself, too minuscule to measure. Official calculations place "agriculture, forestry and fisheries" at the bottom of some 16 Wyoming industries listed in the census. The glory years for mining and oil, the state's biggest industries, ended with the West's "energy bust" in the early '80s; but many political leaders still see Wyoming's economic salvation in terms of aggressive natural resource development. Despite the statistically small role played by timber in the state's economy, the Wyoming Heritage Foundation, a Wyoming Forest Products Industry group, tells us that the timber industry "directly impacts the economies of 26 communities and 16 counties," providing 1,435 jobs and a $23 million payroll in 1989. And of course, these Wyoming communities like "timber-dependent communities" all over the West, live or die according to the flow of National Forest timber, whatever the size of their contribution to the total economy.

During the 1980s, the volume of sawtimber (mostly lodgepole pine) cut annually in Wyoming rose by 39 percent. This was a remarkable increase for a state where, at best, these tall pines can take over a century to mature. As Larry Mehlhaff, of the Sierra Club in Sheridan, puts it: "You must remember that Wyoming has very severe growing conditions—worse than Colorado." As a result of such accelerated cutting, according to Mehlhaff, by the start of the current decade many of Wyoming's National Forests "had flat run out of trees."

Even longtime Wyoming residents were caught off-guard by the accumulating impacts of the logging frenzy of the 1980s—accelerated clearcutting, networks of new roads, scarred slopes and vanishing wildlife habitat. Pat Thrasher, a Forest Service spokesman for the Medicine Bow National Forest, confirms that until about 1985 there was very little public involvement in the Bow's timber management practices. Even news stories about the mill shutdown at Dubois—where everyone *except the timber industry* agreed the trees had certainly run out—didn't alert the public-at-large to the new and troubling timber issues on other Wyoming National Forests. But by the end of the decade, conservation worries, like measles, were suddenly popping up all over Wyoming.

In January, 1990, the Sierra Club won a decisive victory in its lawsuit over planned timber harvest levels on the Big Horn National Forest. A court injunction stopped all further clearcutting of lodgepole pine on the Big Horn. Later, the Sierra Club agreed to a compromise which allowed the Forest Service to sell up to 7 million board feet of timber annually instead of the 14.6 million-board-feet annual sale quantity (ASQ) that Big Horn timber managers had called for in the Big Horn's forest management plan. The Big Horn's forest plan, court documents showed, set annual timber quantity levels *far above* the actual number of trees the forest could produce each year. And, Mehlhaff says, Forest Service documents also showed that forest managers knew "the trees weren't there." Mehlhaff speculates that political pressure may have nudged timber managers to "cook the numbers."

Soon after the Big Horn debacle, Gary Cargill, Rocky Mountain Regional Forester called for a special blue-ribbon panel to evaluate the Medicine Bow's 50-year forest plan. This action, however, wasn't exactly spontaneous. An irate citizens' group from Laramie, which became known as "Friends of the Bow," had taken their frustrations directly to Cargill in Denver. There Cargill, Region 2 head since 1986, and his regional headquarters staff of about 250 (small compared to others such as California's Region 1) oversee 16 National Forests in five states: Colorado, Kansas, Nebraska, South Dakota and Eastern Wyoming.

The panel, chosen by Cargill to review forest management on the Bow was indeed impressive. On the scholarly side, it included two forestry school deans, Dr. Sidney Frissel of the University of Montana and Dr. Jay Hughes of Colorado State University ; Dr.

Robert Lee a forestry professor at the University of Washington; and Dr. Charles Wilkinson, a University of Colorado law school professor and visionary natural resources legal scholar. Dan Perdue, Wyoming's state planning coordinator, along with Tom Thompson, Deputy Regional Forester, rounded out the group.

The team's May, 1990 "Report on the Implementation of the Medicine Bow National Forest Plan," is equally impressive. Couched in ultra-diplomatic language, the report is nevertheless an unmistakable indictment of the Bow's earlier timber management practices. The team concluded that "most of the problem areas (on the Medicine Bow) derive from an emphasis on the production of commercial wood products," a situation "not unique" to the Bow. "In our experience," the panel wrote, "an emphasis on timber production drives the basic decision-making processes in most National Forests in the western United States."

The report charitably suggests Medicine Bow National Forest personnel worked under a variety of handicaps. These included being among the first (in 1985) to complete a forest plan under the new the National Forest Management Act. (Other National Forests, such as the Rio Grande in southern Colorado, have made similar claims about time constraints.) Timber targets that were fixed at a higher, regional level also forced the Bow's managers to put an "emphasis on timber production as a first priority." Finally, FORPLAN, the "timber-oriented" computer program favored by the Forest Service, further skewed the plan toward *Timber First!* management. The Bow, this team said, "should move quickly toward true integrated resource management," and must beware of below-cost timber sales. "These and other federal subsidies to traditional western resource users have received widely-publicized criticism" and will likely continue to rile the public, the panel observed.

The Medicine Bow's review panel found that roadless areas, where future use is still in dispute, were targeted for a total cut of 70 million board feet, close to half of the next 160 million board

95

feet scheduled for harvest on the Bow. Team members suggested this was unwise. "It would seem prudent to consider developing specific guides for evaluating alternative management proposals for such areas," they concluded.

The team's findings touch on another universal Forest Service public land management issue—what these reviewers call the "need for an internal champion" to speak for forest uses other than commercial logging. The leadership "opportunity" they speak of in this report is clearly code for bolder internal agency reform.

Mark Squillace of Laramie, a University of Wyoming law professor, is a founding member of *Friends of the Bow.* Six months after the May, 1990 report, Squillace told me that, while "we're quite pleased with the report," his group is increasingly dismayed over the Forest Service's failure to respond to the report's recommendations. With new timber sales coming up soon, Squillace said *Friends of the Bow* may go directly to the Regional Forester once again, this time asking him to hold up consideration of any new timber sales until Medicine Bow managers address issues raised in the report.

The story Squillace tells is, by now, a familiar one. Louisiana-Pacific is by far the biggest of four timber companies operating in the Laramie area; all four depend on the Medicine Bow National Forest for timber. "L-P has said publicly they will leave if they don't get the 17-18 million board feet" they want each year from the public forest. The Bow's present ASQ (annual sale quantity) is 28.4 million board feet—a figure *Friends of the Bow* says will mean massive clearcutting in the Bow's hotly contested roadless areas. Only five percent of the Bow is now set aside as wilderness and that five percent is heavily used. *Friends of the Bow,* with strong local support, say that the Forest Service should back off plans for heavy logging in these roadless areas.

Friends has no hidden agenda. "We'd just love to see Louisiana-Pacific leave. The forest can't accommodate L-P's insatiable appetite," Squillace says with calm conviction. The Bow, he suggests, could easily support the three smaller timber companies, along with a booming recreation community; but he's not sure Wyoming's leaders, and those in the Forest Service, will come around to that point of view. "We'll either win big—or lose big," this Laramie lawyer allows.

The political clout and ravenous timber appetite of these "big operators" is a recurring theme wherever timber grows in the West. In an effort to increase local "market stability," and insure a ready market for its main commodity, the Forest Service has often encouraged one big operator to move into a certain area. In their book, *The Angry West*, then Colorado Governor Richard Lamm and Michael McCarthy describe this pattern, picturing the American West as a vassal state, largely owned and run by big-time corporate interests:

> "Favoritism was a fact. The government did favor large
> operators over small, and in the process monopoly often
> destroyed free enterprise on the public domain....The federal
> feeling was that monopoly was at least efficient, that cattle kings,
> mining corporations, water-power combines, and lumber
> cartels, operating out of self-interest, would use resources more
> efficiently and more scientifically than small 'cut and run'
> operators."

With timber supplies shrinking not just in Wyoming, but almost everywhere in the West, it looks like the Forest Service's "market stability" strategy may be backfiring.

Wyoming's Game and Fish Department staffers are easy to spot. The state has abandoned the traditional tan or khaki in favor of bold red shirts, giving officers like WG&F wildlife biologist Joe Nemick a friendlier, less regimented look.

Nemick heads wildlife biology in the department's regional office in Lander. The day I looked up Nemick—a fine fall day right in the middle of the hunting season—the Lander office hummed like a command post in combat zone. Nemick, who has 24 years experience with the department as a wildlife biologist,

seems largely unflappable. The department, he says, fights hard
to protect what's left of Wyoming's wildlife habitat, especially
areas with "high wildlife values."

Cutting new roads in previously roadless areas—especially the
wide, heavily graveled boulevards the Forest Service often builds
for timber access, and other claimed "benefits"—is tough on
wildlife. Sports vehicles highballing through the forests mean
increased "road kill." Broken and isolated patches of forest
habitat leave wildlife dangerously exposed.

Big game hunting is big business in Wyoming. In 1988
sportsmen spent almost $200 million here, not including license
fees. Wildlife watching, or "non-consumptive uses," Nemick
points out, contributed even more, a surprising $678 million to
the state's 1986 economy, prompting a new promotional
campaign, "Wyoming Wildlife—Worth the Watching."

While Nemick cheerfully concedes that dealing with the U.S.
Forest Service often involves political gamesmanship, he says: "We
don't roll over and play dead" on National Forest issues. Nemick
produces a copy of "Six-points and two-by-fours —Timber harvest
and elk on National Forests," a piece he wrote for the January,
1989 issue of Wyoming Wildlife. It is a cautious assessment of the
problem, citing efforts to come up with a formula, or forage-to-
cover ratio, which can be applied to wildlife and timber sale
calculations. "As with most questions dealing with wildlife, there
is no one correct answer," he concludes. It's easy to guess that
forest management planners, hunched over their computers,
aren't certain, either, how to feed this sort of problem into
FORPLAN.

Meanwhile, conservation and environmental groups say that
state wildlife biologists all over the West are key behind-the-scenes
players in this strange political game. "A whole revolution is
going on in brown paper envelopes," one environmental
organization staffer told me. Wildlife biologists, the staff person
explains, use the USFS's large brown envelopes to dispatch
important insider information to local watchdog groups. This

revolution, apparently, has yet to touch most state forestry departments, the agencies charged with supervising both state-owned timberland and providing technical advice to owners of private, non-industrial forest land.

Rex Johnson is Wyoming's Forestry Management Utilization/ Marketing Specialist, under the Commissioner of Public Lands. He's been a forester for 30 years and says he has seen these same forest management issues come and go before. Since the turn-of-the-century, he advises me, conservationists have predicted "gloom and doom" over timber supply issues, but adds, "looking at what's out there, I think there's an abundance of natural resources." Johnson is not happy with federal ownership of most of the American West's natural resources, though, because he believes "the public" is an inept manager of those resources. He also laments the fact that much of Wyoming's privately held timberland isn't for sale and generally isn't managed for harvesting timber as a commodity. "In my experience, private ownership of the means of production is best," Johnson tells me in a phone interview. In keeping with that view, he also predicts the revival of the Sagebrush Rebellion, a 1970's movement among disgruntled western ranchers and other natural resource interests, to promote state ownership of the millions of acres of federal land within each state's border. (Wyoming, for example, is 49.5 percent federally owned.)

Like many other traditional foresters, he thinks professional foresters, not the public, should be managing the National Forests. "Unfortunately," he admits, "foresters aren't commanding much respect these days." Moreover, Johnson complains, forestry's national organizations are all headed by lawyers. (The American Society of Foresters is forestry's professional fraternity, but foresters are also active in a whole array of industry groups including the National Forest Products Association and its offspring, The American Forest Resources Alliance.)

Johnson suggests that I talk to Donn Kesselheim of the *Wyoming*

Outdoor Council in Lander, a man Johnson considers
"knowledgeable and not just emotional" about conservation
issues. He was right. Kesselheim, a former educator who is now
the Council's information and outreach person, is certainly no
hot-head. His carefully phrased statements: "In Wyoming, many
people are mistaken about how long it takes trees to grow," and
"The Forest Service has probably the biggest road department in
the world," are devoid of inflammatory rhetoric. Kesselheim
looks very businesslike in understated jacket and slacks as he
argues that Wyoming's conservation community has "a critically
important mission." That mission is to stem rampant resource
development—timbering, oil, and mining on federal lands.

Along with Kesselheim I meet Stephanie Kessler, *Wyoming
Outdoor Council* director. She is a handsome young woman, tall
and trim with long brown hair that defies the corporate look. She
tells me one of her major concerns now is the likelihood of
increased clearcutting in Wyoming's lesser-know forest areas. The
Bridger-Teton, Jackson Hole, and Yellowstone National Park
region in Wyoming's northwest corner thrives on a burgeoning
visitor, resort and upscale rural-retreat lifestyle economy.
Clearcutting in highly visible areas there became a big issue in the
'80s, she says. But in the 1990s, on-going efforts to preserve
National Forests in Wyoming's popular, high-profile northwest
will put increased pressure on National Forest timber targets "in
less scenic areas." She also worries about the fact that "nobody in
Wyoming is talking about managing for old growth." And she
thinks it's patently undemocratic to consider hiking user fees to
hold down overuse of some highly popular wilderness areas.

"I thought the idea was that Americans should *all* have access to
wilderness," regardless of their economic status, Kessler says,
sounding a bit indignant. People in the American West, she
warns, "should beware of European forestry techniques," which
amount to tree farming, complete with chemicals and other 20th-
century wonders. She's also concerned that Americans "don't
[fully] appreciate the wild and diverse forests we have here in the

West." And while Kessler senses a new and "major movement toward sustainable forestry," she's afraid it may not come in time to save Wyoming's remaining roadless federal forestlands which are currently targeted for high yielding clearcuts.

Kessler, who for four years was director of the Alaska Center for the Environment, also says that conservation and environmental groups are now learning the importance of altering the dialogue in what has too often been a forest vs. jobs debate. Kessler points out that citizens groups are now beginning to "talk about people.... Can we move that sector into a new economy" instead of pursuing a confrontational either-or-dialogue—saving trees vs. saving jobs—with all its attendant hostility.

In Wyoming (as elsewhere in the West) changing this dialogue will be a three-way, three-party challenge involving the timber industry, environmental groups and the Forest Service. The USFS once proclaimed, "We harvest timber because it is needed for man's survival." Today, many parties to the dialogue are no longer satisfied with such an oversimplified view.

CLOSEUP

Dubois, Timber Town in Transition

In the American West, town halls and city halls make very different architectural and cultural statements. That's why the bravura of tiny Dubois, Wyoming's surprisingly grand municipal building is so unexpected. Grants paid most of the bills for Dubois's stunning two-story municipal structure—all stone and glass—which seems to emerge defiantly from a hillside above the town's main street. This stylish edifice may be a form of "whistling in the dark" for a Wyoming community struggling to recover from the collapse of its timber-dependent economy.

In 1988, when Dubois (population: about 1067) saw its Louisiana-Pacific mill shut down, nobody was sure if, or how, the town would survive. Two years later, a brochure in the Dubois town hall proclaims, "Wind River—We Mean Business," and town

administrator Pat Neary has become the town's genial and
aggressive sales manager. Dubois, up the road north of Lander
and Riverton in Western Wyoming, sits in the beautiful Wind
River Valley, closely protected on the west by the Wind River
Range. The place, strongly influenced by the same geothermal
system that dominates the Yellowstone region, offers the traveler a
tantalizing preview of Jackson Hole, the Tetons, and Yellowstone
just a few hours away.

But, the idea of a recreation economy for Dubois came mostly
as an afterthought. As Neary says, Dubois's traditional economy is
ranching and timber. A memorial pays tribute to area's
"tiehacks," the pioneer laborers who logged Dubois's lodgepole
pine forests and hacked the logs into railroad ties for tracks that
crossed the west's great empty spaces. When the mill went down
in 1988, cut off by the U.S. Forest Service which said it could no
longer supply the 14 million board feet of public timber L-P said
it must have each year, Dubois was traumatized.

Economists said 35 percent of the community's total income
was directly attributable to L-P, which has been an aggressive
presence in Dubois ever since it took over the mill in 1974. Neary
also explains: "We're one of those unique towns that's completely
dependent on federal policy. We have National Forest on three
sides and an Indian Reservation on the fourth side. We are
literally an island." Dubois, Neary says, once hauled 30 million
board feet a year off the nearby federal forests. But now the
Shoshone National Forest has been picked clean. Massive
clearcuts have scarred the landscape and raised the ire of nearby
Jackson and Pinedale citizens who had already concluded that the
region's face was its fortune. Today, logging in this forest has not
entirely stopped, but continues at a vastly reduced pace; the 1990
harvest is down to a mere 7 million board feet. And local pickup
trucks now sport bumper stickers that say, "Wilderness—the Land
of No Use." (Later, in the Northwest, I saw another bumper
sticker that read: "Wilderness—Land of No Abuse.")

Neary, lean, quick, and just turned 40, doesn't take credit for the fact that after the L-P mill closed down, Dubois "didn't dry up and blow away." The closing followed a bitter two-year court battle and a ruling which said the Forest Service wasn't obliged to manage the National Forest primarily for jobs and the economy. Neary and others give L-P credit for easing the transition, and they give thanks also to various local, state and federal agencies for putting together a strong, self-help survival plan that seems to be working.

Neary occupies a pleasant, airy office in Dubois's spacious town hall. A large window offers a sweeping view of the town and the magnificent Wind River mountains, which he tells me are home to the West's largest herd of big horn sheep. As we talk he leans back in his chair, confidently at ease in Levis (properly broken in) silver-buckled western belt and a crisp white shirt open at the collar. As a member of Dubois volunteer ambulance unit, he also wears a small beeper, or remote paging device, hooked on his belt. It is evidence of the life and death kind of unpaid work that keeps Dubois and other parts of the rural West intact.

Pat Neary seems happy to have shed his former image, that of an assistant vice-president at a Littleton, Colorado, bank. When Colorado's economy went sour, he turned down a job offer in Los Angeles, deciding instead "to move to where I wanted to live and try to make a living there." In the spring of 1988 he arrived in Dubois and spent the summer working as a fly-fishing guide, a skill he had honed during the five years he spent as an instructor with the National Outdoor Leadership School, (or NOLS) based in nearby Lander. (Neary is one of perhaps dozens of NOLS graduates who are poised to become part of the West's new political and economic leadership.)

Pat Neary, once the typical city businessman, is still amused by the idea that he literally found the administrator job when he noticed the town's ad in the local paper. His specialty, financial data processing between banks, didn't fit the town's job description, but his management and administrative expertise certainly did.

While Neary is a confident and poised public manager, he takes care to point out that he should not be credited with the town's successful turnaround. Dubois's recovery "is a bit of a mystery," he muses. Yet, he and other town leaders, such as Dubois Mayor Bob Baker, once L-P's head forester, can easily trace the steps the town has taken during the two years since the mill closed down. Mid-interview the beeper sounds and Neary, grabbing a green down vest, speeds off. He soon returns, seeming buoyant. A false alarm, he explains—an elderly citizen had mistakenly bumped an emergency signal. Our interview continues.

Neary says that immediately after the mill shutdown, the town disbanded its eight-member police department and all the lawyers left town. Two years later, Dubois still didn't have a resident attorney, but Neary says with a sly smile, he doesn't see that as a bad thing.

Wyoming has always been a chic playground for the wealthy, one obvious edge for any community. Neary mentions ranch ownerships that ring with familiarity—Schwinn, Guggenheim, Maytag and Disney. Neary's wife is the office manager for the elegantly upscale Bitterroot Ranch and its "Equitours," or "worldwide riding holidays." After perhaps first brushing up on their horsemanship at the Ranch, tour groups fly off to Ireland, Kenya, and other exotic destinations where patrons will tour on horseback. In Equitour's impressive brochure, riders are shown mounted on beautifully groomed, blue-ribbon steeds, cantering through some of the world's most scenic settings.

So when the mill closed down in the late '80s, Dubois was poised for big-time recreation. Already in place were the area's 5000 ft. airstrip, its nine posh dude ranches, and stunning terrain offering a variety of activities from from big game hunting to hundreds of miles of logging roads so snowmobiling Minnesotans can ride virtually to the top of Whiskey Mountain. Dubois mounted an aggressive advertising campaign, splashing the Wind River Valley's gorgeous attributes all over TV screens in the northern mid-west.

Meanwhile, L-P relocated some of the mill's 105 workers, while others scratched their heads and looked for new ways to make a living in Dubois. A number of L-P people, like town mayor Bob Baker, chose to stay. Two years after the mill closed, the town had lost about 1,000 year-around residents, but Neary says school enrollment is now only seven students less that it was before the shutdown. Local bank deposits, however, have grown an impressive 14 percent in just the last six months, thanks to a booming Dubois real estate market—the result of property priced to sell and a successful ad campaign touting the Wind River valley as a prime vacation spot. Locals say that Californians, fresh from doubling their own investments in that state's booming real estate market, can reinvest in a small but complete ranch outfit (house, 100 acres and horses) starting at $150,000. Snowmobiling, Neary says, is another a growth industry. Wayne Steinert, down at the Dubois Merc, is the state's top snowmobile dealer. And out-of-state snowmobile clubs coming to stay for a week spend an average of $120 a day per person; in contrast, the best summer spenders leave just half that amount.

Neary tells me that one travel and vacation writer recently called Dubois "the Jackson nobody knows." The analysis seems apt. Neary would add the idea, "affordable," too. Dubois motels are $20-$30 a day, RV parks are spacious, and the valley's year-around weather is pleasingly moderate, an enticement for Dubois's growing "active retiree" population. The town's recovery plan called for developing all these diversified but tourist-related economic sectors, while at the same time continuing to nurture a reduced local wood-products industry, expanding from timbering alone into what's known as "value-added processing."

Timber economists are promoting the idea that adding extra value to timber through extended local manufacturing is an important way to boost income in beleaguered, timber-dependent communities. The argument ultimately goes right to the heart of the export issue. In towns like Dubois, additional jobs can be created in milling, crafting, and even marketing wood products locally. Most conservationists I talked to stressed the idea that National Forests from Arizona to the Northwest can indeed support a smaller and healthier local logging industry but cannot and should not be expected to sustain the high production of an industrial timber giant like Weyerhaeuser or Lousiana-Pacific. Some timber management experts, like Dick Behan of Northern Arizona University at Flagstaff, think communities should have a strong hand in deciding how their nearby National Forests should be managed. The question of size and ownership of timber companies might be a good place to start.

Lander legend Tom Bell has dealt with these questions first-hand as founder of the prestigious High Country News. Twenty years ago he began to sound the alarm over environmental abuse in the West. He's written that the town of Dubois, Fremont County, and their citizens "spoke with one voice" in support of keeping L-P going, in spite of the environmental price. So the decision by the U.S. Forest Service to deny L-P the massive timber cut it wanted, represented, according to Bell, "an abrupt turn for the agency, from giving almost carte blanche to logging on the National Forest lands in western Wyoming to an attempt to preserve surviving stands by drastically reducing logging."

In the end, it was a combination of events that forced Dubois to look in other directions for its economic salvation. But while town administrator Neary, and the resort-based economy he's helping to promote, represent the positive side of this radical economic change, the transition from lumbering has been wrenching and painful for many Dubois citizens. As well as anybody, Bob Baker, former chief forester for L-P and current Dubois mayor, exemplifies those who accepted this change with a heavy heart.

Mayor Baker still carries the scars from the five-year battle he led to keep Louisiana-Pacific's stud mill in business here. While waiting to catch Baker the next day at Dubois's Painted Valley Building Supply, the enterprise he now owns and operates, I look around. There's no mistaking the fact that the place is running in high gear. A customer—he sounds like a contractor—is talking to a clerk about an extensive remodeling job for an new resident, which now includes plans for a swimming pool. Baker is bustling around, answering the phone in his office and fielding questions from several people who are looking for supplies. Nevertheless, he is gracious about taking time to talk and we agree to meet at Ziggy's Grub and Tub on the other side of town. Flags, both Wyoming's and the stars and stripes, are flying in front of Ziggy's and just about every other business in town from service station to mini-mart, giving the place a wonderful, festive look. Wyoming, it turns out, is celebrating its centennial, 1890-1990.

It's soon evident that Baker is a natural leader. Before becoming mayor of Dubois, he served three years as a Wyoming state legislator from Fremont County. A Wyoming native, he shows the same Scandinavian heritage people say is a dominant trait in many parts of the Northern Rockies; he is tall, fair, and looks very fit. "It's nice to live here, but it's hard to make a living," he says in answer to flattering remarks I make about the beauty of the valley and the charm of his town. The Mayor's dress is classic Western, a light blue oxford shirt over trim Levis. His bearing is confident.

Baker trained in forest recreation, but working for the Forest Service on the Bridger-Teton Forest convinced the young Baker he was more "interested in growing trees." The Bridger-Teton, to the northwest of Dubois, coincidentally, is the National Forest L-P turned to for logs, once the Shoshone's timber supply was exhausted.

As Louisiana-Pacific's chief forester and a leading Dubois citizen, it was natural for Baker to spearhead the fight to save the L-P operation. "It could have, and should have been a win-win situation for everyone," Baker says. There is genuine regret in his voice, a sound of sadness, almost of tragedy. He worries about the loss of a future for the next generation, in just the same way that conservationists do, only Baker is speaking about jobs, ways for his children and grandchildren to work and live in the West, using what Baker sees as the West's natural gifts, its resources.

If managed properly, he asserts, "Wyoming can have its cake and eat it too." To Baker, the 1988 Yellowstone fire ("the result of the Yellowstone ecosystem concept," he claims) and a windstorm one year that "blew down 50 million board feet of timber" in a National Forest wilderness area, are clear examples of wasted resources. Baker is articulate, authoritative, and likable. But he doesn't know anything about Dr. Jerry Franklin, and this respected and much-discussed researcher's "new forestry," a full ecosystem forest management approach. In response to my question, Baker says Dr. Franklin may well be an expert in the Northwest, but can't pretend to be an expert on the Yellowstone National Park area and the National Forests in Wyoming, Montana, and Idaho which surround it. I'm not surprised to learn that Baker has carried on a running public feud with the powerful *Greater Yellowstone Coalition* folks, and considers them dangerous. (*Coalition* program director, Louisa Willcox, a Yale forestry graduate, an accomplished eco-fighter and a five-foot-two-inch firebrand, later tells me that Baker publicly called her a communist.)

Dubois's lunch crowd now fills the Grub and Tub, and we must speak carefully to be heard above the clatter of dishes and the conversational din. Baker continues. "I am an expert here," he explains, because he has invested years in learning how to grow trees in his part of Wyoming. He understands the lodgepole pine and its "local genetic variations," and how things work on this side (the east side) of the continental divide. His own experience tells him that "management works." Wyoming's big game population is "rebounding" as a result of proper resource management.

Ecosystem management holds no credibility for Baker. It only "perpetuates nature's problems" and fails to include either "people or time" in its scenario. "The Forest Service almost quit selling timber. As I see it, the Forest Service was deliberately forcing L-P out of business," he says bitterly.

In 1980, Baker tells me, Louisiana-Pacific added new

improvements to those made by previous owners of the mill—U.S. Plywood (which later became part of International Champion). The mill was designed to use the high-quality lodgepole pine and Englemann spruce that has historically covered western Wyoming's rising terrain. Upgrading enabled the mill to turn out the same volume of studs using fewer logs. The mill, at its most efficient, could process 24 million board feet of sawlogs each year.

At the same time, however, both the quantity and the quality of National Forest timber began to decline. "We were using less, and the trees were smaller." Yet Baker doesn't seem to understand the reason for that, although it's clear to him that, somehow, wilderness is one of the bogeymen. "Every new and different use, like wilderness, makes the pie smaller." Baker was just one of a number of industry people I talked to who used this term, "pie." Perhaps that is the result of the various ways in which the Forest Service has responded to a 1960 Congressional mandate known as the Multiple Use Sustained Yield Act. Much homage is paid to the multiple use principle, but there is no doubt that in most National Forests selling timber comes first. By 1990, timber issues in the American West were so volatile and the industry was so utterly dependent on a huge public supply that some timber-industry people had begun to talk in terms of simply stabilizing their "share of the pie."

Two years after Louisiana-Pacific's share of Western Wyoming's forest "pie" disappeared, Bob Baker hasn't forgotten his interest in trees. Something of a tree-planting Pied Piper here, Baker has been leading tree-planting outings in Dubois that have proved highly popular. New plantings grace Dubois' showy new municipal building, public parkways and the like. But he still mourns the loss of the mill and worries that Dubois's flirtation with tourism is bringing about what he calls "a false economy." Jobs in the west, he says, have always been "oriented" toward the region's natural resources. While a diverse economy is admirable, Baker says, without digging, cutting, or mining the West's basic resources, "the others can't make it by themselves."

Not surprisingly, he isn't comfortable, either, with the Forest Service's 50-year forest management plans for his region. The agency has begun to pay lip service, at least, to the idea of managing the forest as a whole ecosystem, a concept Baker detests. It simply "limits opportunities," Baker insists, pointing out cases to support his idea that "managing for specific goals [timbering is one] works." Baker cites Wyoming's thriving big game population as an example of successful management. It's easy to understand why Baker and the *Greater Yellowstone Coalition* are warring; the *Coalition* includes the Bridger-Teton Forest in what it defines as the greater Yellowstone ecosystem.

Based on his own experience, Baker is convinced ecosystem management doesn't assure biological diversity either. "When you burn over 700,000 acres of Yellowstone Park, you're gonna convert that all back to lodgepole pine.... It would be a whole lot better if they managed Yellowstone Park so that we preserve not only the lodgepole pine but the Englemann spruce, alpine fir and limber pine," he argues with total conviction. Timber industry leaders everywhere cite the 1988 Yellowstone fire as a blatant example of forest mismanagement. (Others, of course, disagree, saying nothing could have prevented this huge natural event.)

Baker is entirely comfortable with the idea that he is an expert on forestry issues in his locality. When Baker says, "I am an expert here," it doesn't sound immodest or offensive—his voice is pleasant, his tone reasoned. So, it is startling to hear him say that he is not especially concerned about global timber issues. Timber industry newsletters, magazines and other publications are full of information about global timber supplies, the world market, and the log-export issue. Every schoolchild in America seems to knows about the worldwide debate over the fate of tropical rainforests. Bob Baker's pale blue eyes look elsewhere for understanding as he offers this careful explanation:

"I think this is one of those areas where my priorities are different." He pauses. "I am a conservative. I'm one of those people who believe that if I take care of my little piece of America, and you take care of your little piece of America—and we are both responsible people—I don't have to worry about your little piece of America because I know you're going to do a good job. And I'm going to do a good job of taking care of my little piece of America, but I can't really be an expert in global forestry."

Bob Baker pauses again. "I *am* an expert here."

Part III
THE SOUTHWEST AND
THE SOUTHERN ROCKIES

CHAPTER EIGHT

Arizona
Wildlife vs. Timber

The southwestern states are much more than cactus and chaparral struggling for survival in an inhospitable desert environment. Arizona, in particular, produces millions of board feet of highly prized ponderosa pine. To a lesser degree, so does Arizona's neighbor, New Mexico.

The northern reaches of these states, along with parts of Colorado and Utah, are blessed by sweeping, high-elevation pine forests—forests that sustained the region's earliest settlers. Whether cowtown or mining camp, a small, local sawmill outfit could be counted on to furnish timber for frontier entrepreneurs who required everything from mine braces and railroad ties to logs and lumber for cabins and storefronts.

In the last half of this century, commercial logging in the Southwest has consumed hundreds of millions of board feet of this slow-growing timber. Today, foresters agree it's difficult to come up with old-growth ponderosa pine anywhere in this region. Perhaps "virgin" better describes the kind of ancient pine forest that's become virtually extinct. At least, when you ask foresters to pinpoint the location of any remaining old-growth pine stands in Arizona, they just shake their heads and say something like: "Well, let me see. Hmm...you know, it's pretty tough to think of any. There're probably a few isolated pockets...up north."

Timber industry leaders, however, think this is as it should be.

As in every western state, the fight here is over how to manage timber supplies on the National Forests. The forest-products industry owns almost no commercial timberland in either Arizona or New Mexico. Given the vast and often treacherous expanses of deserts, canyons, and badlands that typify the Southwest, this region had neither the abundant forest resources nor the market links that attracted timberland investors like the famous Weyerhaeuser dynasty to other parts of the West. Unlike the situation in Northern California and the Northwest or in the Northern Rockies where the timber industry owns millions of acres of the best timberland, the forest-products industry in Arizona and New Mexico is wholly dependent on publicly owned forestland.

But it has done well. Local markets flourished toward the end of the 1980s. Arizona produced 447 million board feet of lumber in 1988, with a wholesale value of $134.7 million. The Arizona timber-products industry, clearly on a roll, chalked up a 65 percent increase in the value of its wholesale sales during the '80s.

Almost 90 percent of Arizona's sawtimber is ponderosa pine. Conditions on the lofty plateaus of the semi-arid Southwest produce slow growing, high-quality pine lumber that commands a premium price. It comes mostly from the Kaibab and Coconino National Forests in the Flagstaff-Williams region of Northern Arizona and the Apache-Sitgreaves Forests, running to the south and east in a narrow strip of forest highland between the Navajo and Apache Indian reservations. The Navajos and Apaches, who own about a million acres of timberland, are also longtime Arizona lumber operators. Mostly, however, the fierce debate over the level of logging in Arizona centers on National Forest timber.

Arizona timber production rose a staggering 48 percent during the 1980s. Where was all this extra timber coming from? More importantly, how could these ever-increasing timber-harvest levels on Arizona's National Forests be sustained? By the start of the '90s, Flagstaff had become a hotbed of environmental outrage.

But in a state where the main metro areas, Phoenix and Tucson to the south, were more worried about water supplies and electric power to pump blissfully cooled air during 120 degree days and 90 degree nights, Arizona's timber problems seemed as far away as those of Alaska's Tongass National Forest.

Northern Arizona University's School of Forestry in Flagstaff is frequently mentioned as one of the outstanding forestry schools in the West. Others include Humbolt State University in Northern California, the University of Montana, Colorado State University at Fort Collins, along with Oregon and Washington State Universities in the Northwest. (Yale University's forestry school also commands considerable respect, even out West.) As Dean of Northern Arizona's School of Forestry and now a leading professor and researcher of forest policy there, Richard W. Behan has plenty to say about both Arizona's timber management crisis and National Forest management practices all over the West. Behan is widely recognized as a leading voice in these matters. And what he says doesn't always make either the U.S. Forest Service or the timber industry happy.

With Flagstaff nearly dead in its tracks from two feet of wet February snow, Behan took time out to talk to me about Arizona's timber management issues. Would the 1990s be the decade of decision here, as well as for the rest of the West? Behan's answer went straight to the heart of the matter, no jargon, no qualifiers. If we keep on cutting at the rate we're cutting now, Behan says, "in the next 10 years, we'll run out of trees." Foresters, forest managers, and loggers alike, won't have anything left to argue about.

"We're overcutting," Behan declares. Historically, the timber industry has been accused of "cutting out and getting out." Behan is convinced that members of the U.S. Forest Service's "old guard" still see their mission as supplying timber for the nation. In Arizona, the timber industry and USFS forest managers are nearing the point of no return. Like other enlightened western educators, Dick Behan plugs for "forest management in terms of the whole ecosystem." He thinks Northern Arizona University and the Forestry's School's visionary first dean, Charles Minor, were way ahead of others when, in 1972, NAU began teaching and preaching a sort of progressive forestry.

Behan himself preaches and publishes hard hitting stuff about "Multiresource Forest Management," the appropriate successor, he says, to the now failed "sustained yield-multiple use" National Forest management goals. This new way of managing forests has nothing to do with "running out" of timber. Instead, it looks for ways to protect all the forest's resources, balancing timber production, for example, against its impact on the whole system.

Computers are the right tool for this task, but Behan charges that the computer programs now used in the Forest Service are so slanted toward timber production that they further distort the USFS's traditional timber bias. U.S. foresters I talked to generally agreed the agency has a big problem with its computer models. From outdated and inaccurate timber inventory numbers to the USFS's favorite FORPLAN computer-model, they say it's "garbage in, gospel out."

In fact, in the early 1980s, it was Behan who predicted that the National Forest Management Act's forest planning requirements would become a legal and financial nightmare. The Forest Service is now estimated to be spending $2 million to $5 million on planning for each of its 156 forests. Total planning costs will likely exceed $300 million, forest economists predict.

But in Arizona, the state Game and Fish Department saw the new forest planning process as an opportunity to get in on the ground floor. Or, as Bob Weaver, who heads the department's fledgling Habitat Branch, puts it: "Our department went into a very active environmental" stance more than a decade ago. Starting in 1978, the branch, manned by newly hired wildlife biologists and ecologists, began tracking all the land use requests that passed through Arizona's state review process.

So, by the time forest management plans for Arizona's six National Forests came under review in the mid-'80s, the state's

Game and Fish Department was ready. Weaver and his habitat specialists found consistently disturbing "common threads" running through the three forests plans where logging and wildlife met head-to-head—the Kaibab, the Coconino, and the Apache-Sitgreaves. These plans failed to properly follow either the NEPA (National Environmental Planning Act) process or the federal agency's own IRM (Integrated Resource Management) guidelines. Weaver, who sounds more like a trial lawyer than a tree-hugger, says his department joined in formal appeals to all three forest plans. After two years of intense but largely unsuccessful negotiations between the Forest Service, timber industry representatives, Arizona's Game and Fish Department and environmental groups, the Game and Fish people were ready to go to court in early 1990.

And they were talking about it in public. Loud and clear. An unheard of stand for a state wildlife department in the American West. "We took a big, bad stand," says Tom Britt, Game and Fish regional supervisor in Flagstaff. There is no apology, no backing off. Both Britt and Weaver speak with pride and conviction. Righteous conviction.

The Game and Fish Department's February 1990 white paper, "Wildlife Issues with Timber Management on National Forests in Arizona," was a battle flag. It began:

"Many people in Arizona have become aware, to some degree or another, of the controversies surrounding timber management in the Pacific Northwest, especially those conflicts with timber harvest and old-growth dependent wildlife such as the northern spotted owl. However, relatively few Arizonans realize that a battle of similar magnitude is being waged on our state's four primary timber-producing forests, the Coconino, Apache-Sitgreaves, and the Kaibab. These forests are vitally important to Arizona's diverse wildlife populations, as they provide habitat for over 400 species of game and nongame wildlife. They support nearly 90 percent of the state's turkey and elk populations, over 40 percent of the mule deer, and nearly all

the habitat to support sensitive birds of prey, like the goshawk
and Mexican spotted owl."

So, even in the Southwest, loggers and owls are destined to square
off in some sort of public brawl. Like its northern cousin, the
Mexican spotted owl is an "indicator species" used by foresters
and biologists as one measure of the health and ecological
balance of a forest.

The Arizona department's 20-page white paper is a devastating
indictment of federal forest management. As markets improved,
buoyed in part by "the impact of overseas timber exports,"
Arizona companies—the big three here are Stone Forest
Industries, Kaibab Industries and Duke City Lumber Company—
turned to the National Forest for more timber, and forest
managers were quick to oblige. Among other points, the Game
and Fish Department's white paper cites the gross inadequacies of
FORPLAN and ECOSIM, a growth and yield computer program
model "which overestimates growth and yield." USFS inventories,
it turned out, were so far off that in order to meet the forest's ASQ
or annual sale quantity, twice as much acreage as predicted was
required to produce the planned volume of timber.

Even Al Hendricks, who is a forester for the state of Arizona and
a true forestry profession loyalist, expressed shock over the
Coconino's error-filled inventories. Four years into Coconino's
10-year plan, it was apparent even to Hendricks that something
had gone vastly awry in growth and yield model projections. But
in the spring of 1990, Hendricks still had faith in computer
modeling programs. He told me: the important thing is that
federal forest managers were busy "looking at the Coconino now
to see what caused them [the computer programs] to not
accurately predict what happened." Among other things,
Hendricks says the forest planning models didn't "foresee" the
Mexican spotted owl problem. But whatever it was, Hendricks's
loyalty has taken a direct hit. You can hear it in his voice. He says
when he first heard the charges of overcutting, "I didn't believe it
for a minute. But over time, I can now accept that mistakes were

made, some knowingly—and that's inexcusable."

In contrast to Hendricks' doubts about the need for National Forest management reforms, Arizona's Game and Fish Department's white paper didn't pull any punches about the issue of overcutting on the Coconino and the others forests as well. The department argued that an "increasing emphasis...on meeting forest timber-volume targets in response to the demands of the timber industry" could destroy Arizona's lucrative fishing, hunting, and outdoor recreation economy. Quality wildlife habitat, Weavers and company said, couldn't survive the timber onslaught.

Arizona's wildlife managers are finding that mitigation (such as setting aside alternative habitat in another part of the forest, to compensate for loses due to overcutting) just doesn't work. Weaver says it boils down to a "question of quality habitat." The department's February white paper warned that in the case of the Coconino National Forest's 10-year plan, all the administrative appeal options had been "totally exhausted," and the department was heading toward "litigation through the federal court system."

Miraculously, three months later the announcement of a compromise agreement on the Apache-Sitgreaves forest plan caught almost everyone by surprise. Weaver says he believes this agreement brings with it assurances of similar compromises on the Kaibab and Coconino forest plans. Principals to the agreement were representatives of the U.S. Forest Service, Arizona's Fish and Game Department, a state environmental coalition (*The Wilderness Society, the Sierra Club,* and the *Northern Arizona Audubon Society*), a timber industry coalition and the *Arizona Wildlife Federation.*

Of course, one can imagine the political fallout if the department had lost. Arizona's big timber operators appear so cozy with federal timber managers that Arizona wags have dubbed the U.S. Forest Service "the U.S. Logging Service."

Nowhere else in the West has a state wildlife agency taken such a bold stand against threats by logging to its wildlife and natural

habitat, and scored such a success. This landmark 1990
agreement cuts planned timber harvest levels 16 percent during a
new three-year study period. The original 10-year forest
management plan for the Apache-Sitgreaves National Forest
called for a 90 million board feet annual cut in each of the first
five years of the plan. The cut would then have jumped to 108
million board feet annually for the remaining five years. But
during the first two years of the plan (1988,1989) a startling thing
happened. Loggers *couldn't find* 90 million board feet of suitable
timber in the Apache-Sitgreaves National Forest timber sale plots.
Trees were either too small, or otherwise not of commercial
quality. As these disconcerting facts began to emerge, foresters
like the State of Arizona's Al Hendricks did some double takes.

The 1990 settlement directly addresses many of these issues.
Among other things, this Apache-Sitgreaves timber harvest truce
stops plans the Forest Service was considering to *accelerate* timber
sale offerings in order to make up for the two-year shortfall. This
precedent-setting agreement also provides for a first-time
inventory of old growth, scenic, and critical wildlife habitat areas
within the forest. While the agreement is considered a
compromise, it clearly calls for a lighter, more sensitive hand in
timber management, outlawing cable-logging, for example, in
canyon areas with live streams. (Cable-logging involves the use of
aerial cables to haul logs up steep canyonsides.) As part of the
compromise, however, environmentalists gave up their two-year
fight to stop cable-logging in one contested area.

New studies, which began immediately following the May, 1990
settlement, also involve development of old-growth management
plans—in line with Chief Robertson's call for a new view of old-
growth on the National Forests. Also being studied are guidelines
for the survival of the Mexican spotted owl and the recalculation
of the all-important timber ASQ (allowable sale quantity) on the
Apache-Sitgreaves. It sounds like Behan's Multiple Resource
Management manifesto at work.

A press release, dated May 18, 1990, issued by the Arizona

Game and Fish Department, advised that: "This [forthcoming] amendment or revision to the Apache-Sitgreaves National Forest's Forest Plan will result in change to the long-term timber sale schedule and will emphasize silvicultural treatment to obtain multiple resource objectives."

Others were more cautious. Jim Norton, who is the Southwest regional director of *The Wilderness Society*, agrees the Apache-Sitgreaves settlement is a good first step. "The real correction is deferred for three years," Norton told the Arizona Republic moments after the settlement was announced, adding: "We'll be watching to make sure progress is made."

Along with Norton, timber company representatives Jim Matson of Kaibab Industries in Arizona and Bill Stewart of Stone Forest Industries were key participants in the two-year negotiations towards the Apache-Sitgreaves timber settlement. Stewart thinks the Arizona Game and Fish people were uncommonly successful in "putting some harsh constraints" on future timber sales on the Apache-Sitgreaves. But, he says, with a strong market for wood products during the latter part of the 1980s, it was predictable that the timber industry would push for high timber cuts on the federal forests. "Private lands," Stewart explains, "are cut more heavily during poor market times. That's not new." In a reassuring tone, he suggests that this pattern will most likely continue. If the public had truly understood how the wood and fiber products market works, he implies, environmentalists like Norton and the Arizona Game and Fish people wouldn't have been so successful in screwing the lid down on timber sales on the Apache-Sitgreaves.

Stewart further offers the opinion that some environmental groups "would like to cut western timber sales [on public land] by 50 percent." Looking into his own crystal ball, Stewart says that if more constraints are put on the American West's timber production, he foresees an international financial crisis—more trade-deficit and balance-of-payment problems caused by the need to import more lumber and wood products—a whole series

121

of global events similar to what has happened with Middle East oil. I wasn't convinced.

Stewart claims that in New Mexico, where Kaibab and Stone Forest are also major presences, that state's Game and Fish department has had the good sense to "stay within their area of expertise.... They do a good job." He clearly thinks Arizona Game and Fish people are zealots, dangerous extremists who should be watched closely.

CLOSEUP
Forest Supervisor, John Bedell

Forest Supervisor John Bedell is obviously a talented trouble-shooter. Like a Hot Shot fire-fighter, Bedell took over the leadership of the troubled Apache-Sitgreaves National Forest in April, and by mid-May he'd snuffed out the two-year-old fires of dissension and produced an important three-year timber management agreement. While he is appropriately modest ("I just created the climate for four negotiators who wanted a solution,") Bedell also manages to portray himself as one of a new breed of Forest Service leaders. To understand what was going on—why the trees weren't there when the Apache-Sitgreaves timber planners had said they were—Bedell went right to the "people on the ground," in the five out of six Apache-Sitgreaves ranger districts that grow and sell timber. Staff members told him timber numbers were off because they'd been forced—by superiors trying to meet unrealistic timber production targets—to add tree-less brush land to the suitable timberland acreage used to calculate the the allowable annual sale quantity.

Other factors—the newly important Mexican spotted owl, plus what Bedell calls "urban interface" problems such as scenic corridors—hadn't been taken into account in the Apache-Sitgreaves forest plan. He suggests that once these matters were squarely addressed, settlement was virtually assured. The Forest Service, like an autocratic parent, has been disinclined to compromise. To illustrate his point that new attitudes are in order, Bedell says: when the Forest Service wants to resolve an issue through negotiations, "so often the Forest Service enters into a negotiation and they don't want to adjust. They want to educate or convince everyone else that what they originally decided is what they're going to do. If we say we're going to negotiate, that means we're going to change what we do."

And as if that is not enough soul-baring, the Apache-Sitgreaves Forest Supervisor says that we should expect change to be slow. A moment's pause, then: "I'll be the first to admit some of our line officers feel negotiating is a [sign of] weakness," and that admitting a flaw—another pause—"is terrible."

Bedell is far more generous than other foresters in giving some credit to reformers such as Jeff DeBonis, Chris Maser and Randal O'Toole. Critics like these "cause us to look at things in a different light.... Internal examination is always good for us."

Some 90 years ago the fledgling Forest Service began inviting loggers to establish communities on the fringes of National Forests to take care of the timber which would flow from these great forests in an even and sustainable stream. Now the American West's "timber-dependent communities," like the West's once glorious mining towns, face an uncertain future.

Bedell believes the agency's long-standing commitment to keep these logging communities alive and in the logging business "is still a valid policy.... We're looking at sustainability of the industry as well as the forest." And that may require what Bedell calls "an adjustment." Mill capacity could well be outdistancing the federal timber supply, he agrees. "We are not supposed to be liquidating a resource."

As a forest supervisor (he also spent six years as supervisor on the Carson National Forest, near Taos, New Mexico) he claims that he's "never offered a below-cost timber sale," but he acknowledges that such federal timber sales have taken place. The Forest Service "had no business selling" money-losing timber and "we're not going to do that any more." To balance things out, Bedell also makes a point of showing no sympathy for environmental agendas which are clearly aimed at stopping all timbering.

Still, others in Arizona and New Mexico say the day of reckoning may come soon, because the industry, seemingly exploiting its cozy relationship with USFS, has created more mill jobs than federal forests in this region can maintain. Bedell doesn't offer any specific remedies for this or for other federal timber management problems. But he does say he thinks "there is major change in the wind. I can tell you, this is no fad. I expect more change [in this agency] in the next five years than in the last 50 years."

CHAPTER NINE

New Mexico
Land of Adobe and Timber

New Mexico's adobe and piñon landscape seems like improbable timber county. And most of it is. But New Mexico's ponderosa pine, like Arizona's, is described by the timber industry as a "high value" wood. Such ponderosa accounts for about two-thirds of all timber logged in this arid and often harsh southwestern landscape.

Remarkably, in the '80s New Mexico's sawtimber output jumped 74 percent, while showing a 40 percent gain in wholesale value. Over 80 percent of that timber comes from publicly owned land, most of it from New Mexico's five National Forests—the Carson, Cibola, Gila, Lincoln and the Santa Fe. As in other areas of the West, logging on a certain scale has always been an honored part of local tradition. Beautiful wood trim accents Santa Fe's historic adobe architecture. For many, New Mexicans and visitors alike, nothing seems more inviting than a crackling fire in a curving adobe fireplace, gracefully molded into an interior corner of an authentic Santa Fe-style room.

In New Mexico, public interest in National Forest timber policies lay mostly dormant until the 1980s, when a combination of accelerated logging, expanding urban development, and the introduction of the new forest planning process aroused citizen concern over the future of nearby forests. Big-time logging was heading toward the last remnants of New Mexico's old growth, mostly mixed conifers: pine, fir and spruce. As in other western states, the easy-to-get-to timber had already been cut over. The remaining bigger, older trees were only to be found on steep slopes, in remote canyons, in relatively isolated spots. To harvest the last of the New Mexico's old trees, forest managers called for the use of aerial cables, a technique long used in the Northwest to haul timber off steep and inaccessible terrain. Cable-logging practices have become a hot issue in the arid southwest.

Forest economists also say below-cost timber sales are commonplace on New Mexico's federal forests. In 1990, Gila National Forest timber planners prepared New Mexico's first-ever timber-sale Environmental Impact Statement. Critics say two proposed timber sales on the Gila threaten to develop more roadless land than any other timber sale in the Southwest, costing taxpayers far more than the timber is worth, to say nothing of the lost values of sensitive wildlife habitat in virgin forests.

Marlin Hughes, a timber policy spokesperson at U.S. Forest Service Southwest regional headquarters in Albuquerque, says forest management questions in the '90s will center around the conflict between *commodities* (timber, grazing and mining) and *amenities*. Amenities is the bureaucratic term-of-choice signifying recreation, scenic vistas, and certainly in New Mexico, antiquities such as the vast, and uncharted Anasazi Indian ruins in the Jemez Mountains of the Santa Fe National Forest.

Hughes links this new concern over amenities to the advance of urban affluence in New Mexico—historic Santa Fe, for example, is fast becoming ultra-chic and correspondingly expensive. So is the Taos resort area in north central New Mexico. In fact, a first-of-its-kind conference on the future of the Southwest's ancient forests took place in August, 1989 at Taos, sponsored by the Carson National Forest. (John Bedell, then Carson's forest supervisor and clearly one of an new breed of forest managers, had already won plaudits from regional environmentalists for his enlightened views.) The four day gathering featured researcher and writer Chris Maser whose views had been a major inspiration for this pioneering conference. Supervisor Bedell said the conference was planned as the cornerstone for a model forest of the future. Instead of focusing on producing a sustained yield of timber, future forest planners, it was hoped, would work toward a "sustainable forest," a healthy and productive public resource.

But not all New Mexico's forest managers see things the way Bedell does. Some foresters in New Mexico predict prized aspen stands in scenic mountain areas near Santa Fe will succumb to disease, fire or the much touted "conifer invasion" because scenic preservationists there have demanded a "hands-off our aspen" policy.

This "invasion" theory is now well known in western Colorado. It was a key part of a Forest Service campaign in the mid-'80s aimed at convincing Colorado residents that aspen stands, on both National Forests and private lands, required "treatment" (i.e. massive clearcutting) in order to "reinvigorate" their aging beauty. (The fight over western Colorado's aspen forests is ongoing. See Chapter 10.)

In the course of a discussion of New Mexico's traditional sawtimber (pine and mixed conifers), Forest Service spokesperson Hughes, a 30-year Service veteran, says he is convinced USFS policy is already turning away from its previous pro-timber, pro-mining, pro-grazing stance. Even so, he's confident timber planners have been right on target in the past, explaining: "We've been growing at least 20 percent more than we've cut." (Critics, of course, say such claims don't tell the whole story.) Hughes also doesn't see the controversy over Arizona's Apache-Sitgreaves timber sale volume (and the revelations about inflated timber inventories) as any kind of a turning point in Region 3 timber-harvest plans. He says that forest plans in Region 3's federal forests (i.e. in Arizona and New Mexico) were already "calling for a lot less logging," so there is really no connection.

I wasn't surprised. In my interviews with USFS official all over the West, I found a general reluctance to talk about controversies, either recent or not so recent, in real depth. Troubling issues had already been settled, I was assured; perhaps mistakes had taken place, but always on somebody else's forest in some other part of the West. Spokesperson Hughes and other Forest Service personnel were kindly, helpful, and willing to talk at some length about timber matters. But, with few exceptions, these exchanges took on the character of a halting dialogue between a foreign visitor struggling to overcome some kind of language barrier between herself and a weary diplomat who had simply heard it all before.

In parting Hughes tells me that New Mexico is particularly fortunate to have a number of forest-products industry leaders who are progressive, who see the importance of "a balanced [federal forest] program [and] are in it for the long haul." Jim Matson of Kaibab Forest Industries of Albuquerque wins high praise from Hughes, along with Tom Lupinsky, president of Duke City Lumber Co. of Albuquerque.

I found Lupinsky to be pleasant, articulate, and unflappable. Albuquerque, he explains, was named in 1706 for the Duke of Albuquerque, a viceroy of New Spain. Hence the name of his company, Duke City Lumber. Lupinsky is proud of the fact that, through inspired marketing, his company has developed a strong market for products made from Englemann spruce.

Historically, this slow-growing, mid-to-high elevation evergreen has been regarded as a "weed tree." It grows in steep, rough terrain where road construction is difficult, so logging Englemann spruce is costly. That, together with a weak market, had always made this Rocky Mountain monarch "low value" sawtimber. But early in the 1980s, spruce house logs began to find a new and more dependable niche in the wood products market. Soon after that, Duke City successfully developed two important new markets for spruce. One involves "specialized products, such as shelves and interior paneling made from appearance-grade spruce." Lupinsky sounds particularly pleased talking about the second new market, Hokaido, Japan, where Duke City has created a brand new export outlet for products made of Englemann spruce.

Residents of Japan's large northern island (once host to the winter Olympics) were looking for "bright, white" spruce that closely resembled their prized and vanishing native wood. Englemann spruce was perfect.

Thanks to these new products, the market value of southwestern Englemann spruce has jumped 20 percent in just three years. But Lupinsky also claims that logging spruce is an important element in keeping old forests healthy. While the market for spruce house logs provided a cash incentive to harvest "standing dead" spruce, "the real need was to manage green [spruce] stands for elk habitat" and to ward off insect infestations.

Here Lupinsky touched the very core of the debate over forest management and what may or may not constitute a "healthy" forest. The timber industry and many traditional, "commodity-oriented" foresters, see a healthy forest as a high-producing tree farm, where "mature" trees—commercially viable wood—are harvested on a regular basis. Their theory promotes the idea that "managing" (logging) green stands of timber helps control forest fires, insect invasions, and diseases which tends to attack older trees. (In at least one sense they're right: insects, fire and disease can't attack trees that aren't there.)

In contrast, ecologists, environmentalists, and other critics see a "healthy" forest as a well-balanced, biologically diversified ecosystem. Fire is now universally recognized as an important contributor to the natural cycle of a forest. Writing in *High Country News*, George Wuerthner puts it this way: "It is not the forest which is destroyed by fire, blowdown, insect or disease, only the trees' value for timber production." However, development of the American West has left little room for forest wildfires to do their work unimpeded. Forestry experts are now hotly debating the best ways to "manage" both so-called "controlled burns" and natural wildfires across the West.

Wildlife biologists I've talked to also say the Forest Service has so far been unable to document its frequent claim that logging "enhances" wildlife habitat.

Duke City 's Lupinsky, however, has no doubts about the timber industry's contribution to forest health. "We are providing an alternative to uncontrolled fires such as there were in Yellowstone" during the summer of 1988, he asserts. This huge and hugely destructive natural event has become the centerpiece of the wood-products industry's argument for the need to cut older stands of marketable timber. Duke City's president, however, is no one-note ideologue. He acknowledges that the Forest Service stumbled badly trying to grow back logged-over spruce stands in southern Colorado. "We're doing better reforestation now," he says, adding that "everyone has a different answer" to forest management questions, and "no one has a [perfect] solution." Most people, Lupinsky tells me, are intellectually handicapped in dealing with complex forest management questions because "trees have a different [longer] life cycle than humans do." And in New Mexico, the U.S. Forest Service is being "blown around" by the strong new winds of public opinion, causing the agency to be "indecisive."

Santa Fe's Sam Hitt, a zealous forest preservationist, hasn't seen it that way yet. A new/old battle rages at the start of this decade around what Hitt and his organization, *Forest Guardian*, describe as a plan to carry out "the largest logging operation ever in New Mexico [on] pristine Elk Mountain, east of Santa Fe and adjacent to the Pecos Wilderness." Some 25 million board feet of old-growth Englemann spruce would be hauled off the mountain on 65 miles of new logging roads through the Santa Fe National Forest. Die-hard environmentalists, says Hitt, have been fighting for 25 years to protect this area which "contains some of the last remaining large areas of old growth in New Mexico." Generations of New Mexicans have used the area for camping, fishing, grazing and limited selective timbering—including cutting the *vigas* and *latillas* used in Santa Fe's ageless, adobe and exposed-timber construction.

The son of a forester, Hitt, 42, admits to "getting emotional" over old growth, remembering as a lad, fishing deep within

Oregon's perpetually cool ancient forests. "Clearcuts are hot and windy," he observes, and adds: "We're in a real uphill struggle here.... The majority [of the state's residents] are with us but the industry and the Forest Service are very entrenched." My interview with Hitt is via telephone. I've spent months trying to catch up with him, and when I finally do, Hitt tells me he has little time for interviews and none to spare combing his files to help somebody else's research.

His voice is dead serious; this is a true-believer, not a PR man.

CLOSEUP
Forest Owls, Indicator Species and What They Tell Us

Professionally, wildlife biologists lead a precarious existence. For the most part, wildlife researchers and other wildlife specialists work for the government—the U.S. Forest Service and its tiny, but separate sister, the National Forest Systems Research Branch; the U.S. Fish and Wildlife Service; and various state agencies.

Silencing a troublesome wildlife biologist is a simple matter— cut off funding for the work he or she does. "Watch the dollars on the ground," cautions one insider. Political hands, of course, control the public purse strings. During the last 20 years, warnings by passionate and outspoken wildlife researchers have resulted in banishment to some sort of bureaucratic Siberia, or in budget changes which have eliminated the whistleblower's job altogether.

Still, wildlife biologists I've talked to are deeply committed to their work—studying everything from voles and deer mice to goshawks and forest owls. And not just the notorious northern spotted owl, the symbolic touchstone of the fight over the Northwest's old-growth forests, but also the Southwest's Mexican spotted owl, the flammulated owl, the boreal, the northern saw-whet, and the northern pygmy owls.

These same biologists are often jumpy about talking to reporters. Their work involves subtleties, delicate suppositions, and takes years to complete. News stories tend to gloss over these small pieces of the scientific puzzle, and scientists complain that reporters often oversimplify, overstate, or otherwise miss the true essence of the subject. Still, wildlife biologists proved to be generous and enthusiastic sources of information for this project.

Wildlife biologists like Richard Reynolds, of the Rocky Mountain Forest and Range Experiment Station in Laramie, Wyoming, regularly cautioned me about the importance of accurately explaining the function of "indicator species." Particular birds, bugs or animals which are specific to an area are chosen by scientists as "indicator species" for that place: the health and welfare of such critical critters helps scientists to evaluate the ecological conditions—the health and welfare of whole forests, streams, lakes and the like.

The northern spotted owl is used as an indicator species for the great temperate rainforests of the Northwest. The battle cries of besieged logging communities in Washington, Oregon and Northern California, and massive sloganeering ("Jobs vs. Owls") have obscured the fact that the fuss wasn't precisely about saving owls. If the population of an indicator species is declining, that fact serves as a scientific warning about the possible decline of the whole habitat, or some of its critical components.

Wood-products industry people in Idaho told me folks in the Southwest should stop worrying about the fate of the tiny flammulated (flame-tinged) owl, which is doing very well, thank you, in the pine forests of Idaho. But the point isn't whether any of those weird little owls are surviving somewhere, anywhere. Rather the point is that wildlife biologists believe flammulated owls can and should be studied to help assess timber and other management practices in the Southwest's heavily logged ponderosa pine forests.

Wildlife biologist Reynolds writes: "The flammulated owl is limited to forests within the yellow pine belt.... The owl's preference for old-growth pine and associated species—a forest and age class that is extensively managed in the region—and reports that the species is not found in cutover forests point to a critical need to determine the effects of forest management on this owl."

I talked to Reynolds during the summer of 1990, as we climbed together over tangled debris and downed trees in a section of older fir and spruce in a western Colorado forest. He advised me that "indicator species are a very important measure" of the health and balance of a forest. Yet this is just one aspect of wildlife and forest research. Understanding how one indicator species is doing "doesn't show how other important species are faring," he warns. He is clearly pleading with me to write carefully, so readers will understand this ecological web of interdependency. And while laws that protect species which are declared to be "threatened" or "endangered" aren't perfect methods of guaranteeing the health of an ecosystem, "endangered species [laws] are the only ecosystem kind of legislation we have." Reynolds says this with a note of urgency in his voice.

Reynolds, a solidly built man in his middle years with an engaging smile and manner to match, is not your stereotypical, little, old, run-of-the-mill bird watcher. Researchers like Reynolds often speak about "cavity nesters," a term that usually draws a double-take from non-birders and fledgling tree-huggers. Cavity-nesting forest dwelling species are birds (or other critters) that nest and find shelter in the holes in old-growth trees. The small forest owls Reynolds has written about, "are greatly dependent on nest cavities that are excavated by medium to large woodpeckers."

Woodpeckers choose old trees, with their softer, more porous interiors, to peck out a new homesite. Small forest owls search out such hollows and, as "secondary cavity nesters" these woodsy subletors move right in. The northern and the Mexican spotted owls, while larger, are also cavity nesters. Hence their dependence on larger and very old trees (and old forests) for habitat.

By the early 1990s, there was much ado in the Southwest about both the Mexican spotted owl and the goshawk. Keith Fletcher had been named to a new post to coordinate spotted owl programs in Region 3 (Arizona and New Mexico). The U.S. Fish and Wildlife Service was considering whether to include this southwestern owl on its threatened and endangered study schedule. And a suit, filed by conservationists, challenged a federal timber sale, charging that the sale would adversely affect dwindling goshawk populations in old-growth pine stands on the Kaibab National Forest.

Fletcher said in late 1990 that while the Mexican spotted owl has "not yet" been officially listed by the U.S. Fish and Wildlife Service as a threatened species in the Southwest, the Forest Service's Region 3 is concerned about forest owls. "We think the owl is important as a species because it utilizes the characteristics that are often found in old-growth stands—the multi-storied, uneven age stands [with attributes] not usually found in managed forests."

This is typical forestry talk. What it means is simply that by the 1990s so-called "intensive management" for timber production is threatening the Southwest's older pine forests and owl habitat. In a few years, look-alike, "even-age" pine stands may be all that's left. Wildlife is certain to suffer but, in the case of the owls and the goshawks, important new studies are just getting underway which will determine the impact intensive logging is already having, and will have, on these sensitive species.

Reynolds, his voice characteristically intense, says: "So much is new. I teach a lot of field seminars; I do it to get information across. A lot of people [he is speaking here of well-meaning conservationists] don't have a lot of facts.... Facts show we don't know a lot about forest ecology." Reynolds pauses. Sounding almost overwhelmed, he says, "We have a huge task in front of us."

CHAPTER TEN

Colorado
Logging the Roof of the Rockies

Some rural areas in the American West seem like third world countries—economic times are so bad that people will welcome almost any kind of new industry and the paychecks it provides. Colorado is full of such places. And their opposites. Aspen, Colorado, one of the West's premier ski resorts and year-round playground for the rich, is a world away from other western Colorado communities just down the road—towns that, like struggling third-world nations, fight for whatever economic development bones come their way.

Geography also partitions this multi-textured state. A giant, jagged spine, the soaring Rockies run north to south through Colorado, dividing the state into two very distinct territories. On the eastern slope, the mountains of Colorado's "Front Range" provide a stunning backdrop for Denver, the city pioneers dubbed "the Queen City of the Plains." Not entirely a city of the plains, Denver in fact marks the transition from the plains to mountains. Today, Denver dominates a fast-growing urban sprawl that parallels the mountain barriers to its west.

Across the Continental Divide lie Colorado's western slopes—a land of soaring 14,000 ft. peaks and deep canyons. Water from melting snowfields on this flank of the Rockies tumbles west toward the Colorado River and eventually the Pacific. This is a very different world, socially and economically as well as geographically, from Colorado's more metropolitan eastern slope. No major cities have grown up west of the divide. Instead mining towns like Leadville, Crested Butte, Silverton, Aspen and rural ranching hubs such as Grand Junction and Durango give this sparsely populated region its characteristic old-west flavor.

Here, as in so many parts of the rural West, National Forest lands dominate the map, and federal policy decisions can mean economic life or death for local communities. But given Colorado's arid, unforgiving, high-altitude climate, timbering has historically been small and local. Family-owned and operated sawmills, like grocery stores and post offices, were part of Colorado's small-town fabric. Corporate-style logging is a latecomer to the Colorado scene; predictably, new industrial-scale logging operations here often find themselves in conflict with the state's mountain-tourism economy.

In recent years, the U.S. Forest Service has played an aggressive role in rural economic development strategies. John Crowell, the man the Reagan Administration appointed as assistant secretary of agriculture to oversee the Forest Service, had previously been general counsel for the Louisiana-Pacific Corporation, a Portland, Oregon, timber giant with widespread U.S. operations. L-P is not just one of Big Timber's biggest players; analysts say Louisiana-Pacific buys more timber from the Forest Service than any other customer. Crowell's appointment not only helped accelerate timber harvests on the National Forests, it was coincidental to the introduction of Louisiana-Pacific into western Colorado in 1984. Until that time, Chicago-based Stone Container Corp.'s timber operation in southern Colorado was as big as Big Timber got in this state.

Timber production in Colorado is meager at best. Of the 10 western states covered in this book, Colorado is third from last in annual timber output. Utah, with just half Colorado's annual production, is next to last, and Nevada, with virtually no commercial timber production—or forests—is last. In fact Colorado's slow-growing ponderosa pine forests never produced enough volume to have attracted major operators. Englemann spruce accounts for 63 percent of Colorado's timber harvest, but in 1989 the state's total lumber production was a slim 142 million board feet. Of the timberland this high state does possess, 70 percent is found on National Forests.

But Colorado's comparatively small timberland base still supports dozens of small local sawmills, operations that are typical of most communities that border forests in the inland rural West. In addition, the Forest Service over the years has carried out major logging operations in the state, aimed at stemming epidemics of spruce beetles and budworm, and mountain pine beetles in its ponderosa pine forests.

But, until the 1980s the agency had been unable to come up with a program to log and market aspen wood. Aspen forests aren't generally prone to fire or bugs—certainly not in the same way as the other native species, pines, alpine fir and spruce. So, while "salvage" timber sales following forest fires or bug infestations provided ideal opportunities for timber managers to push through grandiose new timber cutting programs on National Forests, Colorado's sweeping alpine aspen groves stood mostly untouched.

Yet because the Forest Service's prime activity is "managing" forests, and because timber programs fatten agency budgets, western Colorado's uncut aspen forests were a natural and enticing target for ambitious federal forest managers. In the early 1980s, U.S. Forest Service officials, with the support of state leaders, quietly made plans to change all that. Louisiana-Pacific was looking for sites to build and operate new waferboard plants. L-P already had similar plants operating in Wisconsin, and western Colorado's mostly virgin aspen forests seemed to offer the perfect source of wood for the chips or "wafers" that L-P would press into manufactured boards. Waferboard, cheaper than traditional plywood, was much in demand and L-P was eager to expand production of this profitable wood product.

The town of Montrose, a small ranching community of about

10,000 in the Uncompahgre River Valley, and a regional hub in west-central Colorado, was aggressively pursuing new economic development. Uranium mining in Montrose County's west end was breathing its last. The county, rural and hungry for better times, was weary of mining's boom-and-bust traumas. But local leaders still regarded exploitation of natural resources as both a birthright and as the region's most dependable economic pathway. The U.S. Forest Service, hand-in-hand with L-P, offered Montrose area leaders a deal they couldn't refuse. Indeed, Montrose area business leaders never seriously questioned the benefits of L-P's new presence. (Kremmling, a coal mining and ranching community in northwest Colorado, eagerly welcomed a companion waferboard-plant proposal.)

Despite warnings of possible trouble ahead from a fledgling, Montrose-based citizens coalition, *Western Colorado Congress,* L-P's new waferboard plant in Montrose County was up and running by 1985. The plant, with its tall exhaust stacks, rose like a rural economic oasis from the adobe flats just outside the little town of Olathe.

Six years later, aspen clearcuts stand out like giant scabs on thousands of acres of National Forest on the high reaches of the Uncompahgre Plateau, a massive tableland cut by mountain rivers plunging west to join the Colorado. And Louisiana-Pacific is poised to clearcut thousands more acres of National Forest aspen timber within a 100-mile radius of the plant.

Families living near the Olathe plant have been forced to abandon their homes, claiming toxic fumes spewing from the plant's stacks made them sick. Workers inside the plant developed similar symptoms. A study by the National Institute of Occupational Safety and Health documented both lax safety standards at L-P's Olathe waferboard plant, as well as an alarming turnover of workers (93 percent) in a single year—many leaving with health problems apparently brought on by toxic materials used in the plant and the inadequate procedures used to deal with them. Stack emissions from L-P's Olathe plant caused mounting public concern, but six years after the plant opened, L-P still hadn't once met state and federal air quality standards. In 1991 the Colorado Department of Health seemed more concerned about keeping the L-P plant open than forcing this wealthy corporation to meet state licensing standards and air pollution rules. Meanwhile, a growing number of Montrose area leaders had come to see Big Timber as a very large can of worms, indeed. Or the modern industrial equivalent of an Trojan horse.

Louisiana-Pacific, its sights fixed firmly on corporate profits, is widely regarded as a timber-industry hard-liner. In California, L-P chairman Harry A. Merlo explained the company's logging practices on its own forests. "We don't log to a 10-inch top, or an 8-inch top, or a 6-inch top. We log to infinity. Because we need it all. It's ours, it's out there, and we want it all. Now." In Western Colorado, environmentalists see evidence that this timber giant views aspen stands in National Forests in much the same way.

If there is a moral to this story, it goes something like this: Do not underestimate Big Timber's political clout or the determination of the Forest Service to cut timber, often in disregard of long-term consequences. Conservationists worry that, with state and federal blessing, L-P will continue to eat away at western Colorado's once glorious aspen forests for years to come. As in some areas of the Northwest, Colorado's scenic highway corridors, such as the Vail-Aspen ski resort area and its approaches along Interstate 70 west of Denver, may be spared. Lesser known but no less scenic aspen forests in other parts of western Colorado, like some third world nations, seemed doomed to become economic "sacrifice areas."

One such area is the Lone Cone mountain region southwest of Telluride. Here aspen forests, both privately-owned and on National Forests, have provided lush grazing for four generations of San Miguel County ranchers. From the earliest times, young cowboys, sheepherders, and other mountain forest habitués have carved their legends into the soft, smooth white outer skin of the aspen trees. These messages, which fall somewhere between

ancient petroglyphs and modern graffiti, bear witness to the
history of the region.

As part of its timber sale preparations, the U.S. Forest Service
thoughtfully decided to document these historically significant
tree carvings. A team of archeologists spent one whole summer
photographing scores of big, message-bearing aspen trees, and
collecting supporting historical information from oldtimers in the
area. Once that was done, the agency apparently had no qualms
about planning to clearcut these fine old aspen forests.

But even without pressure from L-P, the Forest Service in recent
years has been anxious to log aspen on National Forests. A few
years ago, the public hooted down one ill-starred proposal the
agency floated. Billed as a plan to generate more water for
agricultural purposes, the Forest Service claimed that logging
aspen forests in the Glenwood Springs area would cause more
snow to accumulate on the ground, thus increasing run-off.

During my research, foresters frequently told me that sooner or
later fire would destroy Colorado's maturing aspen forests, as well
as aspen forests near scenic Santa Fe, New Mexico, where
clearcutting is for the moment taboo. But environmentalists, as
well as the tourist and vacation industry in these areas, aren't
buying the U.S. Forest Service's theory that massive clearcuts are
the way to keep a forest beautiful.

Clearly, National Forest management decisions have everything
to do with agency goals. Although lumber production in
Colorado showed only a 10 percent increase during the 1980s
(compared to 48 to 65 percent increases in neighboring states),
the Forest Service here has been no less anxious to sell all the
timber it can.

The Rio Grande National Forest on the east side of the
Continental Divide in southern Colorado, shares common
problems with the San Juan National Forest, its neighboring
forest on the west side of the Divide. Both bear scars of logging-
gone wrong in Englemann spruce and subalpine fir forests.

Agency foresters shrug off these atrocities. Clearcutting, these foresters allow, turned out to be the wrong "prescription" for these slow-growing, high-altitude evergreens. Some clearcuts that went to timberline (10,000 ft. and higher) may never grow back, period. In other similarly inhospitable sites, 20 years after clearcutting, healthy seedlings are still hard to find despite repeated attempts at reforestation.

In the October, 1988, issue of Timber Watch, (the newsletter published by the *Colorado Environmental Coalition*), environmental watchdogs toted up a laundry list of abuses on the Rio Grande National Forest. The list is a familiar one. CEC said this high, dry forest could not sustain its planned annual cut of up to 35 million board feet. Clearcuts and shelterwood cuts (staged clearcuts) were poorly designed and unsuitable, said CEC. And because evidence indicated that spruce on the Rio Grande was being cut before it actually matured, CEC said the Forest Service should consider changing the standard rotation age (or cutting cycles) from 160 years to 300 years. Too many roads, skimpy old-growth set-asides, water quality issues and conflicts with other forest "values," also plagued this forest, the watchdogs said.

Three years later, CEC was still calling for citizen action to halt problem-plagued timber sales on the Rio Grande, "the very black sheep of Colorado forestry," as conservationists have dubbed this National Forest. Following a lawsuit, a federal court in 1989 required the Forest to reduce its annual timber harvest to 25 million board feet, a decrease of about 8.5 million board feet. Rio Grande forest managers then began a lengthy forest plan review and updating, in order to come up with a thoroughly revised document.

But when I talked to Phil Anderson, a member of the Rio Grande National Forest's timber staff in May, 1991, I was surprised to learn that Rio Grande timber managers were proposing to slash the allowable sale quantity to 18.2 million board feet per year. Yes, Anderson told me, the Rio Grande had recently discovered that its timber inventories were seriously in error. As a matter of fact timber volume had been overstated by a mind-boggling 45 percent. The Rio Grande National Forest's revised management plan suggests that by 1996 the annual cut could drop to 14.5 million board feet—less than half the volume the forest had targeted for sale in the previous decade.

The story Anderson began telling me was, by now, one I knew by heart. He said in 1985 Rio Grande forest managers were "under the gun" to complete a forest management plan (as required by the 1976 National Forest Management Act). Numbers developed from aerial photographs were stuffed into agency computers and, using the now controversial FORPLAN program, alakazzam!—out came the forest's new annual sale quantity, 33.6 million board feet.

Anderson explains that "a lot of acres that should not have been" included were thus put into the Rio Grande's "timber base." This forest technician is a pleasant, matter-of-fact man, a "just-doing-my-job" sort of government worker. He doesn't seem to take offense when I say that conservationists have labeled the Rio Grande National Forest, "the black sheep of Colorado forestry," and ask him if he thinks the description fits. "Personally, I don't think we've had any more problems than any other forest. We've really had only this one appeal," he says, apparently referring to the last year's lawsuit. In fact, CEC and others such as the *Conejos Concerned Citizens,* as well as the timber industry itself, have challenged a number of timber sales on the Rio Grande.

The Stone Forest Industries mill at South Fork, Colorado, and the 220 jobs it provides, is the biggest timber operation in southern Colorado and the second largest corporate timber presence in the state, just behind Louisiana-Pacific. The South Fork mill is owned by the Stone Container Corporation, with regional offices in Raton, New Mexico, and corporate headquarters in Chicago, Illinois.

The town, and the mill, sit on the western tip of a finger of private land that pokes deep into the Rio Grande National Forest from the east. Some mill workers live in Del Norte, 16 miles to the east but some come from as far away as Pagosa Springs. Famous for the deepest snow in Colorado, 10,850 ft. Wolf Creek Pass separates Pagosa and South Fork, creating a challenging 72 mile commute for Stone Forest Industries mill workers. (Gravel-voiced folk singer and humorist C. W. McCall celebrated this harrowing stretch of road in his 1960's ballad, "Wolf Creek Pass.")

Joe Duda has been a forester with the South Fork mill operation for eight years, four of those for the mill's previous owner, Southwest Forest Industries. He estimates the South Fork mill ("basically a stud mill") presently depends on National Forests in Colorado for most of the 28 to 30 million board feet of timber the mill consumes each year. The nearby Rio Grande National Forest supplies about 50 percent of the mill's yearly timber supply. To fill in the rest, the mill looks north to the Gunnison National Forest, east to the San Isabel and west to the San Juan National Forest on the other side of the Continental Divide, and even as far away as the Pike National Forest near Colorado Springs, an hour's drive south of Denver, and some 200 miles northeast of this southern Colorado timber mill operation.

Profits obviously diminish as trucking distances increase. In some cases, Duda concedes, Stone Forest is hauling federal timber close to 200 miles, a distance that, he allows, "is stretching it." Duda, of course, is talking about the mill's profit margin. So it's not surprising that Stone Forest continues to push hard for more timber sales on the Rio Grande—1.8 million acres of public forest literally in the mill's own backyard.

Below-cost timber sales are also an issue on the Rio Grande. By 1991, according to the Rio Grande's Anderson, timber sales on the Rio Grande National Forest were "within about 95 percent of breaking even." Forest managers had arrived at this "dollars out-dollars in" timber program figure using the new Timber Sale Program Reporting System (or TSPRS) accounting system. Critics say that, while TSPRS makes more sense than the accounting system previously used by the Forest Service, TSPRS is still heavily weighted to make selling below-cost federal timber look like a paying business.

Despite these new Forest Service accounting practices, below-cost federal timber is still a smoldering issue with at least one private timberland manager in southern Colorado. Errol Ryland is in charge of land operations at Forbes Trinchera, an awesome 180,000 acre spread of alpine terrain owned for the last 32 years by the late financier, Malcomb Forbes. In the mid '70s, Ryland says he convinced his boss that careful logging would benefit Forbes Trinchera's thick timberland. Until the last few years, Ryland says, Forbes cut and sold up to 3 million board feet a year, a volume probably unmatched by other private forest holdings in this high, dry region of the American West. Moreover, Rylands points out that Colorado state foresters believe the annual growth on the Forbes 180,000 acre "working ranch" would sustain such an annual timber harvest level indefinitely. (A portion of the original Forbes purchase, acquired from the politically prominent Simms family of Albuquerque, New Mexico, has since been split off into three separate subdivision developments.)

But Ryland goes on to say that Forbes's timber sales dropped to zero in the mid-1980s because they couldn't compete successfully with cheap federal timber sales. "Basically we can't get a decent price for our timber," he told me, because of "the price the Feds sell their timber for. You know," he explains in a disbelieving tone, "they go into negative sales. We really can't compete against them. Some of their timber sales are so cheap it's not worth it [to us] to get rid of it."

Ten to 20 years ago Forbes was selling timber for $65 a thousand board feet. "Now, they [Stone Forest Industries] are offering us $30," says Ryland. He suggests that "cheap" Canadian lumber, along with lack of competition for the locally dominant Stone Forest Industries mill, may also have helped drive down the price offered for privately owned sawtimber.

But when I asked Joe Duda, the South Fork mill official, about prices the mill has offered for Forbes timber, he told me that one of the main problems there involves the haul distance, 100 miles. Minimum prices for National Forest "stumpage," Duda explains, are set according to a variety of factors, including "the distance from the nearest mill." The Rio Grande National Forest, of course, virtually surrounds the Stone Forest's South Fork mill site.

Today Forbes still sells about 1 million board feet a year, but Manager Ryland told me Forbes Trinchera would like to sell more, providing prices were more attractive. He speculates that a proposed drop in the Rio Grande National Forest's ASQ (allowable sale quantity) could help raise prices offered to owners of nearby private timberland, or "woodlots" as the industry calls these private forests.

Rocky Smith of the Colorado Environmental Coalition, a persistent critic of money-losing federal timber sales, defends his organization's claim that the Rio Grande has certainly been "the black sheep of Colorado forestry." Smith says 20 years of "abusive forestry" has left this public forest "looking like hell—it's really hacked up." But by the spring of 1991, Smith was giving major credit to the Rio Grande National Forest's new supervisor, Jim Webb, who, Smith says "is now trying to straighten it out."

Webb turns out to be a cheery, enthusiastic sort. "I can't imagine being happier anywhere else," Webb says of his job. Acknowledging that the Forest Service is struggling with transition within its own agency, Webb says: "We're trying to manage for the year 2000's problems with a 1940's organization." Unlike a number of other Forest Service professionals I talked to in the Southwest, Webb even has a good word to say about Jeff DeBonis and his rebellious *Association of Forest Service Employees for Environmental Ethics* (pronounced "EF-SEE" for short). DeBonis, Webb tells me "is a cool dude. I'm glad he spoke up." And I detect not a trace of sarcasm or animosity in Webb's comments.

Webb, something of a cool dude himself, good-naturedly confesses to being a reformed Forest Service "timber beast," the infamous term used by all sides of the timber debate to describe timber-devouring federal forest managers. He then proudly lists the changes he and his management team are implementing on this National Forest—including a spectacular slash in the Rio Grande's annual timber sales program.

He is bracing for a pitched battle with Stone Forest Industries over the supply issue. Webb says he and South Fork mill manager Kevin Cain have for some time been conducting a sort of public duel, each going to the affected communities in the San Luis Valley presenting their very different views about how much timber this National Forest should supply. Webb says Stone Forest Industries distributes a generally "good" fact sheet supporting its views on Rio Grande National Forest timber issues. He chuckles, though, when he adds that this fact sheet describes timber opponents as "neo-pagans" and "the vocal minority."

Webb maintains that the Rio Grande National Forests does indeed account for about 18 percent of the valley's economic base. But 13 percent of this forest-generated income comes from tourism and recreation, leaving the timber industry a more modest 5 percent share of the valley's total economic base. The Rio Grande's timber program contributes a scant 1.6 percent of the National Forest's share of the area's economic base; grazing accounts for an equally small portion. Webb is convinced he has won public support for the new direction he is charting for this federal forest. "Most folks say, hey, we understand," Webb tells me in the spring of 1991.

Webb has been supervisor of the Rio Grande for four years. With remarkable candor, he points out a major use conflict discussed in the Forest's 1984 forest management plan:

"An assumption was made that we could essentially clear cut about 4000 acres [of spruce] a year on this forest. There is no way that is socially or politically acceptable [now]. People in general who come to the Rio Grande to visit *their* forest expect to see clear water, good scenery, good fishing and hunting. And while they like to drive on the logging roads, they don't want to stare at large clear cuts or seed-tree patches around every corner."

Stone Forest Industries at South Fork stands to be the big loser as the Rio Grande National Forest's timber sale volumes drop steadily over the next five years. But its neighbor, Jackson Lumber Company, South Fork's other, far smaller sawmill business, is confident it will continue to thrive. Bill Rucinski, who has headed this family-owned business for over 15 years, says: "We've never experienced a bad year." The secret of Jacskon Lumber's success is specialization and diversification.

Observers say that Rucinski, 44, is a very savvy businessman. Jackson Lumber's owner says he simply "minds his own business," works long hours right alongside his workers (32 in all) and runs a three-part operation that includes both a wholesale and a retail division as well as a summer greenhouse operation, supervised by his wife, Judy. The nursery and the seedling trees they raise are, like children, a source of great pride. "I like being a conservationist. We plant a lot of trees in the greenhouse." He thinks his most important legacy will be the magnificent trees that will grow from those seedlings.

Jackson Lumber's specialized products include paneling, decking, and tongue-and-grove boards milled from both aspen and spruce. They also "re-saw" lumber, which Rucinski explains produces a finer, more decorative product. "We make items that are in demand [and] we avoid competition" with the "commodity items" big mills produce. These, he tells me, are studs, dimension lumber, and the wood products used by the home construction industry.

In other western states local mills say they can't compete against the big mills and the favoritism Forest Service lavishes on "big business." But in contrast Jackson Lumber has been logging on the Rio Grande National Forest for more than 40 years and expects to continue logging there far into the future. The small business timber sale "set-asides" the U.S. Forest Service is required to reserve for small operators works well for Jackson Lumber. "We couldn't compete without it," Rucinski tells me.

He says the Rio Grande National Forest grows enough timber to supply all the small mills in the San Luis Valley. "If large business wasn't pushing for more, the small mills could get along" well on the reduced volume of timber the Rio Grande expects to harvest in the next five years. High production mills—Rucinski agrees we're talking about his big neighbor, Stone Forest Industries— must push for more and more federal timber. "I can survive on 2 million board feet a year. Large business uses in one year what I would take 18 years to do."

Rucinski is certain the timber industry and federal forests were headed for trouble when, during the last decade, more and more "mills geared up for high speed, high production," turning out billions of board feet of the "commodity items" that feed the building industry. Rucinski, a thoughtful, deliberate man, sounds even more serious when he says: "I think our country is overdeveloped." He thinks that National Forests, even in the Rocky Mountain West, could likely sustain "timbering on a small scale" almost indefinitely.

Rucinski's idea of "minding his own business" includes not running with the pack. He doesn't belong to timber industry organizations. Lobbying and politicking, he suggests, aren't important to his business plan. He says a business should concentrate on its own plan of action. "We're proud of what we do," Rucinski states, adding: "We've got the best safety record in the state." He doesn't envy the difficult job ahead for Rio Grande National Forest Supervisor Jim Webb. "I respect the man," he says, his tone full of foreboding. It will require great skill to balance the new and determined demands on the Rio Grande. On one side are the recreationists who expect a high-quality outdoor experience. (Are these the "neo-pagans" the Stone Forest Industries fact sheet speaks about?) And on the other side, Webb faces intense industry pressure to sustain the volume of federal timber that Stone Forest managers say their mill needs to survive.

Rucinski is betting that Supervisor Webb is equal to this daunting task.

CLOSEUP
"Only the Names Have Been Changed"

The old-time television cop show, *Dragnet*, immortalized the line: "This is a true story. Only the names are changed...to protect the innocent." The episode I am about to relate is true, too. And yes, the names have also been changed...to protect the politically vulnerable. But this story demonstrates clearly that politics—not scientific forestry—often dictates National Forest timber policy.

By now you can guess the background, but for the sake of story telling, let's recapitulate. Call our mythical state El Dorado. Unlike the Northwestern states, El Dorado isn't a major timber-producer. Some ponderosa pine, some spruce—enough to keep small local sawmill operators going, but nothing to attract any of the timber industry's major players. Then one day in 1984, the Board-Foot Corporation, or "B-F," a subsidiary of TIA (for Take It All) Corporation, moved in to harvest the region's aspen trees.

B-F developed a cozy relationship with the U.S. Forest Service and regional economic development honchos, and built a couple of waferboard plants in a remote corner of El Dorado. For this economically depressed area (mining had just hit bottom once again and ranching was wobbly at best), B-F's promise of new jobs was little short of wonderful.

Five years later even B-F's most ardent supporters were conceding that the price the region was paying for those jobs was high. Pollution, poor pay, toxic fumes and sick workers inside the plant were just a few of the negative impacts. And B-F, it turned out, expected to clearcut many thousands of acres of El Dorado's prized aspen forests, mostly in National Forests.

Early on, the U.S. Forest Service trotted out one forester after another to explain to locals how, suddenly, El Dorado's aspen forests were dying, or declining, or being taken over by conifers—the famous "conifer invasion." Luckily, B-F had come on the scene just in time for the needed "treatment." Which, of course, was massive clearcutting of aspen forests hitherto mostly untouched.

The scene fades now to early summer, 1990.

A private meeting is taking place between representatives of *Concerned Local Citizens* (CLC), a couple of regional development types, and a high-level official from the state's Department of Natural Resources. At issue: "the cut." How much publicly-owned aspen timber should B-F be allowed to cut annually? CLC has discovered that the Forest Service "really doesn't know what it's got" in its aspen forests here. Meaning—the Feds just don't have an up-to-date forest inventory.

The Forest Service has, mercifully, backed off the term "treatment." It simply wouldn't fly, and it became a public relations embarrassment. Everyone in this meeting more or less agrees that the issue—how big should the annual cut be—is economic and political. It has everything to do with jobs, economics, and elections (El Dorado's governor is up for re-election in a few months) and very little to do with the health of the forest.

A reporter, who has been following the B-F story, is allowed to sit in on this private meeting. Everything is understood in advance to be off-the-record. Later, that rule is modified to "no naming names."

The talk is candid, to the point. An outfitter, who is also a member of CLC's Forest Management Committee, shows slides— just five or six. They are aerial photos of great patchwork clearcuts, where B-F has literally scalped hundreds of acres of gorgeous high-altitude aspen forests. The outfitter's big-game hunter clients who pay thousands of dollars each for a "remote" experience, weren't pleased about B-F's noisy clearcutting operation right next door to the outfitter's longtime hunting camp site. The site, of course, on a great long forested ridge overlooking a vast mountain panorama, was picked for its beauty. The outfitter says B-F is destroying his business. No one answers this plea.

One business type—a marketing specialist—uses particularly catchy phrases to bad-mouth the Forest Service and B-F. He calls the Forest Service's draft Forest Management Plan and its companion Environmental Impact Statement "mental junk food." He goes on to say: "When B-F got here five years ago, everything changed. Now it's timber vs. tourism." The state has just chosen two routes in the region as scenic byways, but because these mountains are among the highest and most beautiful anywhere, the two routes are called scenic "skyways." A dynamite marketing tool, says Larry, (not his real name, remember.) "Why are we letting this company come in here and wreck all this?" Larry asks the guy from El Dorado's Department of Natural Resources. There is anguish in his voice.

Someone else says the Forest Service's failure to come up with an accurate inventory (how many board feet and where they're located) "is a disservice to both the loggers and the environmental community."

The proposed annual aspen cut has elicited several thousand negative comments. In a rural area where whole county populations number but a few thousand, this is an impressive number. Over a five year period, the cut issue has been appealed, negotiated, facilitated, and endlessly written about.

CLC, who has fought B-F tree by tree for five years, still isn't sure whether it's saved a single tree. B-F wants 3000 new acres of National Forest aspen each year but the CLC says 1200 acres yearly is all the public aspen B-F should be allowed to take. CLC has recently received insider information that El Dorado's governor is now talking about a possible 2000-acre annual cut.

That's what the private meeting is all about. CLC wants to know what Governor Royer (not his real name) is up to and where his Department of Natural Resources stands on all this. The outfitter, no Rambo but a quiet, carefully spoken man, says with considerable conviction that even 1000 acres a year will mean penetration by B-F into every area of this high-altitude plateau. Looking the state guy squarely in the eye, the outfitter adds: "If

B-F wins this, I will become very cynical about the plan." He is speaking of the forest plan, like all those in western National Forests, mandated by the National Forest Management Act of 1976.

The state's Natural Resources man seems to side with CLC. He indicates a low regard for B-F's style of operation and suggests that "it would be a mistake for the Forest Service to look to maintaining or expanding the present timber job base." No one knows just how to take this remark It's awfully clever. He seems to be saying that the state would take a dim view of an expansion of the mill capacity and its jobs, based on an expectation that the National Forest would increase its aspen timber harvest to match.

A few days later, CLC's Mick McSavvy sends out a memo summing up this private meeting. CLC has always approached this issue as a conflict between a profit-hungry outside timber-products corporation and the prosperous, growing tourism/recreation economy that is the lifeblood of local small businesses in this entire region. The state's man, however, has advised CLC that like it or not, B-F too is now an existing business in the town of Obran, implying that the Guv doesn't want any blame for losing jobs in an election year. The prospects look slim for persuading the state to balance those jobs off against jobs lost in other sectors due to B-F—the consummate bad corporate neighbor—and its overcutting.

The day after the meeting, the CLC memo relates, the Guv's guy met with National Forest officials in their regional offices. A few days later a member of the USFS's planning team called CLC to tell them that several alternatives in the draft forest plan had been changed or dropped. On the plus side, planners had scrapped a section that committed the Forest Service to support expansion of existing mill facilities. Less welcome was the news that a prohibition in the draft against below-cost timber sales had been removed.

The Governor's 2000-acre figure would also be added to the plan as a new alternative, and although it won't be selected, it "provides a range of alternatives" for comparison with previously discussed numbers—and makes the Guv look like a good guy to some constituents while not necessarily giving him a black eye with environmental voters. B-F, the memo reminds us, wants a full 3000 acres per year. (Nobody is talking about a cut-off time, so apparently B-F will be allowed to cut the final annual acreage indefinitely.)

Forest planners, however, will toss CLC one small bone. Certain areas CLC considered highly unsuitable for logging were to be "dropped from the suitable timber base." The revised Forest Plan and its new EIS (environmental impact statement) will be released in about five months, to be followed by a 30 day public comment period.

CHAPTER ELEVEN

Utah,
A Rural Economy Under Siege

Utah in the 1950s was best known for the Mormon Tabernacle, the great Mormon cathedral in Salt Lake City. But by 1990, the names of the state's breathtaking National Parks—Canyonlands, Arches, Bryce Canyon, Zion and Capitol Reef—had also become part of the national vocabulary. On almost any day, visitors from all over the world could now be observed, energetically hiking Utah's backcountry trails or admiring grand sandstone formations from designated observation spots.

But the growing fame of Utah's natural wonders has also come into sharp conflict with the state's natural resource-based enterprises—ranching, mining and timbering—industries that have sustained pioneering Utah families for three and four generations. No modern visitor to the state's harsh interior landscapes can fail to appreciate the Mormon's pioneering grit. Yet both sides in Utah's testy and ongoing debate over federal lands argue that this arid land's inhospitable nature and the limitations of Utah's natural resources provide support for their point of view.

Utah's timberland totals a mere 3 million acres, the lowest of any state in the region except for Nevada which has virtually no marketable trees. This fact, however, has not lessened the intensity of the fight over commercial logging on federal forest land within its borders. Instead, Utah's mining, ranching and timbering interests increasingly make common cause, fighting side by side to preserve their traditional rural economy.

Federal land accounts for two-thirds of Utah's timberland. Ownership of the remaining 1 million acres is roughly divided between the state and private non-industrial forests. But the size of the state's timberland has little to do with the demand to harvest those resources. Logging interests in Utah employ the same sort of rhetoric as loggers do in Forks, Washington, the notoriously vocal "Logging Capital of the World."

Five of Utah's seven National Forests (The Wasatch-Cache, the Uinta, the Manti-La Sal, the Fishlake and the Dixie) march from north to south down the state's mountainous central spine. The Ashley National Forest in its Northeast corner surrounds the southern end of spectacular Flaming Gorge; the tiny Sawtooth National Forest hugs the northwest border with Idaho; while a detached pocket of the Manti-La Sal National Forest in the beautiful but little-known La Sal mountains of southeastern Utah rises directly above awesome canyonlands and desert landscapes.

Timber-growing conditions in this high, dry state are generally rated as poor or marginal at best. Still, the Dixie National Forest is the state's major timber-producer. The Dixie is variously described as "the Emerald Jewel of Southern Utah's Golden Circle," (the route linking the region's national parks) and, by Deseret News writer Joseph Bauman, as "a chunk of Alaska floating above the Utah desert."

Escalante, a town of about 800, sits amid the grandeur carved out by Utah's Escalante River as it heads east toward the Colorado and what is now Lake Powell. Stephen Steed is general manager of the sawmill business his father started in Escalante 30 years ago. His brother Sheldon, Steve tells me, is the operation's Resource Manager. In our first encounter, an introductory phone interview, Steve is personable and articulate, and sounds entirely at ease as he describes the history of saw-milling in his region of southern Utah. Timbering, he says, has been going on here since pioneers first settled the area. Until the 1950s perhaps half a dozen small, family operations milled the timber logged and hauled down from the Dixie.

The Steed operation, now Escalante Sawmills, Inc., modernized, grew and flourished and by the 1990s was the single remaining mill in Escalante. In 1975 the mill burned down. Some 50 sawmill jobs also went up in smoke. "Our family, under the advice of both friends and consulting foresters (including the Forest Service) felt there was a need and a demand for a sawmill," Steve explained. Rebuilding began soon and by the next year the Steed mill "was up and going," this time with jobs for 60 workers.

About the same time the U.S. Forest Service began requiring logging operations to post bonds as performance guarantees. Steve Steed says family operations like this one couldn't come up with the $100,000 cash guarantees federal rules demanded. By the end of 1976, the Steed family had sold its Escalante mill to Allied Forest Products Inc. With the acquisition of the Escalante operation, this Portland, Oregon-based company owned four sawmills, with a combined workforce of about 300 employees. Although Allied Forest Products is still small compared to the Weyerhaeusers and the Boise Cascades, the company's larger financial resources meant the Escalante operation could survive. A half dozen years after the sale, the mill was running full tilt, with 120 workers split between two shifts. The mill processed 21 million board feet or more of National Forest timber each year, turning it into studs and other building materials.

Responding to a dwindling National Forest timber supply and changing economic times within the timber and wood products business, Escalante mill managers, like many other western mill operators, saw efficiency as insurance for the future. In 1990, Allied and its managers spent $700,000 upgrading the southern Utah mill. With its new high tech equipment in place, Escalante mill managers dropped the mill's night shift and the 60 workers who manned it, trimming payroll costs by $400,000. Steve Steed credits both the new equipment and an exceptional mill crew with a level of efficiency that's "10 percent better than we expected." The mill now processes about 17-18 million board feet of sawtimber each year.

In 1991, the Escalante mill employed 75 full-time and four part-time workers, amounting to a $1.2 million annual payroll. The operation also pays out about $1.5 million yearly for contract labor—mainly truckers and logging crews.

Although the Steed family no longer owns this mill, Steve Steed is clearly the man in charge. "All four Allied mills are pretty autonomous," he allows. Steve seems born to the role of mill manager in this quiet town where he grew up. He was headed toward a career as a commercial pilot, but soon after the fire he came back to Escalante to help his family rebuild the burned-out mill. He's not sorry he decided to stay on. "This has been a good business—it's been good to a lot of people."

Steve Steed says the Escalante mill certainly *does* have a strong working relationship with the Dixie National Forest. In early 1980s, the Dixie was under siege from a mountain pine beetle epidemic that was leaving dead and dying pine trees across many sections of the Colorado Plateau—the name given to the huge land mass carved out by the Colorado River, most of which isn't actually in Colorado.

Lumber markets in the early '80s were "extremely soft," Steed relates. In fact, times were so bad in the lumber business "some mills had shut down to sit it out." When the Forest Service asked local sawmills to take part in its war against the pine beetle, both Escalante and Kaibab Industries, a big, Arizona-based outfit with a mill in nearby Panguitch, Utah, signed on despite the unfavorable economics of the deal. Both mills lost money on these timber sales, in large part because such sales are designed to clean out bug-infested sites and typically include a considerable number of poor quality trees. "We lost from $10 to $20 per thousand board feet on those lumber sales," he allows, pausing to recall the impact. "That year, 1982, was one of the worst years we've ever experienced in recent times. But we've bounced back and we've done real well for the past five or six years."

Steve Steed's tone is confident. He talks about the "cyclical" nature of the timber business. "In the good times you put money in the bank for the bad times," he explains cheerfully. Escalante is a prime example of a federally dependent logging community. Nearby National Forests (Dixie and Fishlake) are the only source of timber for this mill. In turn, Steed figures the mill and its current $1.2 million payroll "affects 70 percent of the kids in school."

"You can't find a community more dependent than Escalante. People here just don't know anything else [but the timber business]." Steed says the next five years will test just how many of these small timber-dependent communities can survive. In Garfield County, the sprawling southern Utah county which includes the towns of Escalante and Panguitch, no less than seven sawmills were vying for timber sales on National Forests at the beginning of the '80s.

Dramatizing this dilemma, Escalante has been listed by the National Association of Counties as one of 10 towns in the West facing extinction. In 1990, the association drew up its list of "endangered" towns to spotlight the group's view that "federal regulations to save the environment are killing communities," as a story in Salt Lake City's Deseret News put it.

The culprits, according to local folks, are proposed wilderness areas that preserve wildlife habitat at the expense of jobs, and environmentalists who challenge federal timber sales or otherwise disrupt National Forest timber harvest programs. One group, *Friends of the Dixie National Forest* or FOD, sees it another way. In a brochure titled "Forest Rescue," members explain that FOD "grew out of the realization that timber production has become the main emphasis of forest management [on the Dixie] with disastrous effects on wildlife habitat, lakes and streams, aesthetic values and recreational resources."

The conflict is classic.

The Dixie, conservationists declare, is undeniably unique. Both Bryce Canyon National Park and Cedar Breaks National

Monument lie within its two million acres. Capitol Reef National Park borders the Forest to the east, and additional adjoining lands are so wild they've been proposed for wilderness designation. The Dixie is a showcase of contrasts, from scenic deserts and hidden canyons to alpine splendor. Brian Head Resort, a small but popular ski area near Cedar City provides a grand winter playground for desert-bound residents of Las Vegas, Nevada, about three hours south on Interstate 15.

The fight over logging on the Dixie crosses state lines, and points up the "national" aspects of National Forests. The Town of St. George and the Duck Creek areas bordering the Dixie provide a cool haven for burned-out Las Vegas residents; many own summer homes in this wooded part of southwestern Utah.

Friends of the Dixie, three-years-old and growing fast, is an archetypical grassroots citizens organization in the American West. These serious National Forest watchdogs (FOD's 200 plus membership includes a number of active retirees, including its founder and chair Gabriel Moyer) are adept at *realpolitik.* "The National Environmental Protection Act process ," they note, "is being utilized by the group to bring about compliance by the Forest Service with all legal requirements of forest management."

They're fighting the present timber program for the Dixie which, FOD says, anticipates harvesting almost all of the Dixie's marketable trees by 1996.

Nowhere in the American West are conflicts over resource development issues more entrenched than in this part of Utah. No one in southern Utah has forgotten the bitter battle that took place in the early 1970s over the proposed 3000 kilovolt Kaiparowits coal-fired power plant and its massive coal-mining development, or the fact that Escalante residents back then hung environmentalists in effigy to show the world where they stood on the power plant and related coal-mining issue.

In fact, hanging, at least figuratively, seems to be the solution of choice when Escalante area residents talk about their problems with environmentalists. U.S. Representative Wayne Owens, a

Panguitch native, but also one of the state's most conservation-minded elected official, is considered a turncoat. Owens, a Democrat, came out in the spring of 1991 with a plan to create 5.4 million acres of new wilderness in southern Utah.

Escalante grocer Gene Griffin won fleeting national fame when both The Washington Post and Newsweek featured Griffin's remarks that spring about Owens and his wilderness bill. "To sum it up right quick, we'd like to hang him," Griffin reportedly said.

CLOSE-UP
Escalante, an Endangered Town

Escalante's main street is strangely quiet at 9 a.m. on a May morning as I pull up in front of one of the town's two grocery stores—they face each other from opposite sides of Highway 12. With a few exceptions, the town looks like it's going out of business. Munson's, with its spiffed up log front, stands out like a new dress in a second hand shop.

"Wayne Owens is not real popular in this part of the state," Mavis Munson observes when I inquire about Griffin's "hanging" remark. Mavis Munson and her husband, Bob, own and operate "Munson's," a grocery and hardware business. The low, one-story corner structure boasts a frontier-style covered sidewalk, shaded by the building's porch-like roof which, supported by log posts, extends out over the broad public sidewalk.

Mavis Munson is a handsome woman: trim, broad-shouldered, with short, sporty silver hair that sets off her blue eyes and classic features. She wears a blue shirt and wields a feather duster. The store is well stocked; the aisles are narrow. She is cautious and tentative in what she says about this community to a stranger.

Escalante (named for the Spanish priest-explorer Silvestre Escalante who explored the area in 1776) has picked up the battle flag in an environmental war that, one way or the other, it is almost sure to lose. It's been called a "holy war." Wilderness has locked up (or is threatening to lock up) what many Garfield

County residents think may be an untouched treasure trove of coal, oil and minerals in the surrounding area. Garfield County Commissioner Louise Liston complains bitterly: "We've lived with *de facto* wilderness for the past 10 years and have yet to see one instance where it has helped us [economically]."

Still holding her feather duster, Mavis Munson pauses behind the diagonal counter where the cash register is located, as I query her about her town. Escalante has four motels and one RV campground. A second such campground, apparently unfinished, has yet to open, she explains. The town had its best tourist year in 1990 and about two weeks ago Escalante played host to about 250 RVers on a cross-country trek, the biggest event the town has handled, "ever." But two upscale lodge developments south of town on Highway 12 seem to have cornered the lucrative summer visitor trade Utah's great National Parks attract.

She suggests that Escalante was slow to recognize the potential for capturing tourist dollars along Utah's "Golden Circle" route. The town is strategically located on the section of the Golden Circle route along Highway 12 that links Capitol Reef National Park, an hour or so north of Escalante and Bryce Canyon National Park, about 50 miles south. Escalante business leaders have recently joined a new group, a sort of "Highway 12 Chamber of Commerce." A move, Mavis Munson says, that's calculated to improve Escalante's market share of southern Utah's tourist economy.

The Munsons returned to Escalante, where Bob grew up, about two and a half years ago. It is apparent that this couple, who look to be in their 50s, are putting their considerable energies into saving this town from extinction Her husband, Mavis tells me, is a member of Escalante's town board. A big, stocky man with a well-tanned face, glasses, and sandy-colored, thinning hair, pauses to catch the drift of our conversation as he makes his way across the back of the store. This, it becomes clear, is Bob Munson. He amply fills the plaid shirt he's wearing and looks like the kind of expansive, middle-aged sportsman featured in colorful ads for bass fishing boats. However, he does not join in this discussion with still another "outside" reporter. There is no overt hostility, but I begin to feel like a CIA agent.

The Garfield County area "can't make it on farming anymore," Mavis Munson tells me, mostly because "there's not enough water." Typical of this part of Utah, Escalante is a tillable oasis cut off by steep canyons, and the sharp uplands of both the Dixie and the Fishlake National Forests nearby. "If the sawmill goes down, this town won't survive," she says matter-of-factly and without reservation. "People here feel they're being pushed out of what their ancestors made" of this difficult land. She is picking each word cautiously, taking care not to lose control. "I think every voice needs to be heard," Mavis Munson explains, indicating that those who have the closest relationship to this ground count for nothing. She wonders out loud "what happened [in the political debate] to let others get so much power over your lives," so much power over the future of rural communities such as this one.

And she speculates that Wayne Owens, a third-term Congressman representing a metropolitan Salt Lake City district, has perhaps forgotten his roots in Garfield County. People here can't understand how Owens could support more wilderness, a move they consider a Garfield County death sentence.

"I'm all for multiple use," Mavis Munson declares. She senses that "there's plenty of timber " on the nearby Dixie National Forest, but "they just can't get to it." The sawmill is temporarily shut down, and a visitor can pick up on a variety of opinions about why this has occurred. "It's them damn environmentalists," a service station attendant observes. But later mill manager Steve Steed says that a heavy winter snow pack has been slow to melt, delaying access to high-elevation federal timber the mill has already purchased.

During breakfast that morning at the Golden Circle Cafe, the layoff seems to hang like a shroud over the early-morning coffee drinkers. A single pickup truck parks in front of this fading, no-

frills, '50s-style restaurant; a working man emerges, enters the cafe
and slumps into a chair on one side of a table for four, opposite a
second working man. Soon they both cradle coffee cups, but no
amount of coffee seems to pump energy into these disheartened
figures.

The cafe is virtually empty. The clink of every dish or cup
ricochets around the unoccupied interior. It's been four weeks
since the mill last ran, and over coffee these men are consoling
each other. One leaves, and another pickup pulls up. Another
conversation is enjoined over coffee. Sawmill talk. No good
news this week.

A sign in the cafe's front window announces a meeting of *The
Western Association of Land-Users*. Mavis Munson tells me later she
and Bob support the group, which pushes for multiple-use on
public land. Wilderness, of course, is seen here as a single use, a
flagrant trashing of the principle that federal lands should be
available for every sort of purpose. A much broader-based
organization, *People for the West* is gaining some notice nationally.
Supported by ranchers, and timber and mining interests, its aims
are similar to Escalante's local "land-users" group, and both
organizations clearly hark back to the failed Sagebrush Rebellion
in the late 1970s. That drive sought to have states take over vast
federal lands within their borders.

When I meet Steve Steed later that morning at the Escalante
Sawmill, he is all upbeat, friendly, and positive. Ruby's Inn, near
Bryce Canyon, has indeed pioneered a new era in tourism in this
part of Utah, he tells me. In fact, this year-around vacation
complex is now the biggest employer in the region. Escalante, he
concedes, needs to polish itself up—new curbs and gutters, some
new store fronts and welcoming signs on both ends of town—to
win its share of the visitor trade.

Steed, a compact man with a ready smile and trim, brown hair
who is perhaps in his mid-30s, is a polished public-relations
person, as well as a mill manager. A T-shirt hanging like a poster
on a coat hanger at the rear of the mill's main office displays a

recipe for "Logger's Stew" that includes: "4 large well-plucked spotted owls," "3 finely chopped peregrine falcons" and "2 well-beaten environmentalists." Steed and I both ignore the T-shirt's message as we step out into the sunlight and head toward the cluster of low, metal buildings that make up the mill itself. Mountains of stockpiled sawlogs identify most western sawmills. But this mill's log yard is bare.

Leading a tour of the now mostly quiet mill complex, Steed displays an intimate knowledge of every function, explaining the history of changes the mill has gone through, right up to the installation last year of state-of-the-art computerized controls. These, he explains, greatly improve speed and versatility. Steed says, of these costly improvements: "We really stuck our necks out. This is really a commitment to the community. We think we're providing the tools the Forest Service needs" to harvest federal timber in a way that meets newer and higher standards. Steed says things are changing on the National Forest and the Escalante mill is adapting to those changes.

We walk up ramps, peer over at gleaming sawblades, burly conveyor systems that can move heavy logs as easily as matchsticks, and watch a cluster of mechanics performing surgery on some complex mechanical component.

A younger generation of sawmillers (Steed indicates he is one) sees the value in curbing the controversial practice of clearcutting: "They're not against uneven-age management," Steed asserts cheerfully. ("Uneven age management" is the term forest managers use to describe a more "selective" way of harvesting timber.) Steed is proud of the fact he's the fourth generation to be an Escalante area logger. He has just come from a meeting in Salt Lake, attended by Congressman Owens, the Forest Service, and representatives of both the timber industry, and various environmental groups.

Steed implies that this is just one of a series of meetings, and it is apparent that he is putting in considerable time on the front lines during this, perhaps, final battle over the future of Utah's natural resources. He recently took part in a forest workshop conducted by Forest Trust, a Santa Fe, New Mexico-based forestry consulting team. He liked their style. "I felt the environmentalists heard something they didn't want to hear," he tells me.

Steed claims the timber industry and the Forest Service are taking important new steps toward "getting away from old [forest] practices. They understand that they have to do it [logging] in an aesthetically pleasing way." Steed approves of "New Perspectives," a year-old program launched by the Forest Service which seeks to modify the agency's "timber-beast" image.

Steed assures me, however, that on the Dixie National Forest, "the Forest Service has the biological potential to sustain the forest industry in Garfield County" far into the future. On the question of preserving old-growth stands, Steed quotes a Brigham Young University ecologist he's heard recently who points out that old-growth forests are "dynamic" environments which, unlike pickles in a jar, cannot be "preserved." Steed suggests that this is a common misconception among naive environmentalists. (Each side in this debate over National Forest timber management policies frequently infers that the other side is blind to ecological reality.)

Steve Steed admits to being worried about the Dixie National Forest's next 10-year forest management plan, due in 1994. The plan will contain new and more accurate timber inventories. This could mean the Dixie's "suitable timber base," or the area where commercial logging is deemed appropriate, will shrink. Steed's Escalante mill depends on the Dixie National Forest for 90 to 95 percent of its timber supply and he is clearly determined to keep the mill going. The battle over the survival of this mill will be fought, timber sale by timber sale, for the next couple of years. For residents of this "endangered" southern Utah town, fighting for the Escalante sawmill's survival has taken on the proportions of a life and death struggle.

Part IV
THE PACIFIC COAST

CHAPTER TWELVE

Washington
"Big Timber" in Ancient Forests

The forests of the Pacific coastal region—Washington, Oregon
and northern California—are uniquely different from the inland
forests of the American West. This specialness is due to the
nature of things here. Soil, water and weather conditions
influenced by the Pacific Ocean combine to grow giant 400-year-
old Douglas firs in the great rain forests of Washington's Olympic
Peninsula and even larger redwoods in northern California—a
forest environment found nowhere else.

But in addition to the *natural* uniqueness of the Pacific Coast
and its forest ecosystems, two other factors profoundly influence
the timber business here. Unlike much of the West, hundreds of
thousands of acres of the best, most productive timberland in this
region is owned by the timber industry. Thus, the industry here is
not solely dependent on National Forests or other publicly-owned
timberland for a steady supply of sawlogs. And secondly, the
Pacific's convenient coastal ports and high timber production—
facilitated by private ownership of vast timberland—have created
a Pacific Coast timber export explosion.

In 1962, a violent windstorm downed millions of trees on
Washington's Olympic coast. This now famous "blowdown," and
the sudden surplus of wood it left in tangled piles on the ground,
opened the door to new and profitable timber markets in the Far
East.

Twenty years later, exporting timber from the Northwest to
Pacific Rim countries (Japan is a major importer) had become a
modern day Gold Rush. By 1990, quality logs were selling
overseas for premium prices. High-quality, old-growth logs, which
sell for $1.80 a board foot in this country, garner $2.20 on the
export market. "Typically, one old-growth tree is worth $40,000
to $50,000 in log form," one independent logger told me. Fine-
grain woods in Japan sell for $50 a board foot. As a result, even
private non-industrial timberland owners (families, estates, trusts,
and even insurance companies—a new and growing timberland
ownership faction) are selling off long-held old-growth timber
and pocketing windfall profits.

Booming export markets and leveraged buyouts of private
timber companies and their prime forestland have led to a frenzy
of "cut and sell" that has profoundly changed the forest landscape
of the Pacific Coast region, as well as the style and character of the
timber business there. Yet all of this has not lessened the demand
for timber from National Forests in the region—from the high-
producing Willamette National Forest in central Washington to
the Stanislaus National Forest in northern California.

In fact, pressure to cut more and more federal timber in the
Northwest, at an ever increasing rate, ultimately blew the public
lid off the smoldering controversy over U.S. Forest Service timber
management policies. The interrelated issues of endangered
species like the northern spotted owl, and the newly-discovered
importance of ancient forests and their old-growth ecosystems,
finally exploded into national headlines.

But it's really impossible to understand the manifold complexities
of Pacific-coast timber issues without taking a closer look at
frontier history and forest ownership patterns in this remarkable
tree-growing region.

To encourage settlement of the West and to dispose of large
tracts of the public domain following the Civil War, the U.S.
government embarked on a magnificent land giveaway.

Railroads, in particular, received millions of acres of federal land grants, as federal payoffs for expanding rail service to the west coast and to other remote areas of the frontier. These land grants often included highly productive timberland, which the railroads sometimes sold off for handsome profits.

To today's conservationists, the Burlington Northern railroad (formerly the Northern Pacific) and its offspring, Plum Creek Timber Company, are leading corporate villains in the timber melodrama playing itself out now in the American West. The Reagan Administration and its anti-conservation appointees (Interior Department Secretary James Watt leads the list) saw the exploitation of natural resources (from coal to timber) as a gloriously fitting way of life for the West. National policy was retailored to fit this view.

Plum Creek Timber Company owns some 1.5 million acres of timberland in the West. From Bozeman, Montana, to the far side of Washington's Cascade Mountains, Plum Creek is clearcutting its sections of timberland from border to border. Federal land grants in the West were often dispensed as alternating 640-acre squares or "sections." So Plum Creek's checkerboard clearcuts stand out as blatant and ugly symbols of destructive, corporate-style timber management.

Plum Creek is also a leading exporter of American timber, shipping about 1.5 million board feet a year. Weyerhaeuser is said to be the biggest exporter and ITT Rayonier is also a major player in this market. The state of Washington's Department of Natural Resources reportedly exported *over 75 percent of its total annual statewide harvest in 1989.* During the last two decades, overseas sales of timber from state trust lands has generated $1 billion for Washington's schools and colleges. But in 1989, Oregon residents voted (nine to one) to ban the export of logs from state-owned land. Then in September, 1990, new federal legislation restricted the export of logs from federally-owned land, although a companion measure prohibiting the "substitution" of federal timber to replace logs sold overseas is considered patently ineffective by most observers.

The total volume of timber shipped to customers in the Orient more than doubled during the 1980s, reaching 1.7 billion board feet in 1989. Observers say one out of every four logs cut in the Northwest is shipped overseas. It's no wonder then that with U.S. lumber prices the best in years, and log exports paying off like the Mother Lode, corporate Big Timber is cutting at previously unmatched rates. National Forests are being consumed at accelerated rates by what environmentalists see as this industrial forest-eating machine, with reforestation efforts totally unable to keep up with the galloping pace of logging.

Weyerhaeuser, with headquarters in Tacoma, Washington, is the aristocrat of the American timber industry. Weyerhaeuser is also the world's largest private owner of timberland with holdings that include about six million acres in the United States and highly favorable, long-term leases on more than seven millions acres of Crown land in Canada. After more than a century in the timber business, Weyerhaeuser family members (the fifth and sixth generations) are still actively involved in the management of the company—one of the world's five largest producers and marketers of pulp, paper and packaging products.

The Weyerhaeuser family's influence extends well beyond the timber company itself and its interrelated enterprises. Family members and associates have served on the boards of the Potlatch Corporation and Boise Cascade, both major timber-industry players in the American West. Few U.S. youngsters growing up in the mid-20th Century were unaware of Weyerhaeuser, "The Tree Growing Company." National Geographics were a staple in every dental office in America. Invariably, these popular magazines showcased Weyerhaeuser's shiny double-page ads, showing an all-American forester overseeing acres of bushy, brilliantly healthy evergreens.

Ted Nelson, a Weyerhaeuser vice president for timberlands and external affairs, took me in hand the day I stopped by to have a first-hand look at the corporate headquarters of this American timber legend. Nattily dressed in a dark blazer, Nelson, trim and gracious and perhaps in his mid-50s, was tailored to fit the legend. He told me that, despite its huge timberland holdings, the corporation also buys federal timber in the Willamette Valley and in the Klamath Falls region in Oregon.

As a large exporter of logs, Nelson says, Weyerhaeuser "can't directly purchase federal stumpage" (a technical term for timber standing uncut). But federal legislation banning the export of timber from federal forests as well as "substitutes," it turns out, has a convenient loophole. National Forest and BLM timber can be "indirectly" substituted for private logs sent overseas, Nelson explains, when the federal purchase is made by a third party. So Weyerhaeuser, along with other big exporters, regularly buys federal timber through an agent.

The corporation, Nelson says, purchases about 50 million board feet of federal timber each year in Oregon and a lesser 12 million board feet in Washington. Weyerhaeuser and other Big Timber exporters talk about the importance of "free markets" and worry about export restrictions. Banning private timber exports won't save privately held stands of old-growth timber, Nelson explains, because some 80 percent of the logs exported from the Pacific Northwest are already second-growth timber. Besides, a dependable flow of American logs overseas is leading to new markets for finished U.S. wood products abroad. Competitors from New Zealand, Chile, and Russia are ready to grab America's lucrative export markets should the U.S. flow falter.

Timber, I am reminded, is a global game. And Nelson suggests that a dependable flow of federal timber is an essential part of this international competition. Nelson says the timber industry *wants* National Forest managers to make decisions setting aside certain acreage for uses other than timber—recreation, fish habitat, wildlife and the rest. But as part of this dividing process, a significant portion of the public forest "pie" should be set aside for timber production. These acres—the richest and most suitably productive public land—would undergo "intensive management for production" of wood and fiber. We agree this means industrial-scale tree farming.

Our conversation also touches on the "owl" and possible federal action setting aside thousands of acres of the officially threatened bird's old-growth habitat. But such action won't affect this company, Nelson says, claiming that the days of "cut and get out" belong to the past.

Close to a hundred, Company founder Frederick "Dutch Fred" Weyerhaeuser was already a powerful timber baron in the midwest when, in 1899, he turned his sights west. Forests in Wisconsin and elsewhere in the Midwest were being "slicked off," and it was clearly time to move on. Author Keith Ervin writes that "in one bold stroke" Weyerhaeuser and his partners bought 900,000 acres of premium timberland from the Northern Pacific Railroad, part of the railroad's 38 million acres of federal grant lands. Weyerhauser quickly bought up more timberland, including tracts in southern Oregon owned by the Southern Pacific Railroad.

By 1930 Weyerhaeuser had begun its reforesting program in the Northwest and was calling itself "The Tree Growing Company." The company is considered an excellent commercial tree farmer. One independent logger I talked to said, "Weyerhaeuser would go broke if they allowed the soil erosion to take place that the Forest Service does." Washingtonians carry on a very public "love-hate" relationship with the Weyerhaeuser dynasty. Nelson acknowledges this ambivalence, and says that because Weyerhaeuser is a very large presence in the Northwest, "we are a very large target" as well.

Bellingham, Washington, an idyllic port community in the farthest Northwest corner of this remarkable state, is dealing casually with its first rain of the fall season. Even though I live in Western Colorado and deal with harsh Rocky Mountain weather on a daily basis, I grumble about feet that are already wet and cold

as I make my way to Tony's, where I'm supposed to meet a local
environmental leader

Tony's is a cozy, cluttered, college-town bistro, where a number
of earnest-looking academic types are scouring the interior pages
of today's newspapers which appear to be a fixture of the place.
From the first available table (many are old-fashioned "ice cream"
tables and chairs, the kind with loopy wire backs and small,
round, wooden seats) I can monitor the incoming traffic. I'm
looking for Mitch Friedman, a kingpin among environmental
activists in this region. We have no trouble recognizing each
other. He's wearing a blue baseball cap over dark, curly hair and
a beard to match, while I look more like somebody's visiting aunt
than a member of the university set all around me. Bellingham is
home to the University of Western Washington, an institution
distinguished by its Huxley College of Environmental Studies,
where Mitch Friedman was once a student and where he now has
strong allies.

Friedman, who calls himself a "conservation biologist," heads
the *Greater Ecosystem Alliance*, an 18-month old organization he
founded in 1989. Unlike professional eco-fighters I've met in
Montana and Wyoming, Friedman isn't the type you'd see
photographed in *Outside* magazine, promoting back-country
sports or equipment for the super-athlete. He virtually lives in his
office, and gives you to understand that saving the Northwest's
rainforest is so urgent that he seldom allows himself a full night's
sleep.

Although he looks at least 10 years older on this particular day,
Friedman is a mere 27. He is so intense you wonder if he'll last.
But, for all of it, he is warm and generous, both with his time and
with his spirit. For five years he was an Earth First!er, and he has
edited a book, *Forever Wild, Conserving the Greater Cascade Ecosystem*,
which is widely recognized as a good piece of work.

The state of Washington seems to grow great writers. Everyone
in Bellingham is enthused about two new books just out: *Fragile
Majesty—the Battle for North America's Last Great Forest* by Keith

Ervin; and *The Good Rain—Across Time and Terrain in the Pacific Northwest* by Timothy Egan. Both Ervin and Egan are native sons and respected writers. Their part of the West, they write, is awesome and special. It is what must be saved. (But so is my part of the West, I think—so is it all.) Mitch Friedman is fighting to save the same territory. But somehow he also conveys the idea that if the Northwest's forests are saved, the rest of the West's great forests can be saved as well.

But can they be saved? While it is true that in the Northwest's remarkably favorable climate, the Douglas firs, western red cedars, western hemlocks, Sitka spruce, and other forest giants grow bigger and faster than they do elsewhere, timber politics in the Northwest is just as deadlocked as it is in states like Arizona and Idaho.

"Weyerhaeuser and Boeing run Washington," Friedman declares. To compete, eco-warriors here must play political and economic hard-ball both on a local and a national level. So Friedman has changed tactics. During the past year or so, he has backed away from his *Earth First!* role, seeing it as "political baggage" he did not wish to carry. "I'm a bureaucrat, like everybody else," he says over lunch. (Tony's style is upscale vegetarian, sprouts and espresso topped off with elegant little baked things for desert.)

Conservation biology, he advises me, "is a new movement. It is science applied to conservation." He sees himself as a "process-level ecologist." Whatever that may be, Friedman is clearly dedicated to this battle. Recently, he and the *Greater Ecosystem Alliance* conceived and carried out a remarkable propaganda coup, a traveling roadshow involving a single semi-trailer carrying one massive Douglas fir log. Called the Ancient Forest Rescue Expedition, the log and its handlers have twice toured the nation, sounding the call "that help is needed to protect the vanishing and irreplaceable native forests of the Pacific Northwest." Media response has been "incredible," the *Greater Ecosystem Alliance* boasts in its quarterly newsletter, Northwest Conservation, News and Priorities. The expedition was sponsored by 60 conservation and outdoor groups, along with some Indian tribes. In Alabama, "even loggers and mill workers supported our cause." the newsletter reports. "Our present is their past. Forester propaganda will not return the wildlife and great trees to their forests, nor the vitality to their towns."

Freidman's *Alliance* is only one of dozens of environmental groups in the Northwest shouting for attention. Timber industry leaders in the Northwest have acknowledged that their cause lost ground after conservationists successfully drew the national spotlight to the battle over the remaining ancient forests and its now famous inhabitant, the northern spotted owl. But Friedman and his fellow conservationists do not sound like victors.

In addition to the powerful timber industry, Friedman sees all "the agencies" as enemies of conservation. And he includes in this rogues' gallery, the U.S. Fish and Wildlife Service, the U.S. Bureau of Land Management, the U.S. Forest Service and Washington state's own Department of Natural Resources— a bureaucracy which draws special indignation from the Northwest's conservation community. "We don't look for help from any of these agencies," Friedman says with disdain. He speaks of "rampant political corruption," and what he sees as the failure of the federal Environmental Protection Agency as well as the U.S. Fish and Wildlife Service to properly carry out their legally assigned roles as protectors of land, water, and species.

While the size of the annual timber cut will probably go down, "it won't be enough to compensate for all these years of overcutting," says Friedman. "In today's landscape" he says "we face a biological crisis of astronomical proportions." Although few politicians, so far, dare to oppose protection for endangered species, Friedman worries that political deals will result in grossly inadequate "postage-stamp size preserves." Wildlife communities cannot sustain themselves on such tiny islands of forest habitat, biologists tell us.

Biodiversity—the awkward phrase universally used to designate the complex and organic interaction of thousands of varieties of plant and animals in a single region or ecosystem—is Friedman's Holy Grail. He describes himself as "a weird mix of values: a scientist who's sat in front of a bulldozer." In a single month he spent two weeks in the woods, a week in conservation workshops and a fourth week lobbying in Washington, D.C.

Ownership of timberland in Washington, as already noted, is distinctly different from that in other western states, where National Forests often account for 60 percent to 75 percent of all commercially viable timberland. The U.S. Forest Service (with 4.8 million acres) and the timber industry (with only slightly less) rank one and two in ownership of Washington's total 16.8 million acres of timberland. The state of Washington is a strong third with 3.7 million acres. And private (non-timber-industry) ownership accounts for an only slightly smaller 3.6 million acres.

Conservationists assert that Washington's Department of Natural Resources, the agency responsible for state-owned timberland, is the worst sort of land steward, promoting the most blatant "rape and run" style of clearcutting on public land. The reason is simple: money. State agencies administering state-owned land are charged with producing maximum income from these lands. As a result, conservation on state-owned lands in Washington rates little more than lip-service.

"School sections," a familiar term in the rural West, are federal lands (640 acres is a "section") set aside to help support state schools. Fees from timbered school sections, and other state-owned land in Washington, along with huge National Forest payments, (mandated to offset the loss of property tax receipts from non-taxable federal land), are two major sources of income for towns, counties, and school districts in the Northwest. Some school districts here depend on timber-related fees for up to one third of their annual budget. And no one, so far, has come up with an acceptable alternative to this form of traditional, timber-dependency. Ancient forest giants, including 400-year-old

Douglas firs, are being knocked down at record rates. Once they're gone, timber-dependent local budgets will face a major shortfall.

As in neighboring Oregon, conservationists here suggest that state natural resource managers have been wantonly shortsighted. Ruthless clearcutting on steep slopes and drainages is systematically destroying Washington's fabled steelhead trout habitat, and unleashing massive landslides that will render slopes unstable for years to come. In his book, *Fragile Majesty*, author Erwin describes such destruction in grim detail. But he also points out that scientists, until recently, seriously misunderstood the ecology of crucial spawning streams. "Much of the damage done to anadromous [upstream spawning] fish habitat has been the result of ignorance....The Washington Forest Practices Act of 1976 mandated the removal of large debris from streams following logging....During the past decade, biologists have learned that, far from hurting fisheries, logs in streams are [often] helpful," says Erwin.

Curiously, despite the loss of fisheries in Washington and other parts of the Northwest, environmental leaders told me the fishing industry has been slow to make common cause with the environmental community. And while the state of Washington is a major timber-producer—lumber production rose 31 percent during the 1980, while its wholesale value, $1.2 billion, showed a 37 percent increase—it's also significant to note that the timber industry represents less than six percent of this fast-growing state's healthy and diversified economic base.

Still, critics say the current accelerated harvest has ravaged thousands of acres of old-growth forests. Once lush mountainsides now resemble barren, bombed-out graveyards with splintered stumps standing over the wreckage like gravestones. Long held forestry traditions honoring slower, sustained-yield principals, simply gave way to greed in the economic climate of the 1980s. In an atmosphere of fast corporate profits regardless of consequences, timberland in the Northwest took a horrible beating in the '80s.

During this frenzy of harvesting, replanting has become a hit or miss business. State and federal laws requiring cut-over timberland to be replanted within five years haven't guaranteed successful reforestation. Environmentalists say poor growing conditions, especially on steep slopes, coupled with lack of care, have left much former timberland bare even of seedlings. On National Forests, reforestation is a major, and regularly abused, budget category. The 1930 Knudsen-Vandenberg Act allows the Forest Service to hold back funds it earned from timber receipts for replanting following timber sales, instead of turning the money back to the Department of Agriculture. The 1976 National Forest Management Act expanded the use of such K-V funds to include thinning, wildlife habitat improvements and other activities.

Because these so-called K-V funds are what forest economist Randal O'Toole calls "budget-maximizers," agency budget-makers have learned to plan timber sales around the returns these funds will bring to Forest Service budgets. O'Toole cites agency surveys showing that often unnecessary or ill-timed thinning work (spraying herbicides is a Forest Service favorite) was carried out simply to draw more bucks under the K-V rules. Some silviculturists, these surveys noted, admitted to falsifying reforestation and other records to show that they met agency targets. Under the guise of reforestation, millions of dollars have been wasted, along with millions of acres of federal timber.

O'Toole says that the federal budgeting process requires "an even-flow of accomplishments...to maintain a stable [bureaucratic] organization. If trees are not planted in California, a Forest Service official in Washington may not get a desired pay increase. If herbicides are not sprayed in the Klamath National Forest (northern California), an administrator in San Francisco may lose his or her job. Silviculturists are pressured to meet reforestation and similar targets to maintain the flow of cash to high levels of the bureaucracy." Many critics say dropping the

Knudsen-Vandenberg Act should be the first step in any plan to reform the Forest Service.

Washington State and the rest of the Northwest are clearly the epicenter of public furor over forest management in the American West. In book after book, article after article, skilled writers have drawn us into the secrets of these great, temperate rainforests, pleading eloquently with America to understand the magnitude of loss there.

Still, in Washington, some tentative compromises started to take shape in the early 1990s. Author Keith Ervin, writing in High Country News, describes the creation in 1989 of a *Sustainable Forestry Roundtable* by Washington Public Lands Commissioner Brian Boyle. Private forestland owners, environmentalists, tribal leaders and local and state officials ultimately agreed to call for new standards to control erosion and flooding, and for a 10 percent set-aside for wildlife. "Politically," Ervin reports, "the Sustainable Forestry Roundtable and its predecessors represent the most comprehensive effort in the West to open up the management of state and private forestlands to public concerns. Supporters of this consensus-building process say it can now be extended to the National Forests, where the politics of confrontation still prevail," Others like Mitch Friedman and Andy Kerr say too much has been lost already, leaving little or no room for meaningful compromise on critical forest issues.

Leaving Bellingham, I begin a tour south—by bridge, ferry, winding roads, and through some of the thickest, deepest forests imaginable—down the glorious Olympic Peninsula. Writers describe this peninsula as probably the "finest example of rainforest remaining in North America." It feels like Ireland— with evergreens. And the Olympic peninsula boasts its own world champions: a 225 ft.-high Douglas fir that is the world's tallest; and a prize-winning western red cedar, 21 feet in diameter at breast height—room-size. And more.

Despite these Olympian qualities, the Gods have not provided enough forests to suit both the timber industry and conservationists, who successfully battled to win National Park status for a significant portion of the Olympic National Forest, now set aside as Olympic National Park. This handsome piece of public real estate draws over three million visitors each year, the fourth most popular National Park in the U.S. Despite its tourist draw, disgruntled loggers still complain that too much good timber has already been "locked up." The peninsula also is home to what angry, timber-dependent towns here call "the billion-dollar bird"—the now officially endangered northern spotted owl. With new federal court decisions in 1991 clearly supporting the need to set aside thousands of acres of old-growth owl habitat in National Forests here and elsewhere in the Northwest, Washingtonians are bracing themselves for a political eruption of Olympian proportions.

CLOSEUP
Bob Pyle's Willapa Hills

Author and naturalist Robert Michael Pyle, who has written beautifully about his part of Washington, the Willapa Hills in the state's southwest corner, is cautious about the chances for widespread forestry reform. In *Wintergreen*, his prize-winning book about the Willapas, he repeatedly indicts the corporate timber giants for their cold-hearted disregard of the land.

Bob, known affectionately to friends and colleagues as "Butterfly Bob," and his wife, Thea, a graphics and silk screen artist, have gone to some pains to make room in their schedules to meet a stranger who wants to talk about timber issues. And finding Bob and Thea Pyle's hideaway in the Willapa Hills is a glorious and instructive journey.

After driving south from Tacoma, I leave Interstate 5 at Longview, a big, burly mill town on the Columbia River and head west on State Route 4 toward Gray's River. The Columbia River canyon barely accommodates Route 4, forcing it to bend frequently and jam itself against steep, forested slopes that almost overhang the road's inside edge. Each curve in the road is like a curtain rising on an inviting new rural scene. This *feels* like rainforest country. On the other bank of the river lies Oregon.

Washington and other Northwestern states hide the shame of gaping clearcut patchwork forests by leaving the thinnest of forested buffer strips along roads and highways. Like a spy, I snatch views of those forbidden scenes while zooming past at the prescribed late-20th century pace. But, on the way to Bob and Thea's, a detour takes me on a steep and twisting (but still paved) logging road into the very heart of this logging country.

Evergreens grow like rows of corn—Iowa, only with roller-coaster hills. I learn later that this is all state or industry-owned timberland. Much of it is in its third rotation, meaning its third crop of trees. Huge landslides, the result of gross overcutting, keep Route 4 shut down much of the time. The state highway department has spent some $30 million so far on Route 4 road repairs, Bob Pyle tells me later. The value of the timber sale that destabilized this road was only $200,000.

A left turn a couple of miles down the road leads into a wooded sanctuary, where time has softened the outline of a small gray house. An open porch across the front of the house commands a sweeping view of a idyllic meadow; a narrow road disappears under the well-seasoned exterior of a covered bridge.

A sturdy figure in a rocking chair is intently studying the scene and seems not to notice the car's arrival. When, in time, he comes forward, I see a huge, silvering halo of hair and a full beard to match—a Walt Whitman look-alike. Bob Pyle, sometime Oxford scholar and teacher, turns out to be a wonderful hybrid: a hip, outdoor-ish don. My host extends a hand outward as I step up toward the back door. "Watch out for the spider," he cautions anxiously, protecting a dishpan-sized web, complete with a very large, resident spider.

In the living room, books stand shoulder to shoulder, floor to ceiling, on several walls. A smallish TV is arranged for cozy viewing a few feet in front of a generously pillowed sofa. Bob Pyle

confesses to being a movie buff—there's no regular TV reception.
A nearby video cassette is titled, "Bruce Springsteen Anthology."

Pyle, a leading authority on butterflies and an alumnus of both
Yale University and University of Washington forestry
departments, is intimately involved with the forests hereabout.
More public attention, he says, should be given to a continuing
loss of "the invertebrates," which may play a role equal to the
famous owl in the eco-structure of old growth forests. Only
"scraps" of the area's great virgin forests remain.

Virtually all the timberland in this area is owned by the timber
industry. Weyerhaeuser is a big operator here. So is Crown
Zellerbach and Longview Fiber Company, up the road.
Corporate directors not foresters "call the shots" on millions of
acres of industry timberland, says Pyle. The infamous mergers
and leveraged buyouts financed by junk bonds in the money-mad
'80s have further undermined and compromised the Northwest's
regal timberland.

One example: in a corporate-takeover, British financier and
world market player Sir James Goldsmith gobbled up Diamond
International in 1982, along with Crown Zellerbach about the
same time. Goldsmith began breaking up these holdings and sold
off millions of acres of prime timberland to real estate developers
and others who had no interest in keeping this prime forest in
wood production. And the large commercial timberland tracts
Crown Zellerbach still holds in Washington have been brutalized
by overcutting.

Frenzied overcutting to pay off corporate debts has been
commonplace. Logging roads, fragmented forests, ruined soil
that refuses to grow new trees has replaced the primeval forest
legacy of the Willapa Hills. Pyle says some areas have been
replanted six times and success still remains uncertain. He is
clearly a populist who claims that loggers and their families are
victims as well. Weyerhaeuser's "union-busting" put an end to
organized labor in the woods. In fact, the big timber companies
have now distanced themselves from this dangerous end of the

work. Small logging outfits now work in the woods under contract to the big corporations. Wages and benefits have fallen and accident rates are climbing. Pyle says that independent loggers, often with poor equipment and working overtime to make ends meet, are especially at risk. "Plenty of people in this community have been touched by forest deaths," says Pyle, slowly shaking his great mane.

A few year back, he tells me, truckers hauling logs along Route 4 used to "sound their jake-brakes" to show that an alien environmentalist lived in this house. Bob had published his beautiful book of forest essays, *Wintergreen,* in 1986: and in this book he is sharply critical of the big timber companies, but still sympathetic to loggers. Looking pleased, Bob Pyle, the Yale Ph.D., relates that shortly after the book came out "a guy came to the door." By his looks, Pyle figured this stranger could only be a logger, a disgruntled logger; but, as it turned out the man, after some hesitation, had come to ask about buying the book.

Local stores in nearby Skamokawa display signs reading: "This town is supported by timber dollars." Other signs say: "Our Nation is Very Advanced. We prefer owls over families." None of this troubles Pyle. "I tend to get along. I listen to them." Loggers here fear for their future. In spite of the owl talk, they know the old-growth forests are running out, that at present rates of cutting in eight to 10 years—or 20 at the very most—the last of these giants will be gone.

Weyerhaeuser and Crown Zellerbach are the major timberland owners in Pyle's Willapa Hills country. Their brand of intensive forestry ("This is forestry?" Bob Pyle asks out loud.) leaves rivers clogged with slash, soils ruinously compacted by heavy machinery, or destabilized and falling away into streams and over highways. Pyle is concerned that growing hundreds of side-by-side acres of Douglas firs or western hemlock (monoculture tree-farming) disrupts natural "invertebrate communities" as well as the micro-organisms and fungi that make up a healthy forest ecosystem. Aerial spraying, the established weeding practice, is an unpleasant fact of life on these industry tree farms.

Greed has driven big timber companies to maximize profits at the expense of the land. And what's Bob Pyle's answer? "Lower profits." Pyle spreads this message wherever he can. He also believes in building local conservation coalitions. He and others are lobbying hard to save Henderson Canyon, a state-owned patch of very old forest, the last of its kind in Willapa. To his delight, "old-growth spiders" reside in this complex forest environment. The timber companies oppose the idea of creating a special "heritage" reserve, but local support is solid.

Butterfly Bob, the populist, the scholar, and now the realist, thinks citizens have a good chance of saving this small "last, best" ancient cedar forest. He writes in *Wintergreen*, "I personally doubt that those trees will come down without a battle [although] I prefer to arrive at conservation goals through civil means."

CHAPTER THIRTEEN

Oregon,
Where Timber Once Was King

These are bitter times for timber in Oregon. Here more than in any other timber-producing state in the American West, timber has traditionally been king.

But in Oregon today every one of timber management's big and controversial issues—declining timber supplies, treasured but dwindling great old-growth forests, "the owl," mill jobs lost to high-tech efficiency, exports, damage to native fisheries—every one of these timber issues has reached critical proportions. And of course, in both Oregon and neighboring Washington, galloping urbanization and shoulder-to-shoulder crowds in popular National Forest recreation areas are also in growing conflict with timbering.

As in Washington, timberland ownership patterns also play a key role in timber politics in Oregon. Publicly-owned land accounts for about 60 percent of Oregon's 21.7 million acres of forest with commercial timber value. The U.S. Forest Service manages over 10 million acres of federal timberland in Oregon, while the U.S. Bureau of Land Management (BLM) oversees 2.6 million acres of federal timberland in the Pacific Northwest, most of it in western Oregon.

BLM forest management practices draw especially hostile fire these days from Oregon environmentalists who say that forest destruction on these public lands is particularly outrageous. In

1917 this prime timberland reverted to federal ownership after the Oregon and California Railroad and the Coos Bay Wagon Road companies violated the terms of their land grants. As a result, the familiar checkerboard land grant pattern of ownership, found from Montana westward, also distinguishes these federally-owned Douglas fir timberlands along the Coastal Range and the Cascades in western Oregon. Political scientist Paul J. Culhane adds: "Because the bulk of these revested lands were part of the Oregon and California grant, they are commonly called the O&C lands." By statute, BLM was charged with administering these lands for timber production, a mandate environmentalists say is still carried out with a singular disregard for the land itself.

What's left of the BLM's once great old-growth forests in Oregon has now been identified as critical habitat for the northern spotted owl and has been earmarked for preservation by the Jack Ward Thomas team, the committee of distinguished scientists appointed to study and recommend ways to save this threatened bird.

The U.S. Forest Service, nevertheless, is still the major manager of federal forestlands in Oregon.

Mark Hatfield, Oregon's venerable five-term U.S. Senator, looks after Big Timber in his state. Andy Kerr, conservation director of the Oregon Natural Resources Council (ONRC), calls Hatfield "the Godfather" of the Oregon timber industry. Kerr himself has been described by Time magazine as a "terrorist in a white collar," for "masterminding 220 separate [timber sale] appeals in a single month, creating a legal logjam." These kinds of "character assassinations," as author and scientist Chris Maser puts it, are standard ammunition in the battle for the last great forests in the American West.

Timber may technically no longer be king in Oregon, but the industry's political reign has not ended. Hatfield won re-election in 1990, despite a strong challenge from Democrat Harry Lonsdale. Incumbency and financial backing from the still-powerful timber industry helped boost Hatfield over the top. His timber-support record, going back more than 20 years, is indeed impressive. As a co-sponsor of the 1976 National Forest Management Act, he won language allowing the Forest Service to *exceed* sustainable timber sale levels, so that public timber could help fill the gap in the Northwest's supply of private timber.

Starting in 1986, Hatfield and Oregon Representative Les AuCoin teamed up successfully to win timber legislation that, among other things, pushed timber targets even higher in the Northwest, and created a "special timber target in the budget each year for Oregon and Washington National Forests." These and other facts are outlined in The Oregonian's exhaustive, three-part series on timber issues ("The Northwest Forests: Day of Reckoning") that appeared in mid-October, 1990, a few weeks before the November 6 national elections. People I talked to in Oregon that fall considered the Oregonian series the "most comprehensive" look at timber issues in recent years. Hatfield's press secretary, Bill Calder, apparently didn't share that view when I called the Senator's Washington, D.C., office several months later. In fact, Calder's hostility to my questions about timber policies in Oregon caught me quite by surprise.

Calder said the Senator had always sought "a balance" between the needs of the timber industry and concerns about the environment. Summing up the Senator's views about sustaining timber-dependent logging communities "that are in a dire fiscal crisis right now," Calder said Hatfield's bottom line is simply that: "He's concerned about the people." As reporters generally do, I followed up with another question, "More than the forests?" Calder shot back: "Clearly Grace, you've got your mind made up."

Welcome to Oregon timber politics, I thought.

Political analysts agree that national elections in the fall of 1990 were, at best, a draw for environmentalists even though, both in Oregon and elsewhere in the West some pro-environment candidates did well. One of those, Barbara Roberts, Oregon's newly elected governor, got off to a strong start when she increased funding for Oregon's Land and Conservation and

Development Commission, while sharply paring back most other items in the state budget. However, analysts say election results show that voters on the whole are cautious about backing sweeping new environmental controls. Kerr and his allies say that support for the timber industry in Oregon is more a matter of tradition than reasoned conviction. That support is economically outdated, they argue.

"It's as easy as Economics 101," Kerr told me by phone from Portland one January evening in 1991. "Oregon forests are the best fish-growing land. The same land grows fish and trees, but the fish are more valuable. Oregon's remaining trees are more valuable" supporting habitat for the state's six species of salmon than they are as timber producers.

Joining other longtime salmon fisheries activists, Kerr and the ONRC are now redirecting their efforts to save Oregon's ancient forests by focusing on protecting water quality and fish habitat— and the upstream spawning areas of Oregon's native or "wild" salmon. "Everything ends in the creek," Kerr says, over an occasional little crackle in the phone connection.

Oregon newspapers, the previous fall, foretold the dilemma Oregonians would face. Leading off its Oct. 11, 1990, issue, The Oregonian headlined the question: "Anglers, officials ask, 'Where are the salmon?'" And followed up with the subhead: "The state's fishery officials are baffled about the reason for the unexpected decline in the numbers of coho and chinook."

Dams almost everywhere in the Northwest have disrupted spawning patterns, and conservationists believe timbering is further degrading Oregon's salmon habitat. Conservationists in the Northwest have filed petitions with the U.S. Fish and Wildlife Service seeking threatened or endangered species designation for at least two species of native salmon in Oregon.

Unlike "the owl," which for all its notoriety is simply a non-edible forest barometer of sorts, salmon are the heart of a major commercial and sports fishing industry. Future forest battle lines in Oregon could well be drawn over timber jobs vs. salmon industry jobs. Conservationists in the Northwest say that although native salmon now make up only 10 percent or less of the total salmon and steelhead trout runs, their genetic strength is vital to bolster the quality of hatchery-bred species.

Oregon's 1971 Forest Practices Act, designed to protect the state's streams and fisheries from further habitat-destroying timbering, is often ineffective. Landslides plague Oregon's rivers where steep banks have often been shaved clean of trees and other vegetation by logging operations. Rains, the kind these West Coast rainforests are famous for, can turn bare logged-over river drainages into moving walls of mud.

But Senator Hatfield and other leaders in the state were still fighting hard at the beginning of the decade to save timber jobs in rural areas of Oregon. Congressional pressure in the 1980s stopped many a National Forest Supervisor from reducing the amount of timber sold from the forest each year. Forest Service timber managers speak in unhappy tones about "the political cut," meaning the volume of timber Congress sets as the annual timber sale "target" for all the National Forests.

Oregon's Willamette National Forest, the biggest timber-producing forest in the United States, provided the perfect stage for a small revolt within the Forest Service itself. In January, 1989, Jeff DeBonis, then a forest timber sale planner on the Blue River District of the Willamette, wrote a memo on his computer terminal which fed into the Forest Service's internal computer mail system.

"The timber industry's attempt to squeeze every last acre of ancient forest to support a declining industry," he wrote, "is doing so at the expense of the rest of Oregon's economy." Fireworks followed, but DeBonis stayed on for almost a year. During that time he founded the Association of Forest Service Employees for Environmental Ethics and started publication of *Inner Voice*, which draws letters (signed and unsigned) from a wide array of federal agency employees who share DeBonis's frustrations over current public-lands policies.

As the opening salvo in his revolt, DeBonis also published a lengthy letter sent to the U.S. Forest Service Chief on February 4, 1989, pleading for timber reforms. He cited congressional riders granting special favors to the timber industry and subverting court orders involving timber sale challenges, and other congressional moves allowing the Forest Service to "continue our accelerated timber liquidation program."

"Unfortunately," DeBonis told his chief, "we ally ourselves with timber industry and think that the 'environmentalists' are somehow obstructing us with their numerous appeals and lawsuits.... Instead of accepting the obvious merits of their case and rethinking our actions and attitudes, we find ways to circumvent the rulings and continue our business as usual activities." Six months later, DeBonis resigned from the U.S. Forest Service to devote his energies fulltime to the cause of timber management reform.

Meanwhile, some forest supervisors in the inland West were starting to send similar questioning messages to Chief Robertson. Notably absent from those speaking out were forest supervisors from Region 6 (Washington and Oregon) and Region 5 (California). In their 1989 communique to the Chief, National Forest supervisors in the other four of the West's six regions, asked for internal reforms in procedures, working conditions, and policies.

"Public values and personal values of Forest Service employees, including forest supervisors, are changing," they wrote, adding: "We need to be united in a set of common goals intended to regain our status as leaders in natural resource conservation." These supervisors said they were "unified in our support of the Forest Service mission, 'Caring for the Land and the People.'" USFS employees and the public, they went on to say, "strongly support our mission statement, but they do not believe we are doing it." While these statements were welcomed by reformers both inside and outside the Forest Service, they had no discernible effect on agency policy. But a number of Forest

Service people I talked to pointed out that federal bureaucracies have always resisted change. The Forest Service "is slow to respond to [demands for change] but it will respond," one sometime-dissident biologist told me.

But, conservationists worry, can federal forest timber policies possibly change in time to save what's left of the best of the nation's western forests? Timber plans in the Northwest are now calling for a 30 to 40 percent decline in timber harvests. But no one is certain whether these plans will survive the political process intact. And no one underestimates the power of the timber industry to influence Congress, the body that ultimately decides how much timber the federal forests should produce.

An effective timber lobby has successfully pushed National Forest timber targets up and up, despite clear evidence that forests have been ravaged by past orders from Washington, D.C., to cut no matter what the consequences. Now, conservationists are concerned that a growing environmental awareness among the public at large could backfire, bringing about "a legislated cut." They fear that powerful timber industry traditionalists like Oregon's Senator Hatfield and the timber lobby will ultimately pass federal legislation mandating the volume of timber to be cut annually on National Forests.

In political terms the crucial issue is less the fate of the forest than the fate of Oregon's traditional logging jobs and whole communities that have always depended on the forest.

Conservationists say the days of timber-dependent communities are numbered in any case because, at the present rate, the great old-growth trees which mills in these communities depend upon, will be gone in 10 to 20 years. Compromises of all sorts have been proposed, aimed at keeping the federally-dependent timber industry alive. Many conservationists—Andy Kerr is one—say it too late for that, the devastation is too complete. Oregon's new governor is now calling for job-training programs aimed at helping loggers move into other occupations.

Historically, the American timber industry has moved from

place to place, farther and farther west, leaving "slicked-off" forests behind, first in the East, next in the Midwest, and then in the South. No one can say with certainty that this survivalist "cut and run" mentality will fade with the turn of a new century. In fact, the evidence suggests otherwise.

By the summer of 1991, the native salmon issue was sharing center stage with the northern spotted owl in Oregon's high-stakes timber drama. Senator Hatfield and other politicos were hinting that it was high time to amend the federal Endangered Species Act, since any action to save the Northwest's wild salmon might adversely affect dozens of dams and a giant federal hydropower system that in turn affects electric bills as far away as Phoenix, Arizona.

The combined political fallout of dwindling timber jobs and rising electric bills poses a new and alarming threat to the National Forest reform movement. If the U.S. Congress is pushed into gutting the Endangered Species Act, forests everywhere in the American West will face fresh dangers from a newly empowered timber lobby.

CLOSEUP
The Deschutes National Forest

When a National Forest Supervisor moves out from behind his bureaucratic wall, it is a singularly refreshing encounter. So when I found one such official in the Southwest, I asked if he had a counterpart in the Northwest. "Go see Norm Arsenault. He's a neat guy," I was advised.

Arsenault was now supervisor of the Deschutes National Forest at Bend, Oregon, a location that fit nicely within my travel and research loop. Bend lives up to its reputation as an attractive small city high on the eastern slopes of the Cascades in Central Oregon. The lovely Sisters peaks, easily visible to the northwest, are the headwaters for the Metolius River. Bend's college town ambiance and the nearby Mt. Bachelor ski area, along with whitewater rafting, hunting, fishing and an easy, middle-America pace, mute the fact that Bend has for years been considered a logging community, a timber-dependent town. Ponderosa pine and mixed conifer forests (lodgepole and other pines mostly) stand close by. Mills and their huge piles of logs and lumber help visitors make the connection.

Once again, it turned out, I'd managed to show up on an off-day. Both the supervisor and most of the "timber shop" personnel at the Deschutes National Forest headquarters, on the outskirts of Bend, were absent—attending a national training session elsewhere. Besides that, Norm Arsenault had recently moved on (or perhaps up) to a new post in Washington, D.C. His replacement, former deputy Forest Supervisor Joe Cruz, who had just taken over the top management job on the Deschutes, had gone home ill. Reporters, however, seldom give up, so I quickly asked and settled for a public affairs officer.

Public relations skills have recently taken on a new importance in U.S. Forest Service activities. Public Affairs personnel are, for the most part, exceedingly friendly and helpful. Laurie Johnson at the Deschutes National Forest headquarters was particularly adept as she shepherded me through this agency labyrinth. In the reception area, display racks, here as in other Forest Service offices, bulge with literature, advising members of the public about the status of the local Forest Plan, meetings, comment periods, various hunting seasons, and offering an attractive assortment of free recreation guides, visitor information and literature on the National Forest.

Their combined message is a soothing one: all is well on your National Forest. The Deschutes brochure ("Immerse Yourself in the Forest") uses a three-part illustration to show off its new forest management plans: "Wildlife—New standards will increase wildlife and fish habitat; Old-Growth—One-fourth of the Forest will be managed to foster Big 'Ole' Trees and Old-Growth; and Timber—Timber Sales and logging will be reduced 25 percent." This "Ole" business was my first encounter with an official effort

by the agency to be folksy. Forestry professionals regularly write
about the public's inability to comprehend the complexities of
the forest management sciences, but I wasn't prepared for this.

To win public support for the Deschutes' new forest plan, its
brochure stresses recreation and downplays timbering. We learn
that this 1.6 million acres of National Forest is "not only a haven
for Central Oregonians, but it is also a destination playground for
millions of visitors each year." Contained within its boundaries are
five Wilderness areas, the Oregon Cascade Recreation Area and
six National Wild and Scenic Rivers, 500 miles of streams, and
more than 150 lakes.

Finally, Cliff Streeter, a 26-year Forest Service veteran and a
technician with Deschutes timber section, was assigned the chore
of answering my specific questions about timber management.
On his desk was a smallish, bright yellow sign, perhaps 6 by 8
inches; in black letters it said: "Boundary Clear Cut," then "Unit,"
followed by instructions that "this sign faces the clear cut unit."

This was just one of many timber sale identification signs the
Forest Services uses, and it's presence on his desk, Streeter
assured me, did not indicate that clearcutting was the dominant
timber practice on the Deschutes, Streeter explained. In fact, the
Deschutes's new forest plan calls for a return to more "uneven
age" timber management. Nature itself long ago perfected the art
of "uneven-age management," producing forests that contain
trees of all ages, from saplings to ancient monarchs. But
sometimes it sounds as if the Forest Service has reinvented nature.

Clearcutting, once regarded as butchery by any serious forester,
only began to take over as the harvest method of choice in the
1960s. In forestry's jargon-filled parlance, clearcutting is the first
"stage" of a "cycle" that leads to the wholesale replanting of
seedlings which are then "managed" (thinned, sprayed and
fertilized) as an "even-age" stand. Often these young trees are
also a "monoculture," or single-species crop of trees. This
practice has come to be known as tree farming, or "plantation"
forestry; apparently Deschutes timber managers were among the

first to understand that the public saw these tree plantations as
non-forests.

"This Forest is one of the pioneers in going back" to timber
cutting on a selective basis, Streeter told me, a little note of pride
in his otherwise matter-of-fact delivery. Streeter was a pleasant
man, most likely in his late-50s, who wore the tan twill field shirt
favored by the U.S. Forest Service. Dull, government-issue metal
desks, lined up in tight, straight rows, filled his office and several
others like it. Another form of monoculture.

Still, Streeter's candor came as a surprise. The timber industry
knows in its heart, he asserted, that the spotted owl (also a factor
in this National Forest) is not the real issue at the crux of the
timber supply question in the Northwest. "Loggers have to realize
that we were cutting more timber than we were growing," he
offered. During the 1980s, sawtimber volume totals in this state
rose a startling 66 percent. Wholesale value of timber products
shot up 91 percent during the same period.

The Deschutes' recently completed draft forest plan now calls
for a 30 percent reduction in timber harvest levels, a return to
more selective cutting to foster "uneven-age" pine forests, and a
new focus on "managing for old growth." Streeter also
mentioned that a regional group, *Save the Metolius Basin,* has been
highly active in Deschutes National Forest planning affairs. A
Bend conservation activist told me later that, according to a
statewide survey, the Metolius "is the most recognized river in
Oregon," for both fine fishing and rafting, and draws many out-of-
state visitors.

In what Deschutes officials say is a "response to widespread
public opinion," the new forest plan creates 10 unique
management areas in the Metolius Basin," totaling 86,000 acres.
While conservationists were somewhat put off by the plan's
"indulgent, preservationist tone," Bill Marlette, at Bend's *Natural
Resources Center,* said the plan still marks " a new direction" in
forest management in central Oregon.

Cliff Streeter, in the Deschutes National Forest office, credits former Deschutes timber planner Mike Znerold with successfully selling the idea that it was time for the Deschutes to reduce clearcutting its ponderosa pine and to return to a lighter-on-the-land, uneven-age timber management plan.

Znerold, however, had been transferred to the Forest Service's Region 2 office in Lakewood, Colorado, in the Denver metro area. Flipping through the growing piles of information I'd been gathering, Zernold's name and phone number magically rose from a document titled: "Old-Growth—Where Are We Headed in Region 2." The Forest Service, I had learned, churns out such documents—policy and position papers—as if the agency's very life depends on it. Perhaps this practice is the bureaucratic equivalent of academia's "publish or perish" rule for staying on top of the professorial heap.

Znerold, when I contacted him, was both helpful and prompt, sending along a thick packet of position papers and scientific analyses, including his lengthy April, 1990 presentation before a silviculture workshop in Thunder Bay, Ontario, sponsored by the Ontario Ministry of Natural Resources. This paper deals with ponderosa pine and the rise and fall of clearcutting on the Deschutes National Forest. In it Znerold traces the history of "timber management philosophies" since commercial timber sales began on this National Forest in the early 1920s. The paper reads like a scientific confessional—a heartfelt exposé of sincere forest science gone wrong.

Znerold traces the important part fire had played "in the development of these majestic stands on the Deschutes." When timber management practices decreed that fires (either "wild" or man-made) were bad and therefore should be suppressed, forest managers looked for other ways to accomplish the work of fires, which was to get rid of competing plants and trees and old or sickly pines that were favored targets of the dreaded western pine beetle. The method they choose was so-called "selective cutting," a management practice which admirably "met objectives important at the time." The period was the 1930s and 1940s.

Then the post-World War era saw a dramatic change in "the philosophy of forest management," on the Deschutes and throughout the National Forest system. Wood products, Znerold told his Canadian audience, were considered "essential to fuel a growing post-war economy." Pinpointing the switch to wholesale clearcutting that was to mark the character of the Northwest's great forests for the next half of the century, Znerold says:

"On the western slopes of Oregon and Washington stands of overmature Douglas-fir and western hemlock were harvested by clearcutting. State-of-the-art forestry on the western slopes emphasized the management of the stands of timber rather than individual trees. Foresters, supported by local forestry schools, expounded the virtues of even-aged management, and a heavy-handed agricultural approach to forestry."

Later, from his Lakewood, Colorado, office Znerold talked to me about his tenure in Oregon, which began in 1978 on the Willamette National Forest on the western side of the Cascades. Sweet Home, the logging community where Znerold lived, was to become, like Bull Run, Gettysburg, or Antietum, a grim and famous battleground for another kind of civil war—this one over timber and the last of the West's great old-growth forests.

"There was a time when I really thought what the National Forest should stand for was tree farms." Then, after a thoughtful pause, Znerold adds: "That sounds absurd to me today. I look back and realize how inappropriate that was even then." No bravado, no scientific hocus-pocus. Just painful reflections.

In the 1970s, the pine forests of Oregon's central plateau region—the Deschutes, the Fremont, the Ochoco—were ripe for application of the new tree-farming philosophy that had become dogma in leading forest management circles. Znerold says, "We thought we were on the cutting edge" of a great new era in forest management. Seeds were collected from great "super trees," pines that showed genetically "superior" traits. These seeds would be the foundation of new "seed orchards" where the techno-widzardry of forest scientists would lead the way toward the new super-pine plantation forests of the future.

The vision and the program "all crashed" in the mid-1980s. The public, the real owners of the National Forests, wouldn't buy the vision. When the Deschutes Draft Forest Plan came out in 1986, a blizzard of protest letters (1640 of them) told forest managers that clearcutting must go. Deschutes clearcuts looked like "festering sores on the back of a mangy old dog," one critic told shocked Deschutes forest managers. Describing this episode, Znerold speaks of a shift in "values." Recreation and tourism were prospering while timber was undergoing a cyclical downturn.

Clearly, Deschutes forest managers had been handed a new mandate, not from Congress but from their local constituency. "Public pressure was so great," Znerold explained, that even the local timber industry realized, unless changes were made, public opinion could shut down timber sales altogether on this National Forest. But this revelation, it turned out, was pretty well confined to the timber industry on the east side of the Cascades. On the other side of the mountains it was a different story.

By the 1990s, the towns of Sweet Home, Gold Beach, Coos Bay and Roseburg had become familiar names in the western timber war. These are Oregon's historic logging towns on the Pacific side of the Cascades. Each has been torn apart by the continuing battle over timber, and each community is further threatened by the prospect of setting aside thousands of acres of ancient forest (and merchantable timber) as habitat for the threatened, and now infamous, northern spotted owl. No clear resolution is in sight. So far, reform in the Deschutes National Forest has perhaps been the only important victory in the battle to save Oregon's threatened forests.

CHAPTER FOURTEEN

California,
Old Growth on the Cutting Edge

California looms so large in the American scheme of things that even other residents of the West view this huge, diverse Pacific Coast state as another world altogether. And perhaps it is.

To generations of youngsters growing up east of the Mississippi, one photograph in a grade school history book is forever associated with California. In it a tiny man, a 20th Century Lilliputian, stands at the base of a giant sequoia. I, for one, remember this man in dark, ill-shaped work pants and a nondescript shirt, with arms outstretched in an gallant but impossible effort to reach the edges of this monster tree. I quickly understood the picture's message—about how insignificant humans are when measured against this California forest wonder. Along with other young readers, I also believed that California's redwoods would stand forever—America's first and perhaps best "super-tree."

But in 1990, northern California faced "Redwood Summer," a season-long protest action staged by *Earth First!* to tell the nation that California's ancient and glorious redwoods were falling at an alarming and ecologically irresponsible rate. *EarthFirst!* protesters, radical, notorious, and infuriating, were often an embarrassment to other conservation groups that favored more orthodox means of dissent. But even loggers and timber industry pros could not resist hurling insults back when baited by the public antics of these environmental renegades.

Earth First! billed the protests as a non-violent summer of civil disobedience to save old-growth trees. But incidents on both sides of the confrontation pumped up fear, and headlines to match. Modeled after the struggle of freedom riders who converged on the South in the 1960s to fight for civil rights, Redwood Summer was designed to focus public attention on controversial timber practices not on National Forests but on privately-owned timberland. The demonstrations were, in fact, political actions carefully timed to win voter support for "Forest Forever," a sweeping ballot initiative coming up in California's November general election.

In northern California, Big Timber—Pacific Lumber Company, Louisiana-Pacific Corp. and Georgia-Pacific together—is collectively held responsible for runaway clearcutting of company-owned virgin redwood forests, for exporting precious Pacific Coast timber to Pacific Rim countries, and for setting up new mills in Mexico where labor costs are low.

Corporate raiders and leveraged buyouts financed by junk bonds have also had an explosive impact on California's timber industry—as they have in the Pacific Northwest where industry also owns large tracts of the best timberland. In northern California, the story of the Pacific Lumber Company takeover by Houston financier Charles Hurwitz's Maxxam Group is infamous and has been described as a "Texas chainsaw massacre." Logs on Pacific's 190,000-plus acres of timberland are falling at double the previous annual harvest of about 175 million board feet. This massive sell-off of virgin redwoods was triggered to help pay off Maxxam's $680 million debt. Drexel Burnham Lambert, the high-flying Wall Street firm that financed Maxxam Group's takeover of Pacific Lumber in 1985, was to go broke in disgrace five years later.

Pacific Lumber's vast timberlands make up about three-quarters of California's (and the world's) native coastal redwoods—outside those protected by Park designation. They own more redwood forests than all other private timberland owners combined. Pacific Lumber, once the pride of the conservation community, had for years carefully harvested its magnificent forest along "sustained yield" principles. But the new regime—accelerated cutting and clearcutting instead of Pacific's traditional "selective cutting"—imposed by Pacific's new owners, horrified longtime Pacific employees and a growing number of other Californians as well. Lawsuits and legislative proposals slowed the redwood "massacre" somewhat but the redwoods continued to fall.

So partisans of preserving redwoods turned to other tactics; 1990's Redwood Summer and the Forest Forever ballot initiative were among these. The Forest Forever initiative—among its other provisions—sought public funds to buy Pacific Lumber's "Headwater Forest," a magnificent 3,000 acres of company-owned old-growth redwood near Eureka. But California voters narrowly turned down Forest Forever by a margin of 53 to 47 percent. Two other "environmental" initiatives were also defeated. Even so, Forest Forever had sent cold chills down Big Timber's collective spine. The issue was nothing less than public control of private forest lands, the consummate fear of timber industry leaders. The Forest Forever initiative would have raised something over $700 million to buy old-growth forests, phased out clearcutting, boosted protection of streams and fisheries, and would have required timber companies to practice sustained yield harvesting—cutting no more each year than they grew during the same period.

Environmentalists say all three California environmental issues (including Big Green, a catch-all measure controlling pesticides and food products, and a forest-industry counter-initiative) failed because they ignored two fundamental rules for winning political battles: "Keep it simple" and "Keep your enemies divided." Big Green and Forests Forever did neither.

Industry, from agriculture to timber, united to raise millions to campaign against these environmental control measures. But a second round of environmental ballot initiatives designed to curb timber practices on private forests is almost sure to come—as early as California's 1992 election. Big Timber, as owners of millions of acres of prime timberland in northern California and the Northwest, is truly frightened by this prospect. I remember the way Ted Nelson, a Weyerhaeuser vice-president explained in grave, shocked tones that limiting the timber industry's power to make management decisions on its own land was undemocratic and anti-business. And Big Timber is very big business.

California's sheer size and the diversity of its generally robust economy tends to dwarf the fact that California is a major timber producer. By the end of the 1980s California's timber output had surpassed Washington's by more than 1 billion board feet annually. By then, in the American West, only Oregon (at 8.5 billion board feet) topped California's annual lumber production.

In 1989 California produced 5.3 billion board feet of lumber— 65 percent more than the state's 1981 production. Wholesale values jumped a brisk 71 percent during the same period. California's timber industry pegged the wholesale value of its lumber production at $1.75 billion in 1989—yet this timber industry accounts for only about seven percent of California's huge economic base.

But it's important to note here that none of these dazzling industry statistics translate into more jobs for California's timber and mill workers. In a pattern repeated throughout the American West, California timber industry jobs are being lost as old mills are converted to high-efficiency operations, with increasingly automated production.

According to industry figures, federal timberland supplies about 41 percent of California's timber harvest. This is a state where everything runs big. Forest Service officials like Jon Silvius of the Klamath National Forest in northern California take pains to point out that California contains 17 different National Forests, most of which produce marketable timber. Together, California's

National Forests represent about one-tenth of the entire National Forest System.

Four species groups dominate California's timber harvest: Douglas fir and larch (29 percent); ponderosa pine (19.1 percent); hem-fir, a category containing both hemlock and fir much used for home construction (21.9 percent); and redwood (20.5 percent).

Even before the Redwoood Summer of 1990, environmentalists of every persuasion were sounding the call to halt logging on the 13,200 acres within California's Sequoia National Forest where ancient sequoia groves were being invaded at alarming rates. State and National Parks (Yosemite, Sequoia and General Grant/ Kings Canyon) preserve most of the rest of California's ancient sequoias, many over 2500 years old.

Experts are quick to point out that the giant sequoia (Sequoiadendron giganteum) is often confused with its cousin, the coast redwood (Sequoia sempervirens). "Both species are true redwoods, renowned for their gargantuan size," but the coast redwood is the world's *tallest* tree, while the inland giant sequoias "are in fact the biggest trees on Earth."

Who could have imagined that the U.S. Forest Service, in the mid-1980s, would put up for sale, the groves where these giants live? Forest Service officials, in fact, insist the old sequoias themselves weren't being logged, only the pines and other growth surrounding them. Nevertheless, environmentalists saw these timber sales as a disaster with overtones of sacrilege.

California conservationists had long thought the Sequoia National Forest was operating under a self-imposed ban on timber sales within the forest's giant sequoia groves. But in 1982, the agency put up 13 major timber sales in 11 of the forest's sequoia groves. Logging was already underway when local watchdogs (*Save The Redwoods League, Kern Valley Wildlife Association,* plus the *Audubon Society* and the *Sierra Club,* among others) discovered the groves were being trashed.

Commercial logging was wiping out the pines, firs, young sequoias and the lush undergrowth that made these groves a truly splendid forest. No longer part of a sequoia ecosystem with a complex and diverse biology, the giant sequoias, some there since written history began, now stood naked in their own forests. Lawsuits flew. Defending their actions, U.S. Forest Service managers said competition from the pines, firs and cedars, threatened young sequoias and posed a dangerous buildup of "fuel load." Logging the groves, they claimed, was therefore a benefit. Like so many Forest Service claims, few Californians were buying this one. In another celebrated case, the infamous 1986 "Longsaddle" timber sale had created a 30-acre moonscape of barren land, punctuated by giant sequoia stumps and a few solitary, perhaps 2,000-year old sequoia trees, left standing in a bizarre visual parody of land stewardship.

Independent forest economist Randal O'Toole has demonstrated that such sequoia timber sales are Forest Service money-losers. He writes:

"To add economic insult to ecological injury, all of the sequoia grove timber sales to date have drained far more from the U.S. Treasury than they have returned; many have cost even more than Longsaddle. The Peyrone sequoia grove timber sale in California, which decimated one of the largest sequoia groves in the forest, will probably lose the Treasury almost $500,000."

Experts also disagree with Forest Service claims that sequoia groves should be protected from fire. Sequoias survive for centuries (many are 2,000 years old) because their thick bark is virtually fireproof. Fire causes sequoia cones to release their seeds, so sequoias actually flourish after fires sweep through their groves. Longtime forester and author Gordon Robinson writes: "The lowest fire hazard of all the cover types found in our forests occurs in mature, old-growth timber."

Safe from fire perhaps, but not from man. According to the *National Audubon Society*, only about 10 percent of California's 41,000 acres of best old-growth forests are protected by wilderness designation. Under present timber management practices, conservationists predict logging will ruin the rest by the year 2000.

In July, 1990, a coalition of environmentalists enthusiastically proclaimed victory in the battle to protect the groves in the Sequoia National Forest. Others called the settlement, reached after 18 months of often agonizing negotiations, "a sellout."

The agreement involves the Forest's formal land and resource management plan. Louis Lumberg of *The Wilderness Society* believes that although the settlement was a compromise, "most of the environmental community is confident that the new agreement will provide a working model for wise forest management practices over the next 10 years." The *Sierra Club Legal Defense Fund*, which represented seven environmental groups, described the outcome as "an unprecedented settlement agreement governing management of the 1.1-million-acre Sequoia National Forest [and] the first in California for a major timber-producing forest."

Objections and appeals had poured in soon after the Sequoia plan was officially unveiled in 1988. Appellants—the *Sierra Club, The Wilderness Society, Natural Resources Defense Fund, California Trout,* and several other outdoor sports organizations, along with timber industry and grazing representatives—ultimately became parties to the settlement negotiations. The final decision raised new questions about how often a National Forest can be compromised.

Sequoia National Forest timber-program planner Julie Allen agrees that certain parts of the original draft management plan did require more definition but she disagrees with environmentalists (represented by *Sierra Club Legal Defense Fund* attorney Julie McDonald) who claimed that the 1988 plan "was an environmental disaster."

Only in California, perhaps, could battles such as this be led by two powerful "Julies." Planner Julie Allen, a no-nonsense government administrator, graciously describes opponent Julie

McDonald as "a tremendously able lawyer, and a wonderful person."

Key points of the final settlement include: a 26 percent reduction in annual timber harvest levels, a 31 percent reduction in the number of acres that can be logged, and a ban on all logging within giant sequoia groves. The Sierra Club Legal Defense Fund issued a glowing press release, saying the agreement provides "unprecedented protection for streams and meadows," dramatically reduces clearcutting, and represents a complete reversal of the Forest Service's position on logging in giant sequoia groves. Dissident Sierra Club members, however, say there is no room for compromise on this battle-scarred forest.

Forest planner Allen says that while the giant sequoias made this forest plan settlement unique, the other factors (harvest levels, roadless areas and clearcutting, for example) are typical forest and timber management issues faced by most National Forests in the American West. She also points out the settlement binds participants to silence on questions about how the compromise was hammered out.

Julie Allen's days are heavily scheduled. She'd penciled in about 10 minutes for our initial phone conversation, but four people were waiting for her to begin a meeting. Could she call me back? When she did, the next day, it was on her lunch hour. Was this the way California bureaucracies functioned? It certainly wasn't typical of many other government offices I'd dealt with over the years as a reporter. Julie Allen sounds indignant when I mention that a lot of government offices seem to close down after 3 p.m. on Friday afternoons.

Julie is a person of convictions. She tells me immediately where she stands in the national debate over timber policies on National Forests. "My position is: if you live in a wood house and you use toilet paper and you like good printout coming out of your computer, you have to be responsible about being a consumer." Currently, in the United States the demand for timber, for everything from toilet paper to custom kitchen cabinets, Allen tells me, requires 50 billion board feet each year.

About 20 to 25 percent of that total comes from the National Forest. "That's part of the reason I become absolutely infuriated," over efforts by some organizations to "stop all management on public lands." Her voice is intense, full of conviction. She's quite certain these people also use toilet paper, and therefore have taken an "irresponsible" view of commercial timber production on public lands.

Julie Allen, it becomes apparent, is no "woman of the soil." She holds a BA in Political Science, a Master's Degree in City and Regional Planning, and has 20 years of planning experience, 15 of them with the U.S. Forest Service. She is not only a seasoned administrator, but a woman holding her own in what was, until a few years ago, a very male world. Good-naturedly, she admits that, as a woman "life is not always easy when you're in the first phalanx."

Planner Allen talks enthusiastically about hot new satellite techniques being used to improve timber inventory methods— a recently recognized problem on many National Forests in the West. Timber managers here, she tells me, have discovered "a whole set of discrepancies" in the Sequoia's 1989-1990 timber count.

She sounds equally enthusiastic about plans to draw up new and accurate maps of the forest's giant sequoia groves—a major point of the settlement agreement and one she clearly supports. Their boundaries, Allen observes, "were poorly defined." The forest plan appeals and mediation sessions that followed, she admits, produced "better" language on the management of these groves than wording in the original forest management document.

Outsiders, Allen advises me, should understand that these sequoia groves are "very mixed." Within these areas are utility lines and a whole network of roads leading to such things as forest campgrounds and even a Girl Scout Camp. This 1.1-million-acre National Forest sits at the very southern end of the Sierra Nevada Range, east of Bakersfield and Fresno and within easy driving distance of Los Angeles. So the Sequoia is "heavily used for recreation" by nearby Angelenos; but in the Los Angeles tradition, 94 percent of that is "drive-through" activities. Only six percent of Sequoia National Forest visitors seek out its 264,000 acres of wilderness.

Julie Allen's sense of fair play has been sorely strained by environmentalists who fought to stop logging within the sequoia groves. One photograph, showing a single majestic giant sequoia standing alone in the center a barren forest patch—the sort of destruction that foresters sometimes refer to as a landscape that's been "nuked"—was used with devastating effectiveness against Sequoia National Forest's managers. This photo, she suggests, distorted reality. A fire crew had accidentally cut down a sequoia or two; but "specimen trees" were never logged. Yet local folks saw this photo as evidence of on-going logging in the sequoia groves and, Allen complains, "thought we'd betrayed their trust." As an administrator who values precision and integrity, Julie was hurt. Clearly, this wound has not yet healed.

Like so many other forest managers, Julie Allen thinks that owls are something of a non-issue. (Of course, she's speaking about the notorious northern spotted owl, the gentle forest bird whose old-growth habitat is under threat.) She calls such an ecosystem-indicator species "a stalking horse," often used by extremists "who want no management at all" on public forest lands. Present National Forest policy makes sense, she argues, particularly if you consider your role as a responsible consumer. "We're talking about managing some parts [of the National Forest] for commercial use and some parts not for commercial use." To people who oppose what she clearly sees as balanced public resource management, she routinely returns to another favorite image and asks, "Do you use toilet paper? And where *do* you think wood products come from?"

Citizen activist and sequoia champion Charlene Little is on intimate terms with these giant trees. She does not see *any* of them in terms of toilet paper. She calls the negotiated Sequoia National Forest settlement "a sell-out."

It is important, she tells me, for people to understand that, unlike California's northern coastal forests, the Sequoia National Forest is very arid. And, although a temporary moratorium has for the moment banned logging in the sequoia groves themselves, the rest of the National Forest's "beautiful mixed conifer forests" are being cut down at a rate Little describes as "criminal."

Reforestation is poor. In places, sagebrush is replacing the forest. This forest has been so abused, so over-logged, Little explains, that there was simply no room for compromise on how much more timber to sell. Her voice is gentle, but very firm as she says: "This forest needs at least a 100 years' rest, to let it grow back." Growing conditions are so marginal here it takes 140 years to grow a tree eighteen inches in diameter—twice the time in which some forests can produce a new crop of marketable timber.

Kernville is the community nearest to this Sequoia National Forest. And the U.S. Forest Service, Charlene Little tells me, is one of the largest employers in Kernville. A quiet, rural community of about 1500 people, with no stop lights, Kernville sits in the picturesque Kern River valley, buffered by the Sierra foothills, its skyline etched by rising mountains. The Kern River running through the valley has helped turn the town into a resort and retirement enclave. Like local Sierra Clubbers, the community at large is divided over logging practices on the nearby federal forest.

Kern Valley has only one sawmill, a family-owned enterprise, but it provides about 240 jobs. Little points out that this mill depends on the National Forest to supply the flow of sawtimber it needs to keep operating. And the mill has recently been retooled, so it can run even more timber. Little is convinced that the Sequoia National Forest (which can't retool) is being systematically destroyed in order to preserve both mill jobs and the jobs of forest managers determined "to get out the cut."

Unlike some reformers, Charlene Little has a plan. "I feel the

mill workers should be given top priority" for retraining under a
federally-created job-training program. Instead of paying out
some $3 million a year that, on average, the Sequoia National
Forest currently losses on its timber sales, Congress should
allocate that amount to fund such a retraining program. She
hopes federal legislation may eventually set this forest aside as a
natural preserve.

Charlene's dedication to this forest cause is so complete that
her friend and supporter, Roberta Piazza, calls her "St. Charlene,
a true voice crying in the wilderness." This crusader, Roberta
adds, has had to overcome painful shyness to speak publicly
everywhere federal forest issues are debated.

Piazza, a former television news reporter, returned to Kernville
a few years ago to take over operation of the Pine Cone Motel, a
family business. Until recently, she says, the Sequoia was a
"forgotten forest"—ignored by California's environmental
community and largely managed to accommodate the
requirements of several longtime family ranching operations that
each held historic National Forest grazing privileges. (No less
than timbering, grazing in the American West has always enjoyed
a special relationship with the U.S. Forest Service.)

Roberta Piazza recounts how Charlene Little "almost single-
handedly campaigned for Forest Service accountability,"
successfully drawing widespread public attention in the 1980s to
this neglected National Forest and its destructive management
practice—priming the pump for reform.

Former Forest Service timber planner Tricia Hobson looks on her
move back to Florida, where she grew up, as something of a
retreat. She misses the mountains and the West, where she
worked for 10 years as a Forest Service timber planner—the work
she was doing on the Sequoia National Forest when she resigned
in disgust and dismay. She had trained for a career in the Forest
Service. "I'd planned to stay forever. I thought the mission was
right." But things weren't "right" on this National Forest and

when she voiced her concerns about bad timber sales and the doctoring of legal timber-sale documents, she found herself dead-ended and passed over.

Tricia Hobson spent seven years as a timber-sale planner on the Sequoia. As timber supplies dwindled, sale planners began warning their superiors about timber sales that encroached into habitat reserved for the rare and threatened California condor, the giant sequoia groves, or northern spotted owl areas. Timber-sale planners were also required to consider other timber base restrictions, like stream impacts and unstable soil conditions.

"No one was listening," she says. The sadness and the frustration are still fresh. I hear it in her voice which seems still to carry the unspoken question: What else could I have done? Ultimately, Hobson says, Forest timber managers "told us to get out the cut. And if you can't do it, we'll get someone who can."

One incident lingers in her mind like a bad dream: "I had put a red flag on the timber sale EA (Environmental Assessment), saying we had some erosion problems there. The EA was already signed off; this was a legal NEPA [National Environmental Protection Act] document. Someone [who had accessed the computer file] called me up and said the Forest Supervisor had requested we change some of the contents of the EA. From what I gathered they were going to print a new page and slip it in there."

This amounted to possible illegal tampering with an official federal document. Other questionable practices followed. After Charlene Little and other forest activists began to ignite public concern over timber practices on the Sequoia, Tricia Hobson tells me, "the staff was told not to put anything in writing...and to purge the files of anything negative."

Other Forest Service employees, who worked with Hobson at the Sequoia, tell similar stories about conflicts over timber issues, pressure to meet impossible timber targets, and "managers who have to be right." One of Hobson's former co-workers, who is still with the Forest Service in another location and asked not to be named, told me, "The Sequoia was a nightmare."

Hobson wrote a three-page letter of resignation, but no one in the Forest Service ever mentioned the letter or asked her why she'd quit. Soon after she'd left the Forest Service in 1989, Tricia heard about another young timber-sale planner, Jeff DeBonis, who was calling for other Forest Service employees to join him in a push for internal reform.

As we talked in March, 1991, she wondered out loud if she should have stayed on, if she could have worked for reform from within, if she could have stayed with a career she once thought would last a lifetime.

In California and elsewhere in the West, ballot initiatives aren't the only legal action threatening the timber industry's grip on the last great, old-growth forests. The proposed Ancient Forest Protection Act of 1990 is one of several such legislative plans that would ban logging on what's left of old growth forests on National Forests and U.S. Bureau of Land Management land in Washington, Oregon and California. Should Congress pass such a bill, it would likely establish a National Ancient Forest Reserve System to protect essentially all the remaining ancient forests on federals lands in the Pacific Northwest. It would also create a network of "associated forests" to connect these fragmented forests. Tim McKay, with the Northcoast Environmental Center in Arcata, California, is optimistic that Congress will enact such legislation sometime during this decade, perhaps by 1995.

Timber industry leaders say preservationists have already locked up millions of acres of forest within National Parks and wilderness areas. The words "preserve" and "lock-up" powerfully symbolize the gulf in values between those who believe "the best forest is a managed forest" and the other side, environmentalists, who see what's left of ancient forests as ecological treasures. Treasures or not, ancient forests are indisputably rare. It's been estimated that less than two percent of the nation's entire forested area contains stands of trees 150 years old or more.

In the Northwest, an Ancient Forests reserve would likely include and expand the area under consideration for protection as northern spotted owl habitat. Experts have yet to agree on just how much forest the far-ranging spotted owls require, but protecting the owl's ancient forests could put another 3 million acres of timber off-limits to logging.

To counter such a possibility, three members of Oregon's Congressional delegation—Senator Mark Hatfield, and Representatives Les AuCoin and Bob Smith—backed a measure that would limit any decline in annual timber cuts in the Northwest to 2.4 percent per year.

And so it goes. Tit for tat. But such legal and legislative maneuvers demonstrate with great clarity that the real battle over the remnants of ancient federal forests in the American West will ultimately be fought in the U.S. Congress.

CLOSEUP
Timber dependent communities, the real cost

In California, the Forest Service manages 8.7 million acres of federally-owned timberland, roughly half of the commercial timberland in this West Coast state. Some 4.6 million acres are owned by private, non-industrial interests, while the timber industry itself holds about 2.7 million acres. The state of California owns 516,000 acres.

California's most productive timberland lies in the northern part of the state. Its timber towns, Scotia, Ft. Bragg, Eureka and Acadia, the centers for Redwood Summer demonstrations, are far removed from the urban California of movies and TV. LA and southern California are a world away but even in San Francisco, voters are largely out-of-touch with rural life-styles that have made logging a family tradition in the forested regions of northern California. For 90 years, the U.S. Forest Service first fostered, then subsidized that life-style by "inviting mills to set up shop near the National Forests." Family-owned mill operations still exist, but

high-profit Big Timber corporations now dominate the game in
northern California.

The Forest Service, nevertheless, still sticks doggedly to the idea
that its mission includes supporting the economic well-being of
timber-dependent rural communities in the West. Many
independent critics, of course, argue that the Forest Service itself
is timber-dependent, because timber activities—the biggest single
item in its budget—not only fatten the agency's budget but build
careers.

A 1990 study by the Department of Forestry and Resource
Management at the University of California at Berkeley tackles the
timber-dependency issue head on. Prompted by California's
three 1990 ballot propositions, the university's Forest Initiatives
Study Group sponsored this two-part study—*The Human Costs of
the California Forestry Crises.*

In the study, university researcher Jonathan Kusel points out
that both the timber industry and the U.S. Forest Service have
victimized California's timber-dependent communities by
oversimplifying the issues at stake in the fight over timber
resources. "The well-being of human communities in forest
regions has been too narrowly construed," he says. "The timber
industry has cultivated" the idea that a better supplied timber
industry will result in "local community well-being." And so has
the Forest Service. He writes:

"The U.S. Forest Service has helped perpetuate this belief as
well, by guaranteeing an ostensibly stable supply of raw material
for industry while paying lip service to community concerns....
The provision of wood to the timber industry has not directly
led to long-term forest community stability or well-being."

In truth, California's most timber-dependent counties show a
steady decline in the number of timber jobs. In 1948 the state
boasted almost 1000 mills. By 1956, a big timber-harvest year, the
number of mills had declined to 675. In 1990, California's mills
were down to 127 and more shutdowns were expected.

The timber industry is highly competitive. Bigger, more

efficient, and more centrally located mills are replacing small and outdated mills in many traditional logging communities. "Industry concerns about jobs may be real, but it does not include a commitment to local jobs and local community well-being," Kusel states.

Meanwhile, preliminary 1990 census figures show that six of California's eight fastest-growing counties are in the state's central Sierra foothills. These counties also show a near 50 percent rise in population, about twice the rate of growth in the rest of the state during the 1980s. These California forest communities are growing at a remarkable rate for several reasons. Retirees, forest recreation, and "the quality of life attributes the forest offers" are major factors. They also "underscore the changing nature of forest communities [and show that their] well-being cannot be tied to any one specific economic activity."

Real-estate development is also eating up private forest land in California as well, even as harvest levels on the remaining industrial forest lands exceed timber growth by 22 percent. The Forest Service, Kusel warns, "will be asked to take up the slack."

As in Oregon and Washington, school districts in some California forest counties depend on timber fees and related taxes for up to 40 percent of their education costs. "It is troubling that the fiscal health of many school systems in forest counties be tied to the number of trees harvested in national forests," Kusel observes.

The Human Costs of the California Forestry Crisis is the result of a 15-month investigation. In the study, university researchers conclude that Redwood Summer protests and industry counter-measures during the summer of 1990 caused further painful polarization in forest communities. "Frenzied media coverage" dramatically increased local conflicts, focusing on "redneck loggers and hippie environmentalists." But researchers found these stereotypes to be highly misleading and inaccurate. Instead, their studies show that five distinct groups were involved in the Redwood Summer events, and these often overlapped. Local

residents split into three groups: those who were timber industry
workers, a second group who were "environmentally concerned,"
and a third group who "are concerned about the local area,
including forests, but would never consider themselves to be
environmentalists." Groups four and five were "outside
environmental activists" and "multinational timber corporations."

Many forest community residents recognized that locals were
being exploited by both sets of Redwood Summer outsiders "who
would depart the battlefield with their money and their troops
with little concern for local suffering."

The summer-long confrontation, the threat of physical violence,
and insults over "the folklore of stewardship"—or who truly cares
for and sustains the forest—blinded local residents to the
common ground and attitudes they all shared. Researchers found
that California's forest community residents from both sides of
the timber debate believe strongly in "the importance of local
decision-making over local issues," and that "almost all local
people on both sides of the struggle wanted the forest to remain
as forest, not to be turned into condos or toxic waste dumps."

It's important here to note that a startling similarity exists
between the views of these Californians and those of loggers and
mills workers in Montana who overcame their distrust and got
together with local environmentalists to forge the precedent-
setting Lolo-Kootenai Accords. (See chapter 7.) The Montanans
also concluded that they were being "used," particularly by self-
serving politicians who enhanced their own positions by keeping
wilderness and roadless area issues unresolved.

California researchers further said timber industry workers
there "see both the Forest Service and large corporations
following practices that are bad for the land and bad for them."

These California forest communities, the University study
points out, are also "frequently troubled communities," with
growing numbers of rural poor and homeless. Drugs, alcoholism
and spouse abuse rates rival urban numbers. University
researches conclude: "This is a time when rural residents need to

be working together to save the places where they live and the
forests that they all love rather than dissipating their energy on
conflicts." ·

The study suggests that things won't be much better for
California's "timber-dependent" communities any time soon.
Even a newly diversified forest industry with local plants that
manufacture "value-added" wood products (doors, windows,
molding) seems chancy without an "assured" supply of wood. Yet
news stories about California's "Redwood Empire" and the
summer of protest pointed out that, according to state figures, in
1989 lumber companies in Mendocino County logged at a rate
that was *320 times greater* than replanted trees were growing. This
logging frenzy raises troubling questions about future wood
supplies.

The University of California study, outlines with startling clarity
one theme I heard over and over again across the American West.
Logging communities in California, like those in other states, feel
trapped between Big Timber's corporate clout and U.S. Forest
Service policies which kowtow to industry.

The timber-cutting orgy that hit National Forests in the '80s can
be accurately assigned to the Reagan Administration's anti-natural
resource conservation stance. Only scraps—often isolated
patches of the America West's ancient forests—have survived.
California's remaining giant redwoods and Douglas firs now face
a renewed threat. Some timber analysts say the "gap" or shortage
in the supply of sawtimber from industry forests could be even
worse in northern California than anywhere else in the West.
Runaway logging on industry-owned timberland in California has
been so severe—and reforestation so unreliable—that private
timber supplies may take 40 to 60 years to recover.

With Big Timber hungrily eying public forests and California's
timber-dependent communities growing ever more desperate,
forest time is simply running out in the Golden State.

Part V
Looking Ahead

CHAPTER FIFTEEN

Do Public Forests Have a Future?

Historical evidence suggests that Gifford Pinchot and other founding fathers of the National Forest System (sadly, there were no founding mothers) never imagined the voracious appetite for federal trees the timber industry would develop in the 1980s.

These founders never envisioned federal forests 100 years later straining to support a high-tech industry that *demands* 11 billion board feet each year from the nation's public forests. It probably didn't occur to early leaders of the fledgling U.S. Forest Service that one day the timber-dependent communities the service was spawning in the West would become political and economic millstones.

Forest Service founders certainly did not foresee a relentlessly *commodity-oriented* U.S. Forest Service, pushing hard to create a "super-tree" and to turn National Forests in the American West into plantations, full of green clones that exist solely to supply wood fiber—for everything from toilet paper to pressed waferboard.

In 1991, the sheer size of the timber industry in the American West, the aggressive, corporate character of Big Timber and its political power, and Big Timber's growing international trade ambitions, have overwhelmed both the Forest Service and the once glorious federal forests it manages.

Today inner turmoil plagues the U.S. Forest Service. The

agency's professional credibility has been seriously damaged by its obsessive "get out the cut" mentality, its failure to recognize the importance of treating federal forests as holistic systems, and its failure to see the importance of old-growth forests. By 1990, caught in a political crunch by the demands of Congress and the timber industry, this once prestigious federal agency had fallen on hard times.

Pinchot and other federal forest visionaries talked about forest management practices designed to "sustain an even flow of timber." By the year 2000 the flow from western forests may well be reduced to a trickle. The accelerated rate at which federal trees have fallen in the last decade is unprecedented in this century. Federal replanting efforts, in some cases, have been spectacular failures. At present harvest rates, the best of the West's once great old forests will be gone soon, in perhaps 10 to 20 years.

This book has charted these events.

Before the Soviet Union began to crumble in 1989, analysts delighted in saying that the U.S. Forest Service was much like the USSR. With its central management, quasi-military structure and a disciplined, macho brotherhood that stifled independent or creative thinking, the comparison was apt. Women are now taking their place beside men in the Forest Service but, gender aside, conformity is still largely the rule for career success in this bureaucracy.

Who could have imagined that by the late 1980s the Forest Service would be the *world*'s biggest road-builder, or that federal forest managers would be pressured into producing inflated timber inventories, or into "cooking the books" to come up with politically desirable standing timber counts? Or that it had become acceptable to lose millions of dollars on federal timber sales, ostensibly in order to support timber jobs in the rural West, but more accurately to support the timber industry? Or that the U.S. Forest Service would become so expert in creative bookkeeping that it could figure out how to make money-losing timber sales look like money-makers? Even though Americans everywhere realize that the first concern of a government bureaucracy is to sustain itself, many of us simply took it for granted that the Forest Service, refreshed daily by the pure air of its pristine forests, would not stoop to such practices. We were wrong.

I believe critics are right who call for changes in the agency's budget and accounting practices as one of the vital first steps toward reforming the Forest Service and ending timber's tyranny. Conservation activists across the West ultimately discover for themselves that patently illogical Forest Service programs are often motivated by the agency's twisted budget requirements; the current system insures that timber-related activities are generously funded while other activities are neglected.

Jud Wiebe, a friend of mine and a truly committed USFS staffer, plotted like some new-age Shylock, furtively working budget numbers hoping that an unused surplus, most likely earmarked for some timber program activity, could be put to work rebuilding crumbling hiking trails in his district in the San Juan Mountains of southwestern Colorado. Today, the Jud Wiebe Trail high above Telluride—named for Wiebe after his untimely death in 1987—seems to memorialize both Jud's efforts and his Forest Service frustrations.

Younger Forest Service careerists—foresters, wildlife biologists, soil scientists and the rest—all face similar binds. In telephone interviews, they told me in whispered tones how they hope desperately to stay on, doing the work they love while pressing for agency reform from within.

Clearly, they lead a precarious existence. Like clandestine foreign agents, they must play one part, plot another. One such Forest Service regular joked about warnings such as, "How'd ya like the Tongass?"—a reference to agency exile in Alaska's vast and forbidding Tongass National Forest. Service employees who play the game right win transfers to desirable places and better jobs. Wave-makers go nowhere.

A new Forest Service program, appropriately called "New Perspectives," seeks to promote a new way of thinking within the Forest Service itself. The program bears an eerie likeness to the USSR's "Peristroika." Mike Znerold, a new-age agency careerist himself, who coordinates the New Perspectives initiative in the Rocky Mountain Region of the National Forest System, believes New Perspectives could bring about fundamental change.

The program provides incentives and actual cash rewards to Forest Service employees who develop creative, new, on-the-ground strategies for carrying out New Perspective's four principles. In super-bold print, a page from a New Perspectives training manual advises agency workers that this new code for forestry management is based upon: (1) sustainability of resources and ecosystems, (2) participation with the people who are affected, (3) integration of a wider variety of information, and (4) collaboration among all disciplines of the agency.

New Perspectives is highly theoretical. When I ask for specific examples, Znerold says it would be better to talk to someone on the Black Hills National Forest who can describe some efforts on the ground there to implement a New Perspectives "partnership," the collaborative effort that embodies the fourth principle. (Forest Service people are exceptionally adept at redirecting questions to another person, another discipline, or another department. For example, timber specialists duck wildlife questions, and someone in a local office will strongly advise calling Portland or Washington, D.C., "for that information.")

Znerold, optimistically, tells me that New Perspective is a bold way to bring about change. "We're giving them [Forest Service employees] permission to take risks," he assures me. Still, during nearly two years of research for this book, I found almost no newly bold Forest Service risk-takers.

One veteran wildlife biologist begged me to write cautiously so as not to draw attention to his past differences with the Forest Service. The public furor over the northern spotted owl and other threatened forest creatures in the late 1980s had, at last, generated more funding for critically needed wildlife research on National Forests in the West. A dedicated and highly respected researcher, this scientist didn't want to make trouble; he just wanted to get on with the work he passionately cared about.

By the '90s, forestry research in general was coming under fire. University Forestry Schools, for the most part, had long since embraced the idea of National Forests as producers of *commodities*, timber and grazing. University research, funded predominately by the timber industry, predictably focused on timber production. When "ecology" emerged in the 1970s as a legitimate subject for university study, some forestry educators sensed trouble. Forestry, they said, was a science, while "ecology" was a philosophy. The American public knew better.

Twenty years of "Earth Day" celebrations, from 1970 to 1990, have dramatized the country's growing recognition of the earth's limitations as well as its bounties. Bumper stickers now warn: "You Can't Make a Living on a Dead Planet." But the timber industry, backed by university forestry departments, has continued to reassure Americans that science holds the secrets to growing and maintaining great forests. Forestry science, or silviculture, could "mimic nature" in the most exquisite and profound ways. The age of designer forests was at hand.

Official forestry zeal was, and often still is, so strong it reminds me of a remark made about a grandiose new public park, a super forest of exotic greenery. Describing its wonders, the promoters crowed: "This is what God would have built—if He'd had the funding."

Timber managers in the American West have repeatedly told us that "managed forests" could produce ever-increasing volumes of timber, while at the same time forest health would be carefully guarded by forest scientists and computer-equipped public land managers. U.S. Forest Service leaders joined in this chorus of reassurance. Mother Nature became a bad word. The task of university forest research was to make all these rosy predictions come true. And they certainly tried.

The U.S. Forest Service itself has always taken enormous pride in its own research "stations." Yet, Forest Service research apparently hasn't always worked closely with its much bigger sister, the Forest Service itself. One forester told me: "That has been a long standing concern within the National Forest System. The folks in the research are there to serve their own agenda. The problems they were working on weren't the ones we [those out in the woods] needed to solve." Money for research has always been short. U.S. Forest Research Stations, one forest planner said, were busy doing "basic research. What we needed was applied research."

In spite of these problems, by the 1980s forest scientists like Jerry Franklin and Chris Maser in Washington and Oregon (both worked on federal research at various times) were drawing attention to important new evidence about forest "ecosystems" and were advocating a new approach—managing forests as a whole system of interrelated organisms.

A firestorm of controversy erupted in forestry's scientific community. Traditional timber managers fumed. Forest economists sharpened their electronic pencils and started looking for a way around the Franklins and the Masers. By 1990, the Forest Service was scrambling to reclaim its role as the nation's leading public land steward. A flurry of new programs emerged. Besides "New Perspectives" there was "Change on the Range," dealing with grazing reforms, and TSPERS, for "Timber Sale Program Information Reporting System."

TSPERS, introduced in 1989, is the new accounting system the Forest Service (along with the General Accounting Office) developed in answer to mounting public dismay over below-cost timber sales on National Forests. Critics say TSPERS is heavily and unfairly weighted in favor of timber, and yet its results *still* show that most timber sales lose money. The issue of below-cost timber sales on public lands has become a battle of bookkeeping systems. Forest economist Randal O'Toole maintains that tinkering with accounting systems doesn't get to the cause of the problem.

What's needed is full-blown reform of the Forest Service budget and the incentives it provides to sell timber, no matter what the costs.

Conservationists in the Northwest scored a coup when, in the mid-1980s, they successfully alerted the nation to the impending loss of the last of the Northwest's awesome uncut coastal rainforests. Like battle flags, the words "old-growth" and "ancient forests" became symbolic rallying cries for conservationists everywhere who were horrified by acres of clearcuts and runaway timber harvests on western National Forests.

By late 1989, the Forest Service itself was forced to pay lip service to the notion that old-growth forests had inherent value as rich, diverse and irreplaceable ecosystems. The timber industry, along with traditional foresters, fought back. By 1991, little had actually changed and the old trees continued to fall.

Germany is looked upon by many as the cradle of forest science and forest management. By the end of the 18th century, European forests had either been cleared or picked clean. Virgin forests were virtually nonexistent. But by the middle of the next century European foresters had created new forests using an early form of plantation-style management. Germany's "rehabilitated" forests flourished. But these were, for the most part, tough, single-species conifers in "even-age" monoculture forests.

Richard Plochmann, a professor of forest policy at Germany's University of Munich, described these historical events in a 1989 lecture at Oregon State University in Corvallis. He predicted then that America would soon follow Germany's lead in changing the goals of federal forest management. Plochmann told how the German public had finally rejected "forestry solely oriented toward the maximization of profit." By the 1960s "with growing wealth and urbanization came a fear that we might exploit our natural resources and destroy our natural heritage."

Voices from all sides of the American West's timber debate have convinced me that for us the decade of the 1990s is the time of decision.

Remarkably, patches of native forest still stand on federal land
in the West. Even in the rough back country of Northern
Arizona, a few isolated but mostly untouched pine forests still
grow. Strangely, Forest Service timber specialists I talked to
seemed to know little or nothing about these rare snippets of truly
old ponderosa pine forests. Traditional, commodity-oriented
forestry argues that National Parks and wilderness areas already
preserve plenty of old-growth forests. But scientists like Jerry
Franklin say we are just beginning to understand the complexities
of forest ecosystems, and warn that we may be cutting down the
best forest laboratories left on earth.

As I researched this book, I reconsidered the question of
preservation. Are the West's natural resources wasted unless they
are developed, exploited, cut down or otherwise consumed?
Should the value of a public facility—a national park or
monument, a wilderness area, or a federal forest—be judged
primarily by the number of its "visitor days"? Or by how much
money it returns to the national treasury?

This nation sets great value in its national libraries, galleries,
and the housing of its archives and others wonders in the
Smithsonian Institute and the National Gallery in Washington,
D.C. But how many of us ordinary citizens have, indeed, entered
the doors of these magnificent institutions more than one or two
times?

Great federal forests in the West, like libraries, hold our
national secrets, our history. They are a storehouse of forest
"values," like biodiversity, that European forests lost three
centuries ago. Should we measure the worth of public lands that
have been set aside and preserved only by counting the heads of
those who "use" them? If Professor Plochmann is right, the U.S is
beginning to reject such short-sighted views.

In 1990 the U.S. Forest Service employed 29,000 men and women
to manage 191 million acres spread over some 156 separate
National Forest. The agency's budget had swelled to over $3

billion a year. Close to one-third of that was spent on timber sales support, road construction, reforestation, and other timber-related activities.

The timber industry is fighting hard to preserve its special relationship with the Forest Service. An industry publication put it this way: when timber supplies on private forestlands ran short, "Thankfully, there was another timber source—federal forest and state timberland designated by law for multiple use—waiting close by for the right time to go to work."

By state law, most western states must manage state-owned land for the top dollar it will return to that state and its citizens. As a result, thousands of acres of state timberland have been ruthlessly logged. In the Southwest and Rocky Mountain area the state foresters I talked to were, almost to a man, die-hard timber traditionalists. They rated "preservationists" among the lowest forms of life, and at best saw environmentalists as simple-minded do-gooders. Like brain surgery or submarine warfare, state foresters suggested, forest management should only be practiced by trained professionals. I am convinced that any meaningful reform of forest management practices in the American West must include changes in the way each state manages its own timberland.

Restoration forestry is a legitimate new branch of the forestry profession. The term hit me like a thunderbolt, sending messages flashing through my brain. Is "restoration" a confession of failure or simply a new branch of an already fragmented profession? I see it now as an important sign of the powerful theoretical schisms running through the forestry brotherhood. A whole litany of new terms—from "mosaic" to "holistic" and "landscape forestry"— is used to talk about how to improve the eye-appeal of a managed forest. For me, this part of the 1990s forest management debate sounds like a rebellion within a holy order.

But, like other historic reform movements, the U.S. Forest Service and the National Forest System which it manages are buffeted by powerful external forces—the politics of public land management. I've looked diligently for hidden formulas or newer, more effective ways for citizens to break timber's stranglehold on National Forests in the American West. There are none.

The U.S. Congress is the ultimate decision-maker. In this decade, the nation's elected representatives will decide the fate of the last of the West's great forests. Citizens who believe present timber management practices are systematically ruining those forests must make a powerful and convincing noise. I've always hated the finger-pointer who tells us all "to get involved." But I have come to understand during my research for this book, that there is no substitute for the local forest watchdog, the "adopt-a-forest" or "adopt-a-timber sale" group. Citizens who intimately know the local terrain and know where the great trees grow. Or used to grow.

In the American West, timber and mining have historically been cyclical, "boom and bust" industries, critically dependent on the bounty its enormous public lands provided. Today, competing in a global market, the timber industry wants stability. That stability depends, in large part, on securing a dependable supply of federal timber. Timber industry leaders speak of that supply in terms of their "piece of the pie." The industry believes precedent entitles it to a such a share.

One Weyerhaeuser executive defines that claim in this way: the timber industry recognizes the principle of multiple-use of National Forests and is willing to share the forests with a growing number of users, recreationists in particular. But whatever size timber's "piece of the pie" turns out to be, it should forever be set aside for "intensive management for [timber] production." This, we agreed, meant "tree farming."

Speaking about possible National Forest management options, Hal Salwasser, national director of the U.S. Forest Service's New Perspectives program, said in a 1990 speech before the Society of American Foresters: "Tree-crop forestry can be practiced on any ownership.... There is no reason why it should not be available for public lands that are highly productive and close to appropriate markets." This does not ring like a flat-out rejection of what the American public is already rejecting—disfiguring clearcuts and National Forests that look like industrial tree farms.

Environmentalists in the West have long considered Nez Perce National Forest Supervisor Tom Kovalicky "one of the good guys," a reformer. In a November 1990 interview for this book, Kovalicky energetically confessed the agency's past timber sins and called for timber reforms. But, to my surprise, he also strongly supported the idea of setting aside large tracts of National Forests as tree farms for the timber industry. His big, slightly raspy, All-American voice boomed forth with this prescription: Tree farms are indeed "appropriate" parts of a National Forest management plan. But the health of the whole forest should be considered, and tree-farming should take place only on the "best sites," those with rich, stable soil that can support intensive timber management without hurting other forest values.

Kovalicky put his finger on the crux of the debate over National Forest timber policy—the problem of increasingly flagrant conflicts between timber production and "other forest values."

"We have to find a way to get people more interested in what's happening on National Forests. Right now, the [National Forest] system is in the hands of the politicians," this reformer advised me. Three months later, I learned that Kovalicky was retiring. His voice, honest and unembarrassed, will be missed. Or maybe now that he has served out his time as a public lands manager, Kovalicky will help lead the loyal opposition from the other side.

The timber industry knows just where it stands on National Forest timber management issues. Managed forests are the best forests, they tell us. Old forests full of mature trees are simply wasted public resources. They argue that more than enough public land has already been "preserved" for non-development.

Conservationists disagree. Laws such as the 1976 National

Forest Management Act have failed to stop runaway timber-cutting on National Forests in the American West. This is as true in Arizona and the rest of the arid Southwest as it is in the central and northern Rockies and the rain forests of the Pacific Coast region.

So where should this nation grow the trees the timber industry needs to meet America's "demand" for wood products? One Idaho conservationist told me: "They can't grow mountain goats and grizzlies in Georgia. Let them grow the trees, and let Idaho grow what we grow best." The same might be said of other southern states where tree plantations flourish.

This sounds like good common sense. But dividing up the federal forest "pie" is infinitely more complicated. One current suggestion applies what I will call "the cleaver approach." It involves splitting the National Forest and its U.S. Forest Service squarely into two parts—one dedicated to timber production, and the other for all the other "uses."

Many American citizens, however, may not consider that a certain share of their public forest is automatically "owed" to the timber industry. Some 72 percent of this country's *best* timberland is, in fact, *already* in the hands of the private sector, not the federal government. Given the pro-business heritage of both the Reagan and the Bush Administrations, it seems appropriate to suggest that private industry should look for ways to *grow* more trees on private land instead of *harvesting* more trees on public land.

Increasingly, forest reform advocates—*The Wilderness Society* is one—say it is time for the federal government to provide strong incentives, such as tax benefits, which will encourage the expansion of *private* commercial timberland. Unlike other agricultural crops, trees farms will generally have a one-time payoff during the lifetime of a single owner, a fact which discourages private investment. Economist O'Toole even points out that it would be cheaper for the U.S. Government to buy private land and plant trees elsewhere than to continue to replant trees in poor growing conditions on National Forest lands.

Professional foresters argue that most citizens are unable to think in terms of "forest time," and are thus not able to grasp the long term complexities of timber management. They speak of "forest time" as the varying number of decades required to grow timber in a particular location. In the American West, however, citizens can see for themselves evidence which suggests that professional forest managers are seriously abusing "forest time." It's tough to hide hundreds of acres of mistakes and miscalculations that demonstrate a wanton disregard for the land and "forest time" itself.

The science (and the art) of forestry is based on assumptions and probabilities. On National Forests the objective (in theory) is the management of sustainable forests that serve a variety of public uses. As soon-to-retire Nez Perce National Forest Supervisor Kovalicky put it: "We're not supposed to destroy the resource."

Forest Service careers are built on frequent transfers *up* the professional ladder. That means federal timber managers are very often long gone by the time the fruits of bad timber practices have ripened into hard evidence. Accountability—the very core of democracy—is easily lost in a bureaucratic smokescreen, and federal timber managers are forever caught in a forest of half-finished experiments.

Like the medical profession, forest scientists also produce volumes of literature explaining to each other what has happened and what to do next. Until recently, forestry was an insiders' game, all the way.

But, despite the present turmoil within the Forest Service over timber management policy, younger, reform-minded Forest Service professionals say the agency-equivalent of "forest time" is on the side of change. Older career timber managers—the "timber beasts" who have ravaged western National Forests for the last 20 years—are retiring.

No one speaks more passionately about reform than do the younger professionals who have chosen to stay and work for change from within this agency-in-transition. And although no one I talked to dared offer a time frame for those changes, they all agreed—absolutely—on one thing: Congress will act when overwhelming numbers of citizens demand change in the way their National Forests are managed.

It also seems fair to suggest that those citizens must also be voters. The steady decline in the number of Americans who go to the polls gives special interest groups, such as the timber industry, an open field. The industry is there, every day, telling members of Congress how many National Forest trees it wants.

The rise of the environmental movement and the growth of citizens organizations has helped counter industry's political influence. But critics like Northern Arizona University's Dick Behan warn that powerful national environmental organizations, such as the *Sierra Club* (itself afire with internal revolt), *The Wilderness Society* and *The National Wildlife Federation*, are simply a new form of bureaucracy.

Decisions made in Washington, D.C., between government agencies and the Washington-based leaders of national environmental groups may well exclude the desires of a National Forest's "local constituency," says Behan. And that's true. But in the 1990s, literally thousands of local conservation groups and regional organizations all over the nation are working feverishly to make sure that local voices *are* being heard.

Significantly, these grassroots groups cultivate forestry expertise within their own membership. I have seen a number of these citizen-experts in action and the breadth of their knowledge and their political poise is truly impressive. When it comes to forest management and timber cutting, U.S. Forest Service staffers can no longer count on a naive constituency that can easily be pacified by professional hocus-pocus.

These highly informed local forest-reform advocates (including a growing number of newly retired Forest Service personnel, from

District Rangers on up) make powerful allies for like-minded Forest Service professionals. I have not so far been able to discover a perfect formula for reforming timber management policies on National Forests, but this alliance is clearly part of any winning strategy.

High County News Publisher Ed Marston, a highly perceptive observer of western issues—especially conflicts between environmental values and natural-resource development—has rightly drawn attention to the need to understand and assist traditional rural western communities struggling to survive in a changing world. In a thoughtful editorial on this subject, Marsten cautions reformers not to run rough-shod over these threatened communities. He now confesses that his own enlightenment on this subject was somewhat tardy. To conservation leaders he says: "I didn't understand that we couldn't hold the land without the communities. I didn't know that one of our top priorities should have been to work with the communities, however difficult that was."

Another element in a successful public forest reform strategy involves changing the budgetary rules the Forest Service works under. Many in the forest reform movement, from grassroots leaders to national voices, are now uniting behind a drive to dump the Knudsen-Vandenburg (K-V) Act. A lot of these forest reformers believe that changing this law would be the single most effective way to stop the runaway timber programs that threaten to turn National Forests into massive industrial tree farms.

This well-intentioned law, passed in 1930, provides federal funds for reforestation and other timber-related activities. But, as economist O'Toole explains, "The law's poor design encourages Forest Service managers to lose money on timber sales, clearcut fragile land, develop roadless areas" and all the rest. As much as anything, the K-V act laid the foundations for the later adoption of clearcutting on National Forests as the logging method of choice.

Despite the simplicity of this initial strategy, forest management

reform advocates in 1991 seemed certain that a bloody battle was
still ahead. No one discounted the highly potent political power
of the timber industry and its allies in the U.S. Congress.
Conservationists saw two major threats to forest reform on the
legislative horizon: the first was that Congress would simply pass a
law establishing an annual timber cut or harvest volume on
federal forests. The second was that Congress would be
persuaded to turn the policy of supporting so-called "timber-
dependent communities" into law.

Congressional bills, supported by the timber lobby, could also
include bans on lawsuits challenging certain timber management
decisions. And there was the ever-present threat that saving
ancient forests in the Pacific Northwest would result in raids on
little-noticed inland forests. People in Tennessee, Arkansas and
Texas worried that their forests would become "sacrifice areas" in
any legislative trade-off that saves forest owls or goshawks in the
West. I have come to see such tradeoffs or "compromises" as a
modern form of the timber industry's earlier "cut and run" style
of operation.

Even so, environmentalists have reason to be cautiously
optimistic. With the nation's biologists increasingly joining the
public debate on the side of conservation and forest reform,
environmental leaders are certain that recent events, such as a
May, 1991, federal court order halting logging in owl habitat in
the Northwest, show clearly that both science and the courts "are
on our side." Still, Oregon Democrat Harry Lonsdale, the man
who ran hard and did well against the state's powerful Republican
incumbent, U.S. Senator Mark Hatfield in 1990, warns that saving
jobs brings immediate political rewards while saving forests will be
seen as a courageous act by those now too young to vote.
Lonsdale, who is considering a run against Republican Senator
Bob Packwood in 1992, says conservationists must keep "the heat"
on in the U.S. Congress; and he adds, "Congress is full of
cowards."

There is really only one solution. Citizens must give Congress the courage to act promptly and wisely to insure that the last of the West's great forests do indeed survive. Otherwise we will soon be saying our last goodbye to these threatened national treasures. I've written this book as a citizen's guide to the political thickets surrounding federal forest management in the American West and to the possibilities for reforming a failing system. The situation is bleak, but still not hopeless. New voices in forestry science are now beginning to suggest ways we can nurture truly diverse, sustainable forest ecosystems— forests that will thrive well into the 21st Century.

Are enough Americans listening?

SOURCES & ACKNOWLEDGEMENTS

In researching this book I drew on a a very broad range of sources—both in person, in the form of numerous interviews, and in print. My printed sources included many books, hundreds of newspaper and magazine articles, speeches and publications from university scholars, and of course, armloads of material from U.S. Forest Service offices. My own stacks of yellowing issues of High Country News, the highly respected environmental-issues publication covering much of the American West, were a goldmine of background information and inspiration. The timber industry and its representatives provided inportant help: the Western Wood Products Association in Portland, Oregon, was a singularly indispensible and cheerful source. The tiny Norwood, Colorado, public library and the state's superb Pathfinder System reached out to bring in published material from unseen shelves all over the U.S. I am also indebted to conservation and environmental groups and their staff people all over the West who generously provided information, names, phone numbers and other links that breathed life into this project. Important published sources are listed below, by chapter.

INTRODUCTION
Breaking New Ground, by Gifford Pinchot, (reprint) Island Press, 1987.
Nine Nations of North America, by Joel Garreau, Avon, 1982.

CHAPTER 1, ...Enough Timber in the West?
"Importance of Ecological Diversity on Maintaining Long-Term Site Productivity," by Jerry F. Franklin and David A. Perry, in *Forest Watch,* August 1989.
Global Warming: Are We Entering the Greenhouse Century? by Stephen H. Schneider, Sierra Club Books, 1989.
"Concerning Sustained Production of Timber from the National Forest," a March 6, 1990 speech by USFS Chief Dale F. Robertson.

CHAPTER 2, The Environmental Opposition
"War in the Woods," by John G. Mitchell, in *Audubon,* January 1990.
"Owls vs. Man" in *Time,* June 25, 1990.

CHAPTER 3, The Stewards
Timber and the Forest Service, by David Clary, University Press of Kansas, 1986.
Public Lands Policy, by Paul J. Culhane, Johns Hopkins Univ Press, 1981.
Beauty, Health, and Permanance: Environmental Politics of the United States, 1995 – 1985, by Samuel Hays, Cambridge University Press, 1989.

The Angry West, by Richard D. Lamm and Michael McCarthy, Houghton Mifflin, 1982.

Reforming the Forest Service, by Randal O'Toole, Island Press, 1988.

"Wildlife Issues with Timber Management on National Forests in Arizona," an Arizona Game and Fish Department publication, February 1990.

"Multiresource Forest Management with EZ-IMPACT Simulation Models," by R. W. Behan, a research paper from the School of Forestry, Northern Arizona University; Fall, 1989.

"Public Participation in National Forest Planning," by Kevin Williams, a masters' thesis at University of Idaho, 1985.

CHAPTER 4, The Black Hills

Reforming the Forest Service, Randal O'Toole, Island Press, 1988

The Forest and the Trees: a Guide to Excellent Forestry, by Gordon Robinson, Island Press, 1988

CHAPTERS 5 & 6, Idaho & Montana

1989 Statistical Yearbook of the Western Lumber Industry, annual publication of the Western Wood Products, Assn.

"Forest Industry Facts and Issues," a booklet produced by the Intermountain Forest Industry Assn. and the Montana Wood Products Assn.

USFS statistical records on roadless timberland.

Position papers from The American Forest Alliance and The National Forest Products Assn.

"Life Cycles of the Ancient Forest," by Chris Maser, in *Forest Watch,* March, 1990.

Reforming the Forest Service, Randal O'Toole, Island Press, 1988.

The Forest and the Trees: a Guide to Excellent Forestry, by Gordon Robinson, Island Press, 1988.

Land and Resource Planning in the National Forests, by Charles F. Wilkinson and H. Michael Anderson, Island Press, 1987.

CHAPTER 7, Wyoming

Various publications of the Wyoming Heritage Foundation and Wyoming Forest Products Industry.

"Report on the Implementation of the Medicine Bow National Forest Plan," USFS publication, May 1990.

"Six-points and two-by-fours" by Joe Nemick in *Wyoming Wildlife,* January 1989.

"Tourism beats logging in Wyoming," Tom Bell, in *High Country News,* October 10, 1988.

The Angry West, by Richard D. Lamm and Michael McCarthy, Houghton Mifflin, 1982.

CHAPTER 8, Arizona

"Wildlife Issues with Timber Management on National Forests in Arizona," a publication of the Arizona Fish and Game Department; February 1990.

CHAPTER 9, New Mexico

"New Mexico forest takes long-term view," by author, in *High Country News*, September 11, 1989.

"Save the forests: Let them burn," by George Wuerther, in *High Country News*, August 29 1988.

"Forestry Newsspeak prevents us from seeing the ecosystem," by George Wuerther, in *High Country News*, Spring 1990.

"The Nesting Biology of Flammulated Owls in Colorado," a research paper by Richard T. Reynolds and Brian D. Linkhart; February 1987.

"Goshawk Reproduction and Forest Management," by D. Coleman Crocker-Bedford, in *Wildlife Society Bulletin*, 18: 262-269, 1990.

"Distribution and Habitat of Mexican Spotted Owls in Colorado: Preliminary Report," by Richard T. Reynolds, a paper from the Rocky Mountain Forest and Range Experiment Station, Laramie, WY., November 1990.

Reforming the Forest Service, by Randal O'Toole, Island Press, 1988.

CHAPTER 10, Colorado

Much of the information on timber issues in western Colorado came from my own work on news stories which appeared in *Wright's Mesa Review, The Telluride Mountain Journal,* and *The Telluride Times-Journal* during the 1980s and 1990. Other key sources included:

"Growing into a political thicket," by John D. Cox, in *The Sacramento Bee*, April 21, 1991.

Timber Watch, a monthly newsletter of The Colorado Environmental Coalition.

CHAPTER 11, Utah

This chapter is based almost intirely on interviews and background information provided by conservationists and industry leaders, state foresters, and other interested observers. Statistics courtesy of the Western Wood Products Assn. and the USFS.

CHAPTER 12, Washington

Press releases from The Weyerhaeuser Company, public affairs division.

High Country News, special issue on the Northwest, November 19, 1990.

"War in the Woods," by John G. Mitchell, in *Audubon*, January 1990.

"Wall Street and the Great North Woods," *The Amicus Journal*, Winter 1989.

Fragile Majesty – the Battle for North America's Last Great Forest, by Keith Ervin, the Mountaineers, 1989.

238

Reforming the Forest Service, by Randal O'Toole, Island Press, 1988.
Wintergreen, by Robert Michael Pyle, Houghton Mifflin, 1988.

CHAPTER 13, Oregon
"Owls vs. Man" in *Time,* June 25, 1990.
"The Northwest Forests: Day of Reckoning" in *The Oregonian,* October 10,1990;
High Country News, June 5, 1989 and February 26, 1990.
Public Lands Policy, by Paul J. Culhane, Johns Hopkins Univ Press, 1981.

CHAPTER 14, California
"The Largest Trees on Earth," by Catherine A. Dodd, and "They've Been Raping the Giant Sequoias," by Lee Green, in *Audubon,* May 1990.
"Northwest Forests: Day of Reckoning," in *The Oregonian,* October 10 1990.
"Miliken, Junk Bonds and Raping Redwoods," by Bill McKibben, in *Rolling Stone,* August 10, 1989.
"Deforestation hits home–U.S. Forest levels our landscape," by Karen Franklin, in *The New Republic,* January 2, 1989.
"The Forest Service's Catch-22," by Randal O'Toole, in the *Washington Monthly,* January 1990.
The Forest and the Trees: a Guide to Excellent Forestry, by Gordon Robinson, Island Press, 1988.
Reforming the Forest Service, by Randal O'Toole, Island Press, 1988.